Christian Apologetics

Christian Apologetics

An Introduction

Alister E. McGrath

Oxford University

WILEY Blackwell

This edition first published 2024

© 2024 John Wiley & Sons Ltd

The right of Alister E. McGrath to be identified as the author of this work and has been asserted in accordance with law.

Registered Offices

John Wiley & Sons, Inc., 111 River Street, Hoboken, NJ 07030, USA

John Wiley & Sons Ltd, The Atrium, Southern Gate, Chichester, West Sussex, PO19 8SQ, UK

For details of our global editorial offices, customer services, and more information about Wiley products visit us at www.wiley.com.

Wiley also publishes its books in a variety of electronic formats and by print-on-demand. Some content that appears in standard print versions of this book may not be available in other formats.

Library of Congress Cataloging-in-Publication Data applied for

Paperback ISBN: 9781119906933
ePDF ISBN: 9781119906957
ePub ISBN: 9781119906940

Cover Design: Wiley
Cover Image: © St Paul Preaching at Athens by Raphael, 1515. Royal Collection of the United Kingdom//Wikimedia

Set in 10.5/13pt GalliardStd by Straive, Pondicherry, India
Printed and bound by CPI Group (UK) Ltd, Croydon, CR0 4YY

C9781119906933_220324

For my colleagues and students at the Oxford Centre for Christian Apologetics 2004–2013

Contents

How to Use this Book: To the Reader   xi

How to Use this Book: To the Teacher   xiii

1   **Introducing Apologetics**   1
    The Core Elements of Apologetics   3
       Defense: Responding to Questions and Concerns   3
       Explanation: What Christianity is All About   3
       Translation: Unpacking the Language of Faith   4
    Five Types of Apologetics   4
       Evidentialism   5
       Presuppositionalism   5
       Rational Apologetics   5
       Experiential Apologetics   5
       Narrative Apologetics   6
    Why Apologetics Matters – and How it Can go Wrong   6
    Christianity as a "Big Picture"   8
    How Does Apologetics Relate to Evangelism?   11
    How Does Apologetics Relate to Theology?   12
    For Further Reading   13

2   **Apologetics: Some Historical Themes**   15
    Early Christianity   16
    Apologetics in the Early Islamic World   20
    The Middle Ages   22
    The "Age of Reason"   24
    The Twentieth Century   26
    Conclusion   28
    Study Questions   29
    For Further Reading   29

3 The Rationality of Faith   **31**
Setting the Context: Apologetics in a Post-rationalist Age   33
Faith as Justified Belief   35
Faith, Evidence, and Uncertainty: From Clifford to Dawkins   38
Arguments for the Existence of God: Three Approaches   41
    Thomas Aquinas: The Five Ways   41
    Anselm of Canterbury: The Ontological Argument   44
    William Lane Craig: The Kalām Argument   46
What is the Point of Arguments for the Existence of God?   47
Connecting up the Clues: C. S. Lewis and the Argument from Desire   49
Inference to the Best Explanation: Richard Swinburne   51
The Use of Rational Arguments: A Theological Concern   54
The Demand for Proof: The Problem with the "New Atheism"   55
Conclusion   56
Study Questions   57
For Further Reading   57

4 Connecting the Christian Faith with the Human Situation   **60**
Why Facts aren't Enough: Apologetics and the Human Situation   63
Communicating Christian Complexity: Isaac Newton and Mary Midgley   65
Apologetic Aspects of Salvation   67
    Truth and Desire in Apologetics   69
    Christ the Physician: Healing a Wounded and Broken Humanity   70
    Christ the Sacrifice: Entering the Presence of God   72
    Adoption: Believing and Belonging   73
    Liberation: Salvation as Deliverance from Bondage   74
    Explaining the Nature of Sin   75
Apologetic Aspects of the Incarnation   77
    Rethinking the Nature of God   77
    Seeing the Face of God   79
Christianity and the Human Quest for Meaning   81
    Finding a Secure Base in Life   82
    Finding Fulfilment   82
    Inhabiting a Coherent World   82
    A Sense of Self-worth   83
Study Questions   85
For Further Reading   85

5 Exploring Points of Contact for the Christian Faith   **87**
The Concept of a "Point of Contact"   88
Six "Points of Contact": Reflection and Application   90
    A Sense of Longing   90
    The Beauty of the World   93
    The Ordering of Nature   95
    A Sense of Wonder: The Night Sky   97

A Sense of Moral Obligation   98
Existential Anxiety and Alienation   100
Plato's Cave: A Neutral Framework for Framing "Points of Contact"   102
Study Questions   104
For Further Reading   104

6 Narrative Apologetics: Why Telling Stories Matters   106
The Rediscovery of Narrative Apologetics   106
Christianity as a Grand Narrative?   109
Narratives and Apologetics: C. S. Lewis and J. R. R. Tolkien   109
Apologetics as Telling a Better Story   112
The Apologetic Application of Biblical Narratives   115
The Apologetic Application of Narratives: Some Examples   116
    A Biblical Narrative: The Babylonian Exile   116
    A Cultural Narrative: The Relation of Science and Faith   117
    Literary Analogies: Making Theology Real   119
Study Questions   120
For Further Reading   120

7 The Importance of the Audience   122
Greeks and Jews: The New Testament and the Importance of the Audience   124
Apologetics as an Art: The Balcony and the Road   127
Understanding the Audience: Thoughts from C. S. Lewis   129
Seekers and Dwellers: A New Context for Apologetics   131
Apologetics and Audiences: Three Case Studies   132
    Apologetics in Secular Manhattan: Tim Keller   132
    Connecting with Black America: Urban Apologetics   134
    Post-Christian Apologetics in Prague: Tomáš Halík   136
Theological Translation: Explaining Christianity to Secular Audiences   138
    Faith   139
    Salvation   139
    Adoption   140
Study Questions   140
For Further Reading   141

8 Responding to Questions: Some Apologetic Debates   143
God as Wish-fulfilment? Freud's Critique of Faith   143
Is Religion the Cause of Violence?   146
The Problem of Suffering   148
Enlightenment Rationalism: Reason has Displaced God   152
Belief and Proof: The Question of Certainty in Faith   155
The Trinity: An Irrational View of God?   157
Scientism: Only Science Can Answer Life's Big Questions   159
Science and Religious Faith are Incompatible   161
The Question of Miracles   164

Reductionism: Human Beings are Nothing but Atoms   168
Study Questions   169
For Further Reading   170

9   Learning from the Wise: Case Studies in Apologetics   172
George Herbert: Apologetics through Poetry   173
G. K. Chesterton: Christianity as a Hypothesis   175
Dorothy L. Sayers: Apologetics and Detective Novels   178
Francis Schaeffer: Worldview Apologetics   181
Charles Taylor: Apologetics in a Secular Age   185
Conclusion: Moving On   189
Study Questions   191
For Further Reading   191

Acknowledgments   193

Sources of Citations   194

Index   216

How to Use this Book: To the Reader

This book, based on my lectures at the Oxford Centre for Christian Apologetics from 2004–2013, introduces apologetics – the field of Christian thought that focuses on how best to defend and explain the core themes of the Christian faith, and communicate these effectively and faithfully to the wider world. It assumes you, its reader, knows little about the subject, and aims to give you a good working knowledge of the field, and to encourage you to explore it further.

The Greek word *apologia* (which is traditionally translated as "defense") means something like a reasoned case proving the innocence of an accused person in court, or showing that a belief stands up to critical examination. We find this term used in 1 Peter 3:15, which many see as a classic New Testament statement of the importance of apologetics.

> In your hearts set apart Christ as Lord. Always be prepared to give an answer (Greek: *apologia*) to everyone who asks you to give the reason (Greek: *logos*) for the hope that you have. But do this with gentleness and respect.

Yet from the earliest of times, Christian apologetics has been understood more broadly than a mere "defense" of the Christian faith. Many Christian writers thought of apologetics as the explanation, communication, and defense of the core themes of the Christian faith. While older works on apologetics sometimes depict apologetics in primarily argumentative ways, this work reflects the growing recognition that many earlier forms of Christian apologetics appealed to the human reason, imagination, and experience. It thus supplements the rational defense of faith by highlighting the positive appeal of Christianity to the imagination, emotions, and feelings. Francis Spufford's *Unapologetic* (2013) is remarkable on account of its explicit appeal to the emotional rationality of the Christian faith. Spufford shows how emotions that are "deeply ordinary and deeply recognizable to anybody who has ever made their way across the common ground of human experience" lie at the heart of the Christian life, and are given new depth by its structures and practices. For Spufford, apologetics aims to help outsiders grasp what faith feels like from the inside. It's about allowing people to step inside the Christian faith, and experience the quality of life, thought, and experience that it enables.

Apologetics is both a *science* and an *art*. It involves both a solid understanding of the theory of the apologetics, linked to a wise application of this theory in practice. This is reflected in this textbook's consideration of the approaches of some leading practitioners in the field – such as Tim Keller – so that readers can both learn *about* them and learn *from* them, so that they can use them wisely. Although I have my own views on the nature and application of apologetics, this book is primarily concerned to help its readers understand, learn from, and use a range of apologetic approaches developed by leading figures in the field, past and present.

Every effort has been made to ensure that this book is accessible in its presentation, and reliable in its assessments. The book does not tell you what you should think, but rather explores the ideas of leading Christian apologists to help you develop your own thinking on this matter. I will tell you what I have found helpful, in the hope it will help you as well. If you are using this book for private study, you will find it best to read the material in the order in which it is presented. If you are using this book in conjunction with a taught course, you should follow the guidance of the course leader. Most chapters include two concluding sections entitled "Study Questions" (designed to help you check you have understood that chapter's contents) and "For Further Reading," which makes suggestions for works you might find helpful in taking your exploration of these themes further. While many significant studies of apologetic themes were written before 2000, there has been a significant change in momentum and direction of scholarship since then, so that most of the works referenced in these sections date from the twenty-first century. I hope to develop some video and audio resources to supplement this, and these will be freely available through the publisher's website.

Both the author and publisher will welcome feedback from readers of this work, which will help us develop future editions.

Alister E. McGrath
Oxford

How to Use this Book: To the Teacher

This book is based primarily on a series of introductory lectures I gave to student audiences when I was President of the Oxford Centre for Christian Apologetics from 2006 to 2013. The audiences for those original lectures were drawn from a wide variety of nationalities and denominations. These have been substantially rewritten in response to student feedback, and expanded in the light of later lectures I have given on these themes worldwide, particularly an extended course of lectures delivered at Regent College Vancouver in May 2021 (now available to you and your students on my YouTube channel).

The book aims to introduce core apologetic themes and approaches to your students in an accessible and reliable way, allowing you – the course leader or instructor – to supplement these with your own material wherever you feel this is appropriate, or to offer additional viewpoints or perspectives to enrich and expand those that are presented in this work. Apologetics is taught and practiced in a variety of denominational contexts and in the light of a range of informing theological assumptions. In writing this book, I have tried to avoid privileging my own context and assumptions, so that its material can be adapted for a range of Christian denominations and theological perspectives. Like C. S. Lewis before me, I have tried to work within a broad consensual Christian orthodox theological framework, which you can easily adapt and expand for use in Anglican, Baptist, Catholic, evangelical, Lutheran, Methodist, Pentecostal, and Reformed teaching contexts. Specific denominational emphases, exemplars and concerns can easily be grafted onto this generous and vigorous framework.

This textbook encourages you, the teacher, to weave in your own assessments, judgements, and add further material you feel is helpful or appropriate. It is intellectually *permissive* and pedagogically *hospitable*, in that it allows you to add additional material of your choice and adapt it to your own teaching context without in any way compromising its approach. This textbook lays the foundations of a course on apologetics, while encouraging you to build on those foundations in ways you find helpful and appropriate. The book provides you with a scaffolding that has been tried and tested over a period of two decades, to which you can add your own material. You can easily draw on additional writers or preachers who you think connect well with a specific audience to the chapter dealing with "The Importance of the Audience," engage some additional or alternative questions in the chapter on "Responding to Questions," or expand the list of individuals I discuss in Chapter 9 entitled "Learning from the Wise." You can enrich my examples or quotations with ones that you think are more appropriate, or would work particularly well for your students.

The book does not endorse any particular school of apologetics, although it references some of these (particularly presuppositionalism), as well as influential individual writers. The work makes frequent reference to C. S. Lewis, who has emerged as one of the most widely respected and quoted figures within the field at both the popular and academic levels in the past 25 years. Many students now see Lewis as an inspiration for, and a gateway to, the study of apologetics, and this book builds on his accessibility and reputation without limiting its scope or focus. The book is designed to allow you to build your own approach on the foundation laid in this work, enriching it from your own experience and wisdom.

Although I have my own ideas about apologetics, they are not promoted in this work, which rather aims to set out the ideas and approaches of a wide range of representative apologists, to which you are encouraged to add others that you think may be appropriate and helpful. I have tried to introduce and explain these approaches so that readers of this work can decide how to develop their own. You can help with this process of interaction and critical assessment – for example, by weaving into your teaching your own insights, observations, and judgements. You are welcome to add yourself to the group of writers I engage with, which will both extend the range of the book, and help personalize it for the needs of your students.

Finally, I need to emphasize that apologetics is both a *science* and an *art*. This book provides some useful resources for learning about the theory of apologetics, and introduces a generous range of theorists and practitioners to help students develop their understanding of the foundations of apologetics. What this book cannot do is help students develop the *practice* of apologetics, so that they can master apologetics as an *art*. This is where you, the teacher or instructor, have a critically important role to play in helping your students develop good apologetic practice.

For example, one of the tasks I set my students at the Oxford Centre for Christian Apologetics around 2010 was to give a 10-minute talk on a specific apologetic question aimed at a specific audience (such as students). Most students found this helpful in developing their speaking skills and working out how to deal with a complex issue. You will be able to help your students develop the practice of apologetics by setting them practical exercises that will help them move from theory to practice – something that this textbook is sadly not able to do, precisely because mentoring is such an important aspect of the art of apologetics.

Yet despite its limitations, I hope you will find this book a helpful resource in your teaching, and that you will feel able to provide both me and the publisher with any feedback that may be helpful in preparing future editions. While you will want to develop your own teaching resources, the publisher and I intend to produce some accompanying video and audio material that you may find helpful. This will be uploaded to the publisher's website so that you can download it for your own use, free of charge.

Alister E. McGrath
Oxford

1

Introducing Apologetics

This book is a basic introduction to Christian apologetics aimed at students in colleges, seminaries, and church study groups, and those studying this fascinating subject independently. Some Christian apologists offer both defenses of Christianity in general, as well as of one its forms in particular. G. K. Chesterton, for example, defends a broad vision of Christianity, but in his later period offered a defense of Catholicism in particular. This book, however, focusses on *Christian* apologetics. It does not defend any specific form of Christianity, but rather what C. S. Lewis famously described as "mere Christianity" – a consensual vision of the Christian faith, focusing on its core themes and concerns.

Apologetics has a mixed reputation in both the church and the academy. Avery Dulles, one of Catholicism's most distinguished recent apologists, remarked that many people consider an apologist to be an "aggressive, opportunistic person who tries, by fair means or foul, to argue people into joining the church." The best way of countering this impression, Dulles argues, is to study apologetics "at its best," rather than looking at its weak and inadequate representatives and forms. This is the approach we will follow in this book, exploring and examining apologetics at its best down the ages, and asking what can be learned from it by focusing on some of its most significant and influential representatives.

Although apologetics is often understood in terms of developing arguments for the existence of God, it is really a much wider and richer undertaking. While affirming the truth and trustworthiness of the Christian faith, apologetics also aims to communicate the Christian vision of beauty, goodness and truth faithfully and vividly, so that people might grasp and be drawn to the richness and depth of its vision of reality. Truth may *convince* people, yet beauty *attracts* people. This process of explanation and

Christian Apologetics: An Introduction, First Edition. Alister E. McGrath.
© 2024 John Wiley & Sons Ltd. Published 2024 by John Wiley & Sons Ltd.

commendation has become increasingly important as western culture gradually loses contact with the Christian narrative, so that it now often fails to understand its traditional vocabulary, or grasp its spiritual, moral, and existential vision.

As the next chapter in this book will make clear, apologetics has always been an important element of the Christian faith. Refusing to be confined to a Christian ghetto, early apologists considered it important to engage with their critics within the wider culture. Today's critic, they believed, might well turn out to be tomorrow's believer. They realized that, without engaging the wider world, Christianity might remain trapped in a kind of religious ghetto, being incapable of connecting with others beyond the church, or addressing their concerns about it. Recent developments in western culture show a growing disconnection between Christianity and a wider culture. The growing rise of religious "nones" in western culture, which dates from the turn of the millennium, suggests that one of the main reasons for this cultural disconnection with Christianity is a lack of understanding of how it connects up with real-life issues. Christianity is often understood as a rule-based way of life that demands nominal acceptance rather than a deep and transformative embrace. For many apologists, the best *defense* of Christianity is the faithful *explanation* of Christianity, linked with a personal testimony to its capacity to engage and transform human existence.

The Canadian philosopher Charles Taylor, noted for his careful analysis of the nature of secularism, persuasively argues that there is a need for apologetics to move away from a traditional "believers–nonbelievers paradigm" to a new "seekers–dwellers paradigm." This means apologists need to be able to think themselves into other people's ways of thinking. How might an outsider view Christianity? And how might this be sympathetically engaged? How might someone within the church who is struggling with some aspect of faith be helped to understand and embrace it? Part of the art of apologetics is to be able to explain and defend Christianity to an audience that is not familiar with its traditional vocabulary or its practices using terms and images that resonate with this audience. Apologetics is about building bridges from the community of faith to the wider culture, patiently and painstakingly explaining Christian ideas and showing – often by *embodying* them – how these can connect up with the lives and concerns of everyday people.

A second development is the more recent phenomenon of "deconstruction," in which older Christians, often with a long history of church attendance or association, conclude that their faith is no longer *meaningful* or *useful*. In his *Seven Types of Atheism*, the philosopher John Gray argues that atheism is best defined in terms of people feeling that they have "no use" for God. One of the key roles of apologetics is to show the difference that faith makes to life. Why is Christianity *useful*? This topic, among many others, is addressed in this work.

It is helpful to think of apologetics as both a *science* and an *art*. On the one hand, apologetics has a rich intellectual tradition and a distinguished group of practitioners, who are able to inform us about how best to engage questions and debates about faith. On the other, apologetics is a skill – an art that has to be learned through experience and reflection. There is an obvious parallel here with medicine. In healing people, a physician will draw on a rich body of technical medical knowledge, which is regularly updated and expanded; yet in the end, the physician is a practitioner of the art of medicine, which involves understanding patients, learning how to communicate with them, understand their anxieties and fears, and journeying with them through the healing process. While the opening chapters of this work focus mainly on the theoretical aspects of apologetics, later chapters are increasingly concerned with the issue of how apologetics is best practiced, and engagement with its leading practitioners.

The Core Elements of Apologetics

Broadly speaking, there are three main elements to apologetics, set out later, each of which is engaged throughout the analysis provided in this book. Apologetics *engages* challenges to faith, showing that answers can be given to critical questions asked by outsiders; it *explains* what Christianity really is, and the difference it can make to human existence; and it *translates* Christianity's ideas and terms into everyday language.

Defense: Responding to Questions and Concerns

From the earlier times, apologetics has engaged with criticisms, objections, and concerns relating to Christianity from people outside the Christian community. Some of these arise from misunderstandings; early Christian apologists often found that one of the best defenses of Christianity was a simple explanation of its beliefs and practices. Others arise from intellectual difficulties some experience with the Christian faith, such as whether belief in God is consistent with the existence of evil and suffering, or whether the doctrine of the Trinity is fundamentally irrational.

Apologetics requires the cultivation of cultural empathy – in other words, learning about the cultural sensitivities and difficulties that many experience concerning the Christian faith. These may arise from historic issues, such as links between Christianity and colonialism during the eighteenth and nineteenth centuries, or from the dominance of certain cultural values that are seen to be inconsistent with Christianity.

Explanation: What Christianity is All About

A core theme of apologetics is affirming and communicating the attractiveness of the gospel – intellectually, relationally, and imaginatively. Apologetics is grounded in a deep understanding and appreciation of the Christian faith, particularly the difference that it makes to life. This is best done by communicating both the *substance* and the *outcomes* of faith. What do Christians believe? Why do they believe this? And what difference does this make to real life? How does Christianity enable people to find meaning in life? To cope with trauma, suffering, and uncertainty? The apologist needs to have both a good understanding of Christianity, and an ability to make connections with the "ultimate questions" that are so important to many in today's culture.

To draw on an image popularized by the philosopher Hans-Georg Gadamer, the apologist is someone who "bridges horizons," thus enabling the core themes of the Christian faith to be brought into conversation with others outside the community of faith, in order to commend its vision of reality and the quality of life it enables. And, as we shall see, this means being able to translate the vocabulary of faith into the language of the wider culture in general, and specific audiences in particular (pp. 122–40).

This affirmation of the Christian faith can take two forms: *intrinsic* and *comparative*. The first sets out the apologetic virtues of Christianity – its capacity to make sense of things, its empowering vision of life, its grounding of a morally significant life, and so on. This may focus on the ability of Christianity to enable us to cope with suffering, or the transformed vision of the natural world and human nature that it makes possible. The second is more critical, in effect arguing that other worldviews, whether implicit or explicit, have internal contradictions or existential failings. Christianity is then argued to offer a *better* account of reality on these points. This second approach is developed in different ways by C. S. Lewis, Francis Schaeffer, and Tim Keller, and is particularly effective when dealing with audiences that believe their positions (such as secularism or materialism) are simply neutral, and are unaware of the many problematic assumptions embedded within them.

Translation: Unpacking the Language of Faith

The apologist Francis Schaeffer argued that apologetics has two main tasks: "The first is defense. The second is to communicate Christianity in a way that any given generation can understand." Schaeffer rightly notes that a core task of the apologist is to translate the language of the Christian faith into the cultural vernacular. Yet the philosopher and theologian Frederick G. Lawrence has pointed that some traditional ways of expressing the Christian gospel are now seen to be "alien and alienating," partly because of a loss of cultural familiarity with its themes and language.

In today's culture, social unfamiliarity is often equated with irrationality and irrelevance. To many in contemporary culture, the Christian faith seems to be jargon heavy, using a technical religious language that is disconnected from contemporary western culture. Central New Testament terms – such as justification, salvation, and sin – are increasingly likely to be dismissed as antiquated and irrelevant, or at best misunderstood. These terms often need to be translated or *transposed* – that is to say, reframed or re-presented in terms of accessible narratives or images, capable of connecting with a wider audience, while retaining maximum continuity with the Christian tradition. The vocabulary of the Christian faith needs to be unpacked, and re-presented in terms that its intended audiences can understand.

These, then, are the three core elements of apologetics. Each can be amplified considerably, as will be clear from the material presented in this book. Yet before beginning the study of apologetics in any detail, it is important to have a sense of the range of approaches that Christian apologist have developed down the ages.

Five Types of Apologetics

Christianity has developed a range of apologetic approaches and methods over the centuries, often in response to specific challenges and opportunities. While each of these has their own distinct emphasis, they are not incompatible, and are best seen as options that have universal apologetic potential, on their own or in combination with others. In what follows, we shall note five main approaches, to illustrate the range of resources at the apologist's disposal in engaging questions and debates. This list can easily be expanded. While this textbook does not advocate any specific approach to apologetics, each of these is appreciatively referenced and engaged throughout its discussions.

Evidentialism

This approach appeals particularly to the rational and historical evidence supportive of faith, often focusing on the New Testament accounts of the life and ministry of Christ. This approach resonates with a scientific worldview that values inductive reasoning from evidence. It also allows the apologist to engage questions of biblical reliability – for example, in relation to the resurrection of Christ. A good example of this approach is found in John Warwick Montgomery's best-known book, *Faith Founded on Fact*. N. T. Wright's influential work *The Resurrection of the Son of God* can also be seen as a form of evidentialist apologetics.

Presuppositionalism

This form of apologetics is critical, pointing out how the way people reason and the assumptions that they consider to be "natural" or "obvious" are shaped by their under-lying (and often unacknowledged) presuppositions. Writers such as Francis Schaeffer and Tim Keller both point out how there is no neutral or completely objective vantage point from which we see and interpret the world. This approach to apologetics thus aims to identify and criticize these presuppositions, and invite people to see the world through a different set of presuppositions – those of Christianity – and appreciate the new clarity and depth of vision that this brings.

Rational Apologetics

This approach aims to show that good arguments can be made for the truthfulness of Christianity, often using cosmological, teleological, moral, or ontological argu-ments. This form of apologetics became especially important in western culture as a result of the rise of the "Age of Reason," when it was seen to be important to give a rational defense of the Christian faith as a whole, or some of its individual aspects (such as the doctrine of the Trinity). Yet early Christian writers also used rational approaches in challenging the views of Greek philosophers, just as medieval Christian writers used them in meeting the rational criticisms of Christianity originating from Jewish and Islamic writers. They remain important today, despite the waning of rationalism in western culture, particularly in engaging contemporary Da'wah Muslim apologists.

Experiential Apologetics

This form of apologetics argues that Christianity offers a better way of making sense of human experience than its rivals. Augustine of Hippo, Blaise Pascal, and C. S. Lewis all argue that Christianity offers us a new way of understanding our experiences and what these point to. Although this lacks the rigor of rational argument, it connects well with real-life experiences, and offers an important entry point for apologetics through the realm of shared human experience – such as an experience of longing for something of ultimate value, or the sense that this world is incomplete and inadequate for human fulfilment.

Narrative Apologetics

Since the Second World War, there has been growing interest in presenting Christianity as a "better story" that is able to give a better fit with the actualities of life than its secular and religious alternatives. This is seen by many as restoring a proper emphasis to Christianity as a story that is to be lived out, leading to a meaningful and fulfilled life, rather than a series of propositional statements that are to be proved and accepted.

This brief account of some important approaches to apologetics will give readers a sense of the rich range of options at their disposal, as they aim to develop their own approaches. They are not in competition with each other, or inconsistent with each other. They can all become part of a cumulative integrated understanding of apologetics, capable of engaging a wide range of audiences and questions.

Why Apologetics Matters – and How it Can go Wrong

Early Christian apologists were quite clear that they had a major role to play in defending and commending what was widely seen as a maverick new religion in the imperial Roman world. For a start, few outsiders knew very much about Christianity in the second and early third centuries, and rumors abounded about what this new movement believed and practiced. The early Christians were regularly accused of practicing cannibalism and incest during their assemblies. Why? These accusations are generally agreed to reflect cultural misunderstandings of the eucharistic practice of "eating the body of Christ" (which was confused with cannibalism) and early Christian references to a "love-feast (Greek: *agapē*)" (which was confused with an orgy). Early Christian apologists – such as Justin Martyr and Tertullian – responded to these attacks effectively and simply by clearly explaining what Christians actually did.

Yet as Christianity became a more significant presence in late classical antiquity, its critics shifted their attention from its *practices* to its *beliefs*. Christian ideas were subjected to increasing scrutiny, particularly by philosophers who raised questions about their intrinsic rationality. Apologetics now began to focus to clarifying the grounds of Christian belief, providing a defense of beliefs that were seen as problematic – for example, concerning the identity and significance of Christ. Early apologists realized that a failure to defend Christian beliefs would create the impression that these beliefs were indefensible.

The issue of public accountability thus came to play an important role in apologetics. Christian writers aimed to show their many within Judaism and imperial Roman culture that Christianity had excellent rational credentials. As Austin Farrer points out, cultural acceptance often depends on recognition of rational acceptability.

> Though argument does not create conviction, the lack of it destroys belief. What seems to be proved may not be embraced; but what no one shows the ability to defend is quickly abandoned. Rational argument does not create belief, but it maintains a climate in which belief may flourish.

Farrer's point is significant: if you don't defend something that is being criticized, people will simply assume that it is indefensible. Apologetics may not always be well done; yet if it is *not* done, many will assume that it *cannot* be done.

It is helpful to return here to Charles Taylor's analysis of our "secular age," which he argues has led to the "fragilization" of belief. J. K. A. Smith helpfully explains this important idea as follows: "In the face of different options, where people who lead 'normal' lives do not share my faith (and perhaps believe something very different), my own faith commitment becomes fragile – put into question, dubitable." Taylor's point is that all beliefs – religious or otherwise – are now seen as "contestable," in that they are open to challenge and criticism. It is clear that many Christians find this uncomfortable and unsetting.

Two important points, however, need to be made. First, it is not simply *Christian* beliefs that are culturally "fragile." The same problem emerges with any religious, ethical, or political beliefs that lie beyond the worlds of mathematics and logic. And second, apologetics is not about *proving* that core Christian beliefs – such as the doctrine of the Trinity, or the existence of God – are true. Many shallow truths can certainly be proved; yet deeper truths about meaning, value, and purpose in life – whether these are Christian or secular – cannot be proved by science or reason. The rational norms of the "Age of Reason," assumed by some in the middle of the twentieth century to be the guiding principles of Christian apologetics, are now seen as being unrealistic aspirations. Apologetics can certainly give excellent reasons for the hope that lies within us (1 Peter 3:15), but many would now resist the suggestion that it can *prove* Christian beliefs to be true by unaided human reason.

The Canadian apologist and theologian John Stackhouse rightly reminds us of the limits of human reason, and its consequences for apologetics: "given historic Christian teachings regarding the finitude and fallenness of human beings and of our thinking in particular, we must be careful not to claim too much for what we believe." Apologetics can certainly show that there are good reasons for believing in God or other aspects of the Christian faith – but these cannot be *proved* in the strict sense of the term, as I might prove that "2 + 2 = 4," or that "the whole is greater than the part." Epistemological humility is in order here – the realization of the limits placed upon human reasoning by virtue of our sin and finitude.

Apologetics is not merely important in maintaining the plausibility of faith in a wider culture; it is an important aspect of personal faith development, in which individual Christians come to deepen their appreciation of their belief system by gaining a better understanding of (and confidence in) its core themes. Apologetics is part of the process of Christian discipleship, aimed at helping Christians achieve a deeper sense of the interconnectedness of faith, and the coherence of its various aspects.

Yet it is important to recognize that apologetics can go wrong. An example from early Christian apologetics will help make this point clear. Several early Christian apologists – such as Justin Martyr in the second century, and Clement of Alexandria in the third – developed defenses of Christianity against its Platonist critics by using the ideas and language of leading Platonic thinkers (such as Plotinus) to express some core Christian ideas. Yet some scholars suggest that Justin and Clement, in trying to make Christianity acceptable to Platonists, simply ended up making Platonism acceptable to Christians. This problem can, of course, be avoided – but it is important to be alert to this matter.

The Canadian philosopher Charles Taylor, who we have already noted in this work (pp. 2; 7–8), sets out an analysis of the origins of our modern "secular age," which is important for anyone thinking about apologetics. For Taylor, the modern age is characterized by a growing belief that human reason has complete access to the universe, and is able to understand and master its complexities. Many Christian apologists felt that they had to use the tools and methods of this secular age in order to engage it credibly and effectively. Yet in doing so, they often ended up buying into its wider outlook – such as the belief that human beings are the epistemological center of everything, and that there is no need for divine grace in developing arguments for faith. Within this context, apologetics is too easily understood simply as rational persuasion, losing sight of the critically important idea that God is somehow involved in the apologetic enterprise, opening the minds and hearts of people to the Christian gospel.

One of Taylor's many concerns about this impoverished rationalist apologetic is that it seems to have lost contact with the rich theological tradition of the Christian faith. In the early modern period, he suggests, Christian apologetics "barely invoked the saving action of Christ, nor did it dwell on the life of devotion and prayer, although the seventeenth century was rich in this. The arguments turned exclusively on demonstrating God as Creator, and showing his Providence." As Taylor notes, this strategy ends up commending the diminished god of Deism, playing down the particularities of specifically Christian beliefs in order to defend a more generic deity, which was easier to defend rationally – but who increasingly seemed to be a distant irrelevance.

More positively, however, Taylor suggests that we live in "what Heidegger has called 'the Age of the World-Picture.'" Although Taylor has concerns about this development, it can be reframed in a Christian way by thinking of Christianity as setting out a "big picture" of reality – a theme we shall explore in the following section.

Christianity as a "Big Picture"

Christianity offers a rationally plausible and imaginatively compelling "big picture" of reality. It is not so much a collection of isolated individual beliefs, but a web of interconnected beliefs, an "intelligible picture of the world," which gains its strength and appeal partly because of its comprehensiveness, and partly because of its intellectual and imaginative resilience. Francis Spufford is one of many apologists to emphasize Christianity's "imaginative legitimacy" and its rightful place "in the domain of what we all dream, hope, conjecture." The philosopher Keith Yandell offers a good account of the more intellectual aspects of Christian faith, pointing out that this big picture "provides an interpretation of the world and the place of human beings in it, bases an account of how life should be lived given that interpretation, and expresses this interpretation and lifestyle in a set of rituals, institutions and practices."

Christian theology weaves together the threads of biblical truth to disclose a pattern of meaning – like a tapestry, which brings many individual threads together, thus allowing their deeper significance and interconnections to be appreciated. No single thread can show that pattern; it only emerges through the process of weaving the threads together. Yet each individual thread matters. This is a critically important theme in Christian apologetics, and is particularly associated with two of its most influential practitioners – G. K. Chesterton (Figure 1.1) and C. S. Lewis. We will consider Chesterton's approach, as it is particularly engaging and accessible.

After a period of agnosticism during the 1890s, Chesterton found himself returning to Christianity because he realized that it offered an intelligible picture of the world. In

Figure 1.1   The journalist and apologist G. K. Chesterton (1874–1936) as depicted in the London magazine *Vanity Fair*, noted for its witty prose and caricatures of famous figures in Victorian and Edwardian society. Adobe Stock Images 162279309.

his famous 1903 essay "The Return of the Angels," celebrating his return to faith, Chesterton pointed out that it was not any individual aspect of Christianity he found particularly persuasive, but rather the overall "big picture" of reality – what he called the "spiritual theory" – that it offered. For Chesterton, it is the Christian vision of reality *as a whole* – rather than any of its individual components – that proves compelling. Christianity provides the cement that links aspects of reality together into a coherent whole, offering "an arrangement of the pieces by which they remain related, as do the stones arranged in an arch." Like a scientific theory, it was to be judged by how much sense it made of observation and experience. "We have returned to [Christianity] because it is an intelligible picture of the world. We have returned to it because, by the rejection of rationalism, the world becomes suddenly rational." Individual observations of nature, Chesterton declares, do not "prove" Christianity to be true; rather, Christianity validates itself by its ability to make overall sense of those observations. "The phenomenon does not prove religion, but religion explains the phenomenon."

The importance of a "big picture" can, however, be explored by considering other writers, such as the secular philosopher of science W. V. O. Quine. In his landmark essay "Two Dogmas of Empiricism," Quine suggests that what really matters is the ability of a theory *as a whole* to make sense of the world. Our beliefs are linked in an interconnected web that relates to sensory experience at its boundaries, not at its core. The only valid test of a belief, Quine argued, is thus whether it fits into a web of connected beliefs that makes sense of our experience in its totality.

The point that both Chesterton and Quine make (though in different ways) is central to Christian apologetics. The apologist can zoom *in* on individual aspects of the Christian faith, showing how each is illuminating and transformative, and how it might be defended and commended. In my own case, for example, I found the distinctively Christian idea of incarnation to be of critical importance in grasping both what Christianity was all about, but also why it had such importance in relation to revelation and redemption, to the illumination and transformation of our lives. The incarnation spoke to me of a God who chose to inhabit history; who chose to come to the place that I inhabited as one of us; who suffered, as I and so many others did – but who also chose to make that same suffering the basis of our salvation. In short, I discovered a God who journeyed to my place of exile, in order to bring me home. The biblical affirmation that the "word became flesh and lived among us" (John 1:14) speaks of God, not as a passive distant observer of the human situation, but rather as an active fellow traveler and constant companion within the historical process. God is someone we can know and address in worship and prayer.

The apologist can also zoom *out*, however, and focus on the grander vision of the Christian faith as a whole – the "big picture," which reassures us that we can adopt and inhabit a way of thinking and living that celebrates the coherence of reality, and is able to enfold and accommodate the many aspects of life. For many apologists – including Chesterton and Lewis – the task of the apologist is to show how this "big picture" is able to fit in what we observe in our world and experience within ourselves more effectively and plausibly than its rivals. Lewis's landmark statement, with which he concluded an Oxford lecture of 1945, is widely cited as one of the finest (and most succinct) summaries of this apologetic point: "I believe in Christianity as I believe that the Sun has risen, not only because I see it, but because by it I see everything else."

This strongly visual image helps us to appreciate how the Christian faith is able to weave together the threads of Scripture and human experience and observation to provide a reliable and satisfying account of life. Lewis is one of many writers to use images of illumination – such as the sun lighting up a landscape – to help convey the capacity of the Christian faith to make sense of things. A similar point was made by the US apologist Francis Schaeffer, who argued that Christianity was able to affirm "the unity of thought. It provides a unified answer for the whole of life."

Yet there are other ways of expressing the explanatory capaciousness of the Christian faith, including stories, which we shall consider in Chapter 5. Lewis's own rich understanding of Christianity was ultimately based on its fundamentally narrative character. Christian doctrines, for Lewis, are "translations into our *concepts* and *ideas*" of that which God has already expressed in a "more adequate" language – namely, the "grand narrative" of the Christian faith itself.

How Does Apologetics Relate to Evangelism?

Apologetics and evangelism can certainly be distinguished in theory; it is, however, hard to separate them in practice. Many people find it helpful to think of apologetics as clearing the ground for evangelism, just as the synoptic gospels tell how John the Baptist prepared the way for the coming of Jesus Christ. Apologetics is about ground clearing, removing roadblocks to faith. We could say that apologetics aims to establish the plausibility of the proclamation of salvation in Christ – for example, by developing an intellectual case based on cultural history for the fallenness or sinfulness of humanity, or by appealing to the experience of spiritual longing as a sign of alienation from God and our true destiny.

A rough working definition of evangelism might be "inviting someone to become a Christian." Apologetics would then be clearing the ground for that invitation, so that it is more likely to receive a positive response. Evangelism is often said to be like offering someone bread. Apologetics would then be about persuading people that there is bread on offer in the first place, and that it is good to eat in the second – thus preparing the ground for an invitation to receive this bread.

Where apologetics is often *dialogical*, evangelism tends to be *invitational*. David Bosch's definition of evangelism as "invitation" has found wide acceptance, and helps clarify how this can be distinguished – but not *separated* – from apologetics:

> Evangelism is the proclamation of salvation in Christ to those who do not believe in him, calling them to repentance and conversion, announcing forgiveness of sins, and inviting them to become living members of Christ's earthly community and to begin a life of service to others in the power of the Holy Spirit.

Apologetics thus prepares the way for evangelism, acting like a base camp along the road to faith. It reassures people that they are not abandoning rationality in embracing faith, and helps them overcome some roadblocks along the way.

Put simply, this book aims to introduce the basics of Christian apologetics. It is not concerned with the defense or justification of any specific form of Christianity – such as

Anglicanism, evangelicalism, Catholicism, or Lutheranism. It is perfectly possible to imagine, for example, an "Anglican apologetics," which might include defense of an episcopal form of church government. This work, however, focusses on *Christian* apologetics, understood as the more general defense and justification of common shared Christian themes across Christian denominations, particularly in relation to the questions and challenges they face today – rather like C. S. Lewis's idea of the generous consensual orthodoxy he named "mere Christianity." It does this by:

1. explaining how Christian writers and churches have understood apologetics down the ages;
2. exploring and assessing the various approaches to apologetics that have emerged within the Christian tradition, taking care to ensure a proper representation of major theological and confessional constituencies;
3. introducing representative apologetic responses to objections and concerns that are raised concerning aspects of Christian belief; and
4. considering how the theory of apologetics can be put into practice, focusing particularly on the difference that the Christian faith makes to life, the best ways of explaining its core themes., and the apologetic *practices* of some significant individuals.

How Does Apologetics Relate to Theology?

Some forms of rationalist apologetics that emerged in the twentieth century saw the art of apologetics as a purely human undertaking, which involved mastering the techniques of persuasion and rhetorical manipulation to win arguments. Yet Christian theology has always recognized that conversion is something in which God is involved. Apologetics may help remove obstacles to faith, as someone might open a shutter so that sunlight can stream into a dark room. But apologetics does not *create* faith, any more than opening a shutter creates sunlight.

Yet while traditional rhetorical skills, such as those set out in the classical period by Aristotle, are significant in any form of human communication, there is an essential *theological* dimension to Christian apologetics. It is helpful to contrast Christian and Marxist apologetics at this point. The latter is an attempt to persuade people that Marxism is true, and then invite them to become part of this political movement. Christian apologetics might initially seem similar: it might be described as an attempt to persuade people that Christianity is true, and invite them to become part of this community.

Yet this comparison is deeply misleading. Christianity and Marxism are not equivalent systems of thought, in that Christianity considers itself as a response to God's self-disclosure in Christ. God is thus not only the goal of Christian apologetics; God is seen as an active participant in the apologetic process. Christianity has never understood faith simply as rational acceptance of core Christian beliefs. For Christian theology, the opening of human minds and hearts to the truths of faith is not something that can be secured by human rhetorical skills alone; it arises through the work of the Holy Spirit, which can be seen as accompanying, enabling, and amplifying the skills of the apologist.

Christian theology thus frames the apologetic task within a framework of divine revelation and grace, by which the process of responding to the Christian proclamation and growing in faith is seen as resting on God's grace. Paul makes this point to the Christians in Corinth in explaining his role in their conversion: "I planted the seed, Apollos watered it, but God has been making it grow. So neither the one who plants nor the one who waters is anything, but only God, who makes things grow" (1 Corinthians 3:6–7). The sixteenth century Genevan theologian John Calvin speaks for the Christian tradition as a whole when he declares that faith is "both revealed to our minds and sealed in our hearts by the Holy Spirit" (pp. 36–8).

Apologetics can open someone's mind by helping them to grasp the richness and relevance of the Christian faith; it can also help reduce or remove barriers and obstacles to faith. Yet it is God who initiates and sustains the process of transformation and renewal that is widely known as "conversion." Theologically, there is an important role for human agents in apologetics – but Christian theologians would insist that the apologist is in some way aided and energized by divine grace and, just as the Holy Spirit may open the minds or prepare the hearts of an audience. The American Anglican theologian Mark McIntosh makes this point well: "The power of God's story is not from the inanimate effect of words. It is the very Spirit of God who comes to dwell within us, giving us ears to hear the Word and tongues to share with others the meaning it has for life."

Christian apologists rightly believe that the task of defending, explaining, and commending the gospel is aided, encouraged, and motivated by the same God who is proclaimed. It is God who converts, not the apologist. Apologetics, like preaching, is a work in which human agents see themselves as guided and empowered by the God they are proclaiming. While Christian theologians may differ on how grace and human action are related, most would agree that Christian apologetics is about opening hearts and minds to God's transforming grace.

We shall have more to say about how theology enables apologetics later in this work (see, for example, pp. 67–81). In the next chapter, we shall look at some important episodes in the history of Christian apologetics, before we move on to consider specific apologetic questions in more detail in later chapters.

For Further Reading

Bailey, Justin Ariel. *Reimagining Apologetics: The Beauty of Faith in a Secular Age.* Downers Grove, IL: InterVarsity, 2020.

Baucham, Voddie. *Expository Apologetics: Answering Objections with the Power of the Word.* Wheaton, IL: Crossway, 2015.

Chatraw, Josh. *Telling a Better Story: How to Talk about God in a Skeptical Age.* Grand Rapids, MI: Zondervan, 2020.

Chatraw, Josh, and Mark D. Allen. *Apologetics at the Cross: An Introduction for Christian Witness.* Grand Rapids, MI: Zondervan, 2018.

Copan, Paul, and William Lane Craig. *Come Let Us Reason: New Essays in Christian Apologetics.* Nashville, TN: B & H Academic, 2012.

Cowan, Steven B., and William Lane Craig. *Five Views on Apologetics.* Counterpoints. Grand Rapids, MI: Zondervan, 2000.

Craig, William Lane. *Reasonable Faith: Christian Truth and Apologetics.* 3rd ed. Wheaton, IL: Crossway Books, 2008.

Davison, Andrew, ed. *Imaginative Apologetics: Theology,* Philosophy and the Catholic Tradition. London: SCM Press, 2011.

Dulles, Avery. *A History of Apologetics*. 2nd ed. San Francisco, CA: Ignatius Press, 2005.

Fenton, Joseph C. *Laying the Foundation: A Handbook of Catholic Apologetics*. Steubenville, OH: Emmaus Road Publishers, 2016.

Fesko, J. V. *Reforming Apologetics: Retrieving the Classic Reformed Approach to Defending the Faith*. Grand Rapids, MI: Baker, 2019.

Geisler, Norman. *Christian Apologetics*. 2nd ed. Grand Rapids, MI: Baker, 2013.

Gould, Paul M. *Cultural Apologetics: Renewing the Christian Voice, Conscience, and Imagination in a Disenchanted World*. Grand Rapids, MI: Zondervan, 2019.

Keller, Timothy. *Making Sense of God: Finding God in the Modern World*. New York, NY: Penguin Books, 2018.

Kinghorn, Kevin, and Jerry L. Walls. "The Spirit and the Bride Say 'Come:' Apologetics and the Witness of the Holy Spirit." In *The Testimony of the Spirit: New Essays*, edited by R. Douglas Geivett and Paul K. Moser, 223–43. New York, NY: Oxford University Press, 2017.

Kreeft, Peter. *Fundamentals of the Faith: Essays in Christian Apologetics*. San Francisco: Ignatius Press, 1988.

Kreeft, Peter, and Ronald K. Tacelli. *Handbook of Catholic Apologetics: Reasoned Answers to Questions of Faith*. San Francisco: Ignatius Press, 2009.

McGowan, Andrew. "Eating People: Accusations of Cannibalism against Christians in the Second Century." *Journal of Early Christian Studies* 2, no. 4 (1994): 413–42

McGrath, Alister E. *Mere Apologetics:How to Help Seekers and Skeptics Find Faith*. Grand Rapids, MI: Baker Books, 2011.

McGrath, Alister E. *Narrative Apologetics: Sharing the Relevance, Joy, and Wonder of the Christian Faith*. Grand Rapids, MI: Baker Books, 2019.

McGrath, Alister E. *Through A Glass Darkly: Journeys through Science, Faith, and Doubt*. London: Hodder & Stoughton, 2020.

McLaughlin, Rebecca. *Confronting Christianity: 12 Hard Questions for the World's Largest Religion*. Wheaton, IL: Crossway, 2019.

Morley, Brian. *Mapping Apologetics: Comparing Contemporary Approaches*. Downers Grove, IL: IVP Academic, 2015.

Nicholi, Armand M. *The Question of God: C. S. Lewis and Sigmund Freud Debate God, Love, Sex, and the Meaning of Life*. New York, NY: Free Press, 2003.

Ordway, Holly. *Apologetics and the Christian Imagination: An Integrated Approach to Defending the Faith*. Living Faith. Steubenville: Emmaus Road Publishing, 2017.

Quist, Allen. *The Reason I Believe: The Basics of Christian Apologetics*. Saint Louis, MO: Concordia Publishing House, 2017.

Sire, James W. *A Little Primer on Humble Apologetics*. Downers Grove, IL: InterVarsity Press, 2006.

Sire, James W. *Apologetics Beyond Reason: Why Seeing Really Is Believing*. Downers Grove, IL: InterVarsity Press, 2014.

Spufford, Francis. *Unapologetic*. London: Faber and Faber, 2012.

Stackhouse, John G. *Humble Apologetics: Defending the Faith Today*. Oxford: Oxford University Press, 2002.

Stackhouse, John G. *Can I Believe? Christianity for the Hesitant*. Oxford: Oxford University Press, 2020.

Sweis, Khaldoun A., and Chad V. Meister. *Christian Apologetics: An Anthology of Primary Sources*. Grand Rapids, MI: Zondervan, 2012.

Taylor, James E. *Introducing Apologetics: Cultivating Christian Commitment*. Grand Rapids, MI: Baker Academic, 2006.

Toren, Bernard van den. *Christian Apologetics as Cross-Cultural Dialogue*. London: T&T Clark, 2011.

Weir, Todd H., and Hugh McLeod, eds. *Defending the Faith: Global Histories of Apologetics and Politics in the Twentieth Century*. Oxford: Oxford University Press for the British Academy, 2021.

2

Apologetics
Some Historical Themes

In studying apologetics, you are stepping into a conversation that has been going on for nearly 2,000 years. It helps to know the history of this conversation! This chapter tracks some of its themes and leading representatives. Although the term "apologetics" was not used within the early Christian community until it was introduced by Eusebius of Caesarea in the first half of the fourth century, it is clear that what is now known as "apologetics" can be traced back to the time of the New Testament itself. While its forms and approaches vary from one historical location to another, apologetics has been an integral task of the Christian community of faith throughout its history. The New Testament itself offers some important examples of apologetic approaches, and well as commending the practice of explaining and defending the Christian faith. Although some leaders of the early church – such as its bishops – played important apologetic roles, many early Christian apologists were lay people.

In this opening chapter, we shall briefly consider some historical themes in Christian apologetics. This is not a comprehensive account of the overall historical development of apologetics, but is rather a series of snapshots to illustrate some important episodes in this process, especially in the period of the early church and the past few centuries, and to help readers to get a sense of the kind of issues that apologetics has had to engage with. Each historical period and context give rise to its own distinct apologetic concerns, and it is important to be able to use that past to inform and resource our engagement with the present.

While many readers of this work will be anxious to get straight into the discussion of apologetic methods, approaches, and strategies, it is nevertheless helpful to get a sense of how Christianity has understood and practiced apologetics over its history. This is not a distraction from present-day concerns, but helps set today's apologetic concerns

Christian Apologetics: An Introduction, First Edition. Alister E. McGrath.
© 2024 John Wiley & Sons Ltd. Published 2024 by John Wiley & Sons Ltd.

and approaches in context, as well as offering resources to apologists today. In recent years, there has been growing interest in an "apologetics of retrieval," which reclaims the approaches of early Christian writers (such as Augustine of Hippo) and applies them to contemporary concerns and issues. We begin by considering the emergence of apologetics in early Christian thought and practice.

Early Christianity

Apologetics was clearly significant during the apostolic period, during which the New Testament emerged. Indeed, the New Testament scholar F. F. Bruce noted that most of the main early Christian approaches to apologetics had their roots in the New Testament, particularly in the Acts of the Apostles.

> Of three main types of Christian apologetic in the second century Luke provides first-century prototypes: apologetic in relation to pagan religion (Christianity is true; paganism is false); apologetic in relation to Judaism (Christianity represents the fulfilment of true Judaism); apologetic in relation to the political authorities (Christianity is innocent of any offence against Roman law).

The Acts of the Apostles includes some significant examples of apologetic speeches, including Peter's Pentecost sermon (Acts 2:14–36), which argues that Christ represents the fulfilment of Judaism, and Paul's address at the Areopagus (or "Mars Hill") in Athens (Acts 17:22–31), in which he argues that Christ discloses the true meaning of things. We will consider the apologetic importance of both these addresses later in this work (pp. 124–26). The first letter of Peter urges Christians to respond to questions they are asked about their faith: "Always be ready to make your defense to anyone who demands from you an accounting for the hope that is in you; 16 yet do it with gentleness and reverence" (1 Peter 3:15–16).

This concern for apologetics continued during the early Christian age, sometimes still known as the "patristic period." This is usually understood to enfold the period between the final works of the New Testament and the Council of Chalcedon (451). This was a remarkably creative and important stage in the development of Christianity in the Mediterranean world, during which leading Christian thinkers set out to consolidate the core ideas of their faith, as set out in the New Testament, leading to the formulation of definitive statements about the identity and significance of Jesus Christ, and the distinctively Christian understanding of God. The period saw an emerging consensus on the sources of theology, particularly through the fixing of the canon of Scripture. These internal challenges led to a remarkably creative period of theological reflection within the church.

Yet the early church also faced external challenges during this period, most notably the need to respond to growing hostility towards Christianity on the part of other religious and philosophical movements in the Greco-Roman world, particularly from Judaism, Greek philosophy, and traditional Roman religion. While theological clarification was of major importance in protecting the church's identity, the early Christian communities also had to define and justify themselves in the face of competing religious and cultural alternatives. Four major forms of apologetic writing emerged at this time in response to these challenges.

1. Works that challenge and correct pagan charges of immorality or sedition on the part of the Christian faith, or the Christian community. Early Christianity was widely misunderstood within imperial Roman culture, and these apologetic works aimed to correct misunderstandings and misrepresentations. Most of these works date from the second and early third centuries, and include the *Apology* of Aristides of Athens, the *Letter to Diognetus*, the *First and Second Apologies* of Justin Martyr, and the *Apology* of Tertullian. Justin Martyr wrote a particularly significant apologetic work responding to Jewish criticisms of Christianity. His *Dialogue with Trypho*, thought to date from 155–160, argued that Christianity was the fulfilment of Jewish life and thought.

2. Critiques of rival systems of thought in late classical antiquity, including Judaism, Greek philosophy, and Roman civil religion. In his second-century homily *On Pascha*, Melito of Sardis argues that Christ is the *logos* (Greek: "word") whose crucifixion and resurrection fulfills the law of Israel – and in doing so, brings it to an end. The coming of Christ thus both fulfils the Old Testament law and makes it redundant. Tatian of Assyria's *Oration to the Greeks*, which also dates from the second century, takes the form of a critique of the rhetorical pretensions of Greek philosophy. Arnobius of Sicca's *Against the Nations* was probably written in the first decade of the fourth century at the time of the Diocletian persecution. This work ridiculed the idea, widespread during the late third and early fourth centuries, that the gods had withdrawn their favor from the Roman Empire because of the rise of Christianity.

3. A third group of writings were aimed at individual critics of Christianity, aiming to engage their concerns and show them to be misplaced or overstated. The most famous of these is Origen's *Against Celsus*, written in the middle of the third century. Celsus, whose criticisms of Christianity were first set out in the late second century, argued that Christianity was little more than a garbled and philosophically unsophisticated version of Judaism. In responding to this charge, Origen offered a detailed account of some central Christian themes, noting particularly how Celsus has failed to find the hermeneutical key that would help him to make sense of the Hebrew Bible. For Origen, while Christianity is rooted in the Hebrew Bible, it uses a different interpretative framework than Judaism, and thus understands this text and its significance in a new way.

4. A fourth set of apologetic works avoid polemics and criticism, and instead provide constructive expositions of the Christian faith, on the basis of the assumption that the best defense of Christianity is a proper explanation of its ideas and practices. Clement of Alexandria wrote his *Stromata* (Greek: "miscellanies") to explain Christianity to Greek philosophers, and to persuade Christians that philosophy could be taken seriously (Figure 2.1). Yet perhaps the most important of these works was Augustine of Hippo's *City of God*, which offers a compendious account of Christian theology in refuting the pagan charge that Rome's desertion of her traditional religion led to the humiliating "Sack of Rome" in 410 by the Visigoths, an event that is often regarded as marking the beginning of the end of the Western Roman Empire.

Figure 2.1   The remains of the ancient city of Alexandria, an important center for early Christian apologetics, showing Pompey's Pillar, built between 298–302 CE. Adobe Stock Image 214265799.

So what issues were explored in early Christian apologetics? We shall consider some representative examples to get a sense of the topics with which we are engaged. One of these is the rise of Gnosticism in the second century, which posed a particularly significant challenge to Christianity. Although we only have a partial understanding of the origins and distinct ideas of this movement, it is clear that it posed a significant threat to the church by proposing alternative ideas of salvation, which were verbally similar to those of the gospel, or by respecting the New Testament, while interpreting it in some distinctly un-Christian ways. Irenaeus of Lyons was one of the most effective critics of Gnosticism in the second century. His *Against the Heresies* provided a powerful critique of Gnosticism's internal coherence and historic roots, along with a lucid account of core Christian beliefs that emphasized their interconnectedness and their superiority to their pagan rivals.

As Rome's political and military power began to decline in the late second century, many blamed the rise of Christianity for weakening the hold of traditional Roman religion, which was seen as essential to the wellbeing of the empire. This concern about the rise of Christianity being the primary cause of the decline of traditional Roman religion, on which the stability of its empire depended, peaked in the Latin west around 250, marking the 1000th anniversary of the founding of Rome. Christians now came to be referred to as "atheists," in that they did not conform to the polytheism of Roman civil religion. (While this use of the term "atheism" may puzzle some modern readers, given that early Christians clearly placed belief in God at the center of their faith, it is helpful to remember that the Greek philosopher Socrates was also denounced as an "atheist" because of his criticisms of traditional Greek religion.)

By this time, a significant apologetic tradition had been established within the western Latin-speaking church. One of the most important of the early Latin apologists was Tertullian, a third-century orator generally thought to have been based in the great Roman North African city of Carthage. Tertullian debated the fundamental truths of faith with a number of significant cultural movements, including secular philosophy, Gnosticism, and Judaism. Tertullian is often associated with the Latin phase *Credo quia absurdum est* ("I believe because it is absurd"), which is often cited in debates about the rationality of religious belief. Scholars of early Christianity have shown that Tertullian never actually used this phrase, which is in any case inconsistent with his approach to the reasonableness of faith. As Peter Harrison points out, this false quotation was regularly seized on by eighteenth century rationalists who wanted to portray religion as irrational, and faith as an epistemic vice. Tertullian's attitude to reason is summed up definitively in the following quotation:

> For reason is a property of God's, since there is nothing which God, the creator of all things, has not foreseen, arranged and determined by reason. Furthermore, there is nothing God does not wish to be investigated and understood by reason.

For Tertullian, Christianity is a reasonable faith, and there are no limits to what may be "investigated and understood by reason." The same God who created humanity with the capacity to reason expects that reason to be used in the exploration and representation of the world – in the expectation that this will lead the reasoner to find God.

The Greek-speaking eastern church developed its own distinct apologetic approach, particularly in the great Egyptian city of Alexandria. Origen's detailed rebuttal of Celsus's philosophical, moral, and religious criticisms of Christianity, noted above, is widely agreed to be one of the most important works of early Christian apologetics, showing that a Christian philosopher was able to hold his own against an educated pagan critic. This third-century work demonstrates a remarkable confidence in the intellectual and moral credentials of the gospel. Origen's approach was developed in the fourth century by other Alexandrian writers, as well as writers based in the region of Cappadocia, such as Gregory of Nyssa. Athanasius of Alexandria, one of the most important apologists of the fourth century, placed considerable emphasis on the internal coherency and consistency of the Christian faith, offering the basis of a defense of the Christian faith to both Jewish and Greco-Roman audiences.

For Athanasius, the Christian belief that humanity is created in the image of God is taken to mean that human rationality has the ability to reflect the mind of God. The truth of Christianity can thus be ascertained by close inspection of the world of nature, such as the night sky. Athanasius develops this idea in his important treatise *On the Incarnation*: "Humanity could look up into the immensity of heaven, and by pondering the harmony of creation, come to know its Ruler, the Word of the Father, whose sovereign providence makes the Father known to all."

Although the conversion of Constantine in or around 312 led to Christianity becoming culturally acceptable and eventually politically dominant within the Roman Empire the second half of the fourth century, later patristic theologians rightly saw that this did not necessarily secure rational acceptance of the gospel. This is evident in the writings of the greatest apologist of the Latin west, Augustine of Hippo, whose conversion to Christianity in August 386 is widely regarded as a landmark in the development of western Christianity.

Augustine's contribution to apologetics was significant at several levels, including the philosophical defense of the rationality of the Christian faith, the appeal to divine illumination in securing reliable human knowledge of God, and the importance of the subjective world of memory and feeling in matters of faith. Augustine's substantial theological output laid a robust conceptual foundation for apologetics, recognizing the role of divine grace and illumination in conversation, while at the same time highlighting the importance of human agency in the apologetic task. Perhaps most importantly, Augustine recognized the vulnerability of the Western Roman Empire, and began to strategize about how Christianity could prosper in the radically changed world that lay ahead. It was a prophetic vision. During the second half of the fifth century, the central Roman state finally collapsed, setting the scene for the rise of Christianity in western Europe, with Augustine being widely recognized as one of its most important theological and apologetic resources.

Apologetics in the Early Islamic World

The collapse of the Roman Empire in the western Mediterranean led to significant changes in the situation of western Christianity, which could no longer rely on the protection of the Roman state. In the eastern Mediterranean, however, the situation was significantly different. In 324, Constantine declared that the ancient city of Byzantium was to be the new capital of the Roman Empire. In 330, it was renamed "Constantinople" (from the Greek words for "the city of Constantine"). Constantinople remained the capital of the eastern Empire, which survived the collapse of the western Empire, and continued until the fall of the city to Islamic forces in 1453. During this period Christian theology in Greece and Asia Minor (modern-day Turkey) developed its own distinct agendas, often loosely described as "Byzantine" theology. Perhaps the most important apologist of this age was the fourteenth-century theologian Gregory Palamas (c. 1296–1359), whose arguments for the direct perception of God – rather than an undue reliance on rational argument – continues to be important in some schools of apologetics and spirituality.

The fall of the Roman Empire in the west had brought about major political instability in this region. In the east, however, the Roman Empire remained functional, with Constantinople emerging as the "New Rome." However, a new force emerged in this region through the rise of Islam in the Arabian peninsula during the seventh century. During the period following the death of Mohammad in 632, Islam expanded rapidly by military conquest. By 640, the "Caliphate" (a region under Islamic control) had been extended to Mesopotamia, Syria, and Palestine; by 642, to Egypt; and by 643, to the Persian Empire. Many of these areas were former strongholds of Christianity – such as the cities of Damascus, Alexandria, and Antioch. Islamic expansion in this region continued in subsequent centuries, until the great eastern Christian stronghold of Constantinople was finally conquered in 1453 (Figure 2.2). Although Ottoman armies besieged the city of Vienna in 1529, the city was able to resist this attack, which is generally considered to mark the end of Islamic expansion in Europe.

The rise and growing military power of Islam made it clear to Christian apologists that they were confronted with a new intellectual and cultural rival in the east. The Islamic emphasis on the absolute "oneness (Arabic: *tawhid*)" of God led to Islamic apologists calling into question both the Christian doctrine of the Trinity and the

Figure 2.2 The Byzantine mosaic of *Christos Pantocrator* in the south dome of Chora Church in Constantinople. Adobe Stock Image 86320002.

divinity of Christ. Christian apologists in Islamic regions set out to defend the consistency and intelligibility of their faith, especially in relation to the doctrines of the incarnation and Trinity.

John of Damascus (c. 675–749) was the first significant Christian theologian to build intellectual bridges to Islam, and demonstrate the rational credibility of the gospel in the light of Islamic critiques of its teachings. As a high-ranking civil servant in the court of the Caliph of Damascus during the eighth century, John gained a good understanding of Islamic theology, allowing him to develop significant defenses of the divinity of Christ that would carry weight with an Islamic audience. Around the same time, the patriarch Timothy I of Seleucia-Ctesiphon (often known simply as "Timothy of Baghdad") produced his *Apology* – a defense of Christianity in response to questions raised by Mahdi, the Caliph of Baghdad in 781. This document was widely used as a training manual by the ninth-century church on how to respond to Islamic concerns about the gospel.

By the ninth century, Arabic was firmly established as the public language of many parts of the Islamic world, including Syria. Christian apologists realized the need for apologetic works in Arabic, which were able to engage Islamic writers in constructive dialogue, and offer a demonstration of the rationality of the Christian faith. The northern Syrian bishop Theodore Abū Qurrah (c. 750–c. 825) was one of the first Christian writers to use Arabic as his primary language. In his apologetic works, he set out a significant defense of Christian beliefs. Islam regarded the idea of the incarnation as blasphemous; Abū Qurrah, however, argued that it was necessary for God to assume a human existence and experience suffering in order to free human beings from their sins. Some of Abū Qurrah's works were later translated into Greek, where they influenced mainline Christian responses to Islam.

The Middle Ages

Christianity in western Europe had survived the collapse of the Roman Empire in this region, and played a major role in reestablishing centers of learning. By the eleventh century, some degree of political stability had been restored to western Europe, leading to the emergence of universities and an increasingly sophisticated urban culture. Although the rise of "Christendom" as a settled Christian region in Europe reduced the importance of apologetics in the life of the western church, it is clear that some significant writers of the medieval period recognized the need for the effective and persuasive presentation of Christian ideas across religious and cultural boundaries.

Monasteries became the spiritual and intellectual powerhouses of Christianity in the early Middle Ages. The Benedictine monastery of Bec in Normandy was particularly significant in this respect. Anselm of Canterbury (Figure 2.3) – an eleventh century Archbishop of Canterbury who was originally a monk at Bec – championed an intellectual renewal of Christian theology, showing how core beliefs, such as the incarnation and atonement, could be affirmed and defended rationally. For Anselm, the inherently rational character of Christian doctrines meant that they were capable of public defense.

The University of Paris emerged as one of the most significant centers of learning in western Europe, attracting large numbers of Christian, Jewish, and Islamic scholars. Thomas Aquinas, one of the most important thirteenth-century theologians, was a major presence at Paris, and recognized the importance of offering a rational defense of Christianity to Jewish and Islamic readers. Like Anselm before him, Aquinas held that Christian beliefs were fundamentally rational, even if they transcended the limits of reason, and were thus able to form a coherent and rationally defensible system. Aquinas's *Summa contra Gentiles*, written between 1259 and 1265, is clearly apologetic in both its general tone and approach. Whereas Aquinas's best-known work, the *Summa Theologiae*, is a detailed compendium of Christian theology, clearly written with the needs and concerns of Christian readers in mind, the *Summa contra Gentiles* anticipates questions that might be raised by Jewish, Islamic, or secular audiences. It remains an important resource for modern apologists, not least on account of its thoughtful defense and articulation of core beliefs.

Figure 2.3 Anselm of Canterbury (left), depicted on the altar of Münsterschwarzach Abbey, Bavaria, Germany. Anselm is depicted holding his work *Cur Deus homo*, which set out an influential account of the rationality of the incarnation. Adobe Stock Image 291704035.

Neither Anselm nor Aquinas, however, appear to have had significant experiences of *direct* cultural and intellectual encounter with representatives of alternative religious traditions, such as Judaism or Islam. Like many medieval writers, their knowledge of such rival religious beliefs was generally indirect. The fourteenth-century writer Ramon Llull is of particular importance in that he had direct contact with alternative religious outlooks, particularly Islam, in the Kingdom of Majorca during the thirteenth century. Medieval Spain became a significant center for dialogue between Christian and Islamic theologians at this time. This is reflected in Llull's apologetic writings, such as *The Book of the Gentile and the Three Wise Men*, which sets out a general rational defense of Christianity, while being attentive towards the concerns of an Islamic readership.

Figure 2.4   Engraving by Athanasius Kircher (1602–1680) showing the Jesuit missionary Matteo Ricci on the left and the first Chinese convert to Christianity, Xu Guangqi, on the right. Adobe Stock Image 53564586.

Although the European Reformation of the early sixteenth century was significant theologically, it had limited interest in questions of apologetics. Leading Protestant reformers such as Martin Luther and John Calvin were primarily concerned with the reform and renewal of the Christian churches of western Europe, and did not engage significantly with the missiological or apologetic questions involved in reaching beyond the established Christian world. Most of the important apologetic activity and reflection in the later sixteenth and early seventeenth centuries took place within Catholicism, as the great voyages of discovery of Spanish and Portuguese navigators opened up the worlds of thought of South America, India, and China, and thus identified apologetic questions that had to be engaged. A good example of the forms of apologetic that emerged during this period can be seen in the work of Michele Ruggieri (1543–1607) and Matteo Ricci (1452–1610) in south-eastern China during the 1580s (Figure 2.4). Ricci's *True Record of the Lord of Heaven* (1585) is an excellent example of an apologetic work setting out basic Christian ideas in a way that made them accessible to Confucian readers.

The "Age of Reason"

Although the period of the European Reformation was very significant theologically, introducing important new debates about the nature of the church and the interpretation of the Bible, apologetic issues did not feature prominently in its agenda. During the later sixteenth century, Protestants and Catholics developed ways of defending their different understandings of Christianity against each other. Yet at this time, there was little attempt made to defend Christianity as a coherent belief system in the face of other ways of thinking. Debates tended to take place between different forms of Christianity – such as Calvinism, Catholicism, and Lutheranism – focusing on which specific form of Christianity could claim to be the most authentic. This represents a form of *denominational* apologetics, concerned with the defense of a particular version of Christianity, rather than a more general *Christian* apologetics, which focused on whether Christianity itself was defensible.

This began to change during the "Age of Reason" – a term often used, alongside "the Enlightenment" to refer to the increasingly rationalist culture that emerged in western Europe and North America during the course of the "long eighteenth century" (1685–1815). The "Enlightenment" was a complex phenomenon, which placed growing emphasis on the ability of unaided human reason to resolve religious, social, and political questions. It is probably best seen as a family of movements that emerged following the European Wars of Religion, reflecting a growing consensus that human reason offered a more reliable basis for communal decision making than religion. Enlightenment thinkers argued that human reason was the only reliable source of knowledge, and called into question many traditional cultural and religious ideas that were held to be open to rational critique. These included the doctrine of the Trinity and the concept of original sin.

This period created new challenges for the Christian churches, and led to the development of apologetic approaches to cope with the increasingly rationalist cultural mood in most parts of western Europe. In his *De veritate* ("On Truth"), the Dutch jurist and apologist Hugo Grotius set out to demonstrate the superiority of Christianity over rival religions, specifically paganism, Judaism, and Islam. In doing so, he set out reasons for his assertion that he believed met the criteria now expected for rational acceptance of a specific religious tradition. The use of such rational criteria was now, of course, without risks. One concern that critics of the approach noted was that it risked reducing Christianity to a rational philosophy, and failed to safeguard its spiritual and affective aspects.

This concern was addressed by Blaise Pascal, a prominent French theologian and mathematician. As the result of a spiritual experience during the night of 23 November 1654, Pascal spoke of his faith in "God of Abraham, God of Isaac, God of Jacob – not of the philosophers and scholars." While Pascal's apologetics are eminently reasonable, he emphasizes the limited capacity of reason to grasp reality, and the importance of the human heart in discovering religious faith. "The heart has its reasons of which reason knows nothing. It is the heart which perceives God and not the reason." Pascal does not endorse irrationalism here, but rather highlights the importance of the emotions and intuitions in perceiving God. Many recent apologists have found Pascal's approach helpful, and he remains one of the most influential contributors to the development of apologetics.

In England, the rise of the movement known as "Deism" led to growing interest in minimally counterintuitive forms of religion during the eighteenth century. Deism, by limiting God's role to the act of creation of the universe and the provision of human moral guidance, seemed to offer educated English society a form of religion that avoided what were seen as the rational difficulties of traditional Christian ideas such as the doctrine of the Trinity, or the divinity of Christ. The "scientific revolution" of the late seventeenth century led some to suggest that the universe was simply a machine that did not depend on God for its functioning.

The modern period also witnessed the emergence of a distinctively American approach to apologetics, especially in the writings of Jonathan Edwards (1703–1758). Although Edwards was remarkably well informed about trends in European philosophy, his apologetic approach is clearly grounded in the cultural realities of the American colonies. Edwards developed several apologetic strategies, mingling rational and affective approaches. He argued that the signs of beauty, design, and unity in the world were an indication of divine design, yet also emphasized the importance of engaging "religious affections," rather than merely offering "external arguments" for faith.

The early modern period saw apologetics become increasingly important, as the cultural mood became more critical of religious faith. Although external challenges – such as other religions – remained an important motivation for apologetics, these were supplemented by growing skepticism about certain core themes of Christianity within western culture. This trend continued in the nineteenth century, resulting in increasing attention being paid to apologetic issues in most major Christian denominations, both in western Europe and North America. Although the "Age of Reason" adopted an approach to rationality that is seen as problematic in the twenty-first century (see pp. 33–5), it remains important to show that the Christian faith is reasonable.

The Twentieth Century

In the opening decade of the twentieth century, apologetics was widely viewed with suspicion by many within the Christian churches. In 1907, the German liberal theologian Martin Rade argued that the term "apologetics" was a liability, and ought to be abandoned. Others, however, disagreed. In the first decades of the twentieth century, the English writer G. K. Chesterton developed an approach to apologetics that appealed to the imagination, showing how the core themes of the Christian faith – such as the incarnation – resonated deeply with human intuitions. For Chesterton, however, the appeal of Christianity lay not so much in any of its individual ideas, but in the overall greater picture of reality that resulted when these were woven together. As a journalist, Chesterton recognized the importance of good communicative skills, which were particularly well deployed in his "Father Brown" detective novels (published between 1910 and 1936), which became bestsellers during the "Golden Age of Detective Fiction." Where Arthur Conan Doyle's fictional detective Sherlock Holmes used purely rational approaches to solving cases, Father Brown used methods that were more intuitive and imaginative.

A similar approach is found in the writings of the novelist Dorothy L. Sayers, who held that Christianity was able to disclose and illuminate the deeper patterns of reality. Sayers authored some of the best-known British detective novels of the late 1920s and early 1930s, featuring her aristocratic amateur sleuth Lord Peter Wimsey. For Sayers, a detective discovering a pattern lying behind observed events is analogous to the tasks of Christian apologetics (pp. 178–81). Both tried to reach beyond outward appearances, and discover the deeper patterns of truth that lie behind them.

Chesterton established an important precedent in twentieth-century apologetics – the rise of a talented individual apologist, who stood outside church authority structures. Others in this tradition include J. R. R. Tolkien, C. S. Lewis, Sayers, and Marilynne Robinson, who saw themselves as called to use their literary gifts to defend and commend their faith. Lewis's principled advocation of "mere Christianity" – a consensual orthodoxy, which downplayed its institutional aspects – proved important in securing a growing acceptance of the importance of apologetics across denominational boundaries. Although there are points at which Lewis demonstrates a strongly rational approach to apologetics (such as sections of *Mere Christianity*), his more general approach is to hold together an appeal to the imagination, the use of stories to demonstrate how faith can change individual lives, and a reassurance that Christianity makes sense of what we observe in the world and experience within us.

After the Second World War, US voices began to play an increasingly important role in a conversation that had hitherto been dominated by European writers. This is to be seen as the natural outcome of the large number of seminaries and Christian colleges that emerged in the United States, and a concern for Christian higher education that is particularly – though not uniquely – characteristic of US Protestantism. The rise of what are sometimes termed "culture wars" in the United States are clearly of importance here, in that certain cultural shifts were seen to require an apologetic response on the part of Christian pastors and academics. Writers such as Cornelius van Til, Francis A. Schaeffer, Edward John Carnell, John Warwick Montgomery, and R. C. Sproul developed apologetic approaches and ministries that secured a significant and continuing place for apologetics both in Christian higher education and the life of the churches.

In the past fifty years, interest in apologetics has increased significantly within western Christianity, partly reflecting a growing awareness of the need to respond to secular challenges to religious belief on the one hand, and an increasing realization of its importance for Christian discipleship on the other. Where US apologetics of the second half of the twentieth century tended to be shaped by specific schools or methods – such as "evidentialism" and "presuppositionalism" – this has gradually given way to a more diverse range of approaches, often developed by individual apologists with their own specific concerns and ministries in mind. One of best examples is Timothy Keller, founding pastor of Redeemer Presbyterian Church, New York City, who developed an apologetic ministry in response to the questions raised by members of his young professional congregation (pp. 132–34). His best-selling *Reason for God* (2008) represents a strongly relational and pastoral response to these questions, engaging the person as a whole, aiming to demonstrate that the Christian faith is both truthful and transformative.

The surge in fortunes of Christian philosophy since the 1970s, often seen as reflecting the work of the Reformed philosopher Alvin Plantinga, did more than restore theism's legitimacy within the philosophical community; it also created a new interest in deploying philosophical defenses of faith in apologetics. The British philosopher Richard Swinburne has also achieved wide recognition for his defense of the rationality of faith, particularly his argument that the simplicity of theistic belief is an indication of its plausibility. Swinburne's landmark works *The Coherence of Theism* and *The Existence of God* remain widely cited, and have had a significant impact on many younger apologists. William Lane Craig's wide-ranging defense of Christianity has been very influential, particularly in student circles. Perhaps his most significant achievement has been the revitalization and redirection of the Kalām argument for the existence of God, which has arguably been given new significance through developments in scientific cosmology (pp. 46–7).

Two of the most significant – and possibly interconnected – forces in western culture are secularism and the natural sciences. How should apologetics relate to these trends? Many have drawn on the work of the Canadian social philosopher Charles Taylor, whose analysis of the nature and origins of secularism has been deeply influential. Taylor's *Secular Age* (2006) challenged the then-dominant model of secularization that holds that religion has gradually diminished in social influence and significance, arguing instead that the modern world is not characterized by the disappearance of religion but rather by its diversification and in many places its growth. The novelist and apologist Marilynne Robinson takes a different approach, arguing that the aesthetically and existentially limited account of our universe offered by modern naturalism fails to make sense of who we are, and is not warranted by the "evidence" that is cited in its support. "The modern world, insofar as it is proposed to humankind as its habitation, is too small, too dull, too meager for us. After all, we are very remarkable. We alone among the creatures have learned a bit of the grammar of the universe." We need a bigger, more satisfying view of reality, which acknowledges both the successes of the natural sciences, while at the same time recognizing its failure to answer life's deepest questions.

The natural sciences continue to be apologetically significant, not least because of the persistence of the "warfare" narrative of the relation of science and faith, which lies at the heart of the "New Atheism" of writers such as Richard Dawkins and Sam Harris in the first decade of the twenty-first century. John Lennox and Alister McGrath have both countered this atheist weaponizing of science, and developed apologetic approaches that challenge the "scientism" that underlies the "New Atheism."

It is clear that the apologetic scene has changed significantly in the west in the past two generations, both in terms of the questions being asked and the manner in which answers are given. Many apologists have noted that traditional questions (such as those concerning the authority of the Bible), though remaining important, seem to have receded in perceived significance on account of the rise of interest in more relational or existential questions (such as how to live, or the meaning of life). Further shifts may be expected in the future. Yet the diversity of approaches and responses are clear evidence of the ability of the ongoing importance of apologetics in helping ensure the churches are able to engage and answer life's deepest questions in ways that are theologically faithful and culturally relevant.

Conclusion

This chapter has offered a brief survey of some major themes in Christian apologetics, setting the context for more detailed discussion of these themes in the remainder of this work. While many readers will feel that engaging history has limited value, it is important to appreciate two points. First, Christian apologists have been present and active throughout the history of the church, defending faith against its critics, and exploring how faith connects with individuals and communities. And second, we can learn from these past approaches, offering an "apologetics of retrieval" that draws on the wisdom of the past by applying it to the present. At many points in this work, we shall reach into the past, dust off some older ways doing apologetics, and explore how they can have a new lease of life in today's situation. In the next chapter, we shall turn to consider one of the great themes of apologetics – the rationality of faith.

Study Questions

1. Each chapter ends with four "study questions" that are intended to help you review your understanding of this chapter and take your thinking further.
2. What were the three main apologetic concerns of New Testament writers?
3. What pressures seem to have caused the emergence of apologetics within early Christianity?
4. Why was apologetics seen as unimportant during the Reformation period?
5. Many twentieth-century British apologists were individuals with no positions of authority within any of the churches. How significant is this observation? What might it tell us about the place and role of apologists?

For Further Reading

Antonova, Stamenka Emilova. *Barbarian or Greek? The Charge of Barbarism and Early Christian Apologetics.* Leiden: Brill, 2019.

Baker, Deane. "Charles Taylor's 'Sources of the Self:' A Transcendental Apologetic?" *International Journal for Philosophy of Religion* 47, no. 3 (2000): 155–74.

Bruce, F. F. *The Defense of the Gospel in the New Testament.* Grand Rapids, MI: Eerdmans, 1977.

Craig, William Lane. *Reasonable Faith: Christian Truth and Apologetics.* 3rd ed. Wheaton, Ill.: Crossway Books, 2008.

Dulles, Avery. *A History of Apologetics.* 2nd ed. San Francisco, CA: Ignatius Press, 2005.

Edwards, Mark J., ed. *The Routledge Handbook of Early Christian Philosophy.* London: Routledge, 2021.

Edwards, Mark J., Martin Goodman, Simon R. F. Price, and Christopher Rowland, eds. *Apologetics in the Roman Empire: Pagans,*

Jews, Christians. Oxford: Oxford University Press, 1999.

Fontana, Michela. *Matteo Ricci: A Jesuit in the Ming Court.* London: Rowman & Littlefield, 2011.

Forrest, Benjamin K., Joshua D. Chatraw, and Alister E. McGrath, eds. *History of Apologetics: A Biographical and Methodological Introduction.* Grand Rapids, MI: Zondervan, 2020.

Gregerman, Adam. *Building on the Ruins of the Temple: Apologetics and Polemics in Early Christianity and Rabbinic Judaism.* Tübingen: Mohr Siebeck, 2016.

Gschwandtner, Christina M. *Postmodern Apologetics? Arguments for God in Contemporary Philosophy.* New York, NY: Fordham University Press, 2013.

Harrison, Peter. "'I Believe Because it is Absurd': The Enlightenment Invention of Tertullian's *Credo*." *Church History* 86, no. 2 (2017): 339–64.

Jacobsen, Anders-Christian, and Jörg Ulrich, eds. *Three Greek Apologists: Origen, Eusebius and Athanasius*. Frankfurt: Peter Lang, 2007.

Jacobsen, Anders-Christian. "The Apologists," in *The Early Christian World*, edited by Philip F. Esler, 547–64. 2nd ed. New York, NY: Routledge, 2017.

Janosik, Daniel, and Peter G. Riddell. *John of Damascus, First Apologist to the Muslims: The Trinity and Christian Apologetics in the Early Islamic Period*. Eugene, OR: Pickwick Publications, 2016.

Keating, Sandra Toenies. *Defending the "People of Truth" in the Early Islamic Period: The Christian Apologies of Abū Rā'iṭah*. Leiden: Brill, 2006.

Keener, Craig S. "Paul and Sedition: Pauline Apologetic in Acts." *Bulletin for Biblical Research* 22, no. 2 (2012): 201–24.

Louth, Andrew. (1970). "Reason and Revelation in Saint Athanasius." *Scottish Journal of Theology* 23, no. 4 (1970): 385–96.

Mihai, Constantin-Ionuţ. "Gregory Thaumaturgus and Early Christian Apologetics." *Vigiliae Christianae* 75, no. 2 (2021): 185–204.

Morris, Thomas V. *Making Sense of It All: Pascal and the Meaning of Life*. Grand Rapids, MI: Eerdmans, 1992.

Nielsen, Jørgen S., and Khalil Samir. *Christian Arabic Apologetics During the Abbasid Period (750–1258)*. Leiden: Brill, 1994.

Palmer, Daryl W. "Atheism, Apologetic and Negative Theology in the Greek Apologists of the Second Century." *Vigiliae Christianae* 37 (1983): 234–59.

Rade, Martin. "Bedenken gegen die Termini 'Apologetik' und 'christliche Weltanschauung.'" *Zeitschrift für Theologie und Kirche* 17 (1907): 423–35.

Rassi, Salam. *Christian Thought in the Medieval Islamicate World: Abdīshō of Nisibis and the Apologetic Tradition*. Oxford: Oxford University Press, 2022.

Ronan, Charles E., and Bonnie B. C. Oh, eds. *East Meets West: The Jesuits in China, 1582–1773*. Chicago: Loyola University Press, 1988.

Standaert, Nicolas. *Methodology in View of Contact Between Cultures: The China Case in the 17th Century*. Hong Kong: Chinese University of Hong Kong, 2002.

Wang, Xiaochao. *Christianity and Imperial Culture: Chinese Christian Apologetics in the Seventeenth Century and their Latin Patristic Equivalent*. Leiden: Brill, 1998.

Weir, Todd H., and Hugh McLeod, eds. *Defending the Faith: Global Histories of Apologetics and Politics in the 20th Century*. Oxford: Oxford University Press, 2021.

Williams, Daniel H. *Defending and Defining the Faith: An Introduction to Early Christian Apologetic Literature*. New York, NY: Oxford University Press, 2020.

3

The Rationality of Faith

A central task of Christian apologetics is to show the reasonableness of faith. So what does it mean to declare that an individual belief or a belief system is "rational"? Two main answers can be given to this question. First, a theory is "rational" if it is *evidenced* – that is to say, that the evidence demands or compels it. And second, a theory is "rational" if it is able to connect and coordinate a series of observations better than its rivals. Both these understandings of rationality have been widely used within Christian apologetics, and have their parallels in other forms of human reflection – such as the natural sciences.

Most Christian apologists believe it is important to *affirm* and to *demonstrate* that Christianity is rational, both in the sense that good reasons may be given for its core beliefs, and that the Christian faith is able to make sense of the world of observation and experience. These two are seen as interconnected, in that the ability of Christianity to make sense of experience and observation is seen as an indication of its truth. A good example of this lies in the novelist Dorothy L. Sayers, one of the most influential British apologists of the twentieth century. Sayers was quite clear why she was drawn to Christianity. Her faith gave her a tool by which she might "make sense of the universe," disclosing hidden patterns and allowing meaning to be discerned within its otherwise opaque mysteries. Many share Sayers's desire to be able to make sense of their world and their lives.

Yet Christianity is not simply a rational belief system, something that is true which changes the way we *think*. It is something that can create and sustain a meaningful mode of *living*. There is no necessary connection between something being *true* and being *transformative* – think, for example, of the complex absence of any existential payload to the true statements "2 + 2 = 4" and "the whole is greater than the part."

Christian Apologetics: An Introduction, First Edition. Alister E. McGrath.
© 2024 John Wiley & Sons Ltd. Published 2024 by John Wiley & Sons Ltd.

The French classical scholar Pierre Hadot has pointed out that most schools of ancient philosophy saw their cultural role as extending far beyond intellectual reflection to include the development of a "way of life" that integrated belief and practice. Philosophy in the ancient world was more than intellectual doctrines; it was also a summons to live out the good life by articulating a certain ideal of the good, and equipping people to pursue it. A philosopher was thus understood to be "a person who has made a certain life-choice and accepted a certain way of life."

Early Christianity was thus seen as a form of wisdom that could be lived out – a conceptual or imaginative framework that made sense of the human quest for identity, purpose, meaning, truth, and beauty on the one hand, and showed how these goals might be achieved, despite the many failings and foibles of human nature, on the other. Christianity helped its followers to understand the nature of the world and to live with integrity within it, always conscious of the need for divine grace in achieving its goals. The appeal of early Christianity to late classical antiquity was grounded partly in its perceived ability to transform lives and create people of character. Christianity offered a way of *coping* with suffering, rather than offering intellectual explanations for its presence (pp. 129; 151–52).

Many now argue that we live in a post-rationalist age, in which the deficits and limits of human reason are generally conceded, especially among younger people. Richard Dawkins (Figure 3.1) and other writers associated with the "New Atheism" seem to be locked into an outdated rationalism with their demands that believers "prove" the existence of God (while conveniently overlooking their own inability to "prove" that

Figure 3.1   The British evolutionary biologist Richard Dawkins and celebrity atheist, author of *The God Delusion* (2006). Alamy Image GBBDW7.

there is no God). Francis Spufford expresses this cultural suspicion of slick "rational" arguments for and against the existence of God in his influential work *Unapologetic* (2013): "I don't know if there's a God. (And neither do you, and neither does Professor Richard Dawkins, and neither does anybody. It isn't the kind of thing you can know. It isn't a knowable item.)"

Spufford isn't advocating irrationalism, but simply warning us against a naïve overreliance on human reason. Like any tool, reason needs to be calibrated and checked out. "Rationalism" is basically an overreliance on reason to answer all our questions, just as "emotionalism" represents an excessive dependence on our feelings. Yet reason and feelings both have a proper and valuable place in apologetics.

In this chapter, we explore the rationality of the Christian faith. Yet first, we need to set the context for this discussion. Why is it important apologetically to show that Christianity is rational?

Setting the Context: Apologetics in a Post-rationalist Age

As we noted in the previous chapter, the rise of the "Age of Reason" in the eighteenth century created new challenges for Christian theology in western Europe, North America, and Australasia – but not, it must be stressed, in Africa, Asia, or Latin America. The rise of rationalism in western culture was partly precipitated by the destructiveness of the European Wars of Religion, particularly the Thirty Years War (which lasted from 1618 to 1648), which led to growing cultural suspicion of organized religion, raising questions about its social role and rationality. Descartes' *Discourse on Method* (1637) and Spinoza's *Ethics* (1677) helped create a philosophical culture that gave priority to human reason in establishing and validating beliefs. Many scholars now argue that the defining characteristic of modern philosophy is that it tries to establish its beliefs with certitude, without recourse to God, on the basis of the necessary truths of reason.

The phrase "The Age of Reason," often used as a synonym for the Enlightenment, is misleading, as it implies that reason had been ignored or marginalized up to this point. Yet the Middle Ages can quite legitimately be thought of as an "Age of Reason" in its own terms, developing sophisticated rational defenses of religious belief, including Thomas Aquinas's "Five Ways," which we shall consider later in this chapter. Yet there is a significant difference here: where medieval writers saw human reason primarily as a *critical tool* in developing knowledge (for example, by reflecting on the truths of revelation and their implications), the Enlightenment considered that unaided human reason was the *foundation* of reliable human knowledge. "Rationalism" thus came to designate ideas that were derived and justified by pure reason. Western European rational norms were treated as universally valid, independent of location and history. Patterns of human reasoning are partly shaped by their historical context. What was in effect a "local" rationality was thus treated as being universally valid.

Some Christian apologists responded to the rise of the "Age of Reason" by developing rigorously logical or argumentative approaches to faith. Yet, while it is important to show the rationality of faith, apologetics can too easily become little more than a technique for winning arguments with people outside the community of faith (pp. 1; 54–5). There is a danger that using such strongly argumentative approaches traps us in the mentality of a bygone age, in effect imprisoning us within what Max Weber famously described as the "iron cage" of rationalism. Furthermore, emphasizing the rationality of Christianity can lead to the cultural perception that Christianity is simply about *ideas*. As Marilynne Robinson rightly points out, these "arguments" often seem spiritually thin and epistemologically simplistic. "I think the attempt to defend belief can unsettle it, in fact, because there is always an inadequacy in argument about ultimate things."

Recent philosophical critics of the Enlightenment – such as Alasdair MacIntyre or John Gray – have argued that its quest for a universal foundation and criterion of knowledge collapsed under the weight of a massive accumulation of counterevidence. The vision of a single universal rationality simply could not be defended or achieved. As human beings, we have no choice but to realize we must live in the absence of any clear, unambiguous, absolute, and purely rational truths. We must indeed articulate and defend criteria by which our beliefs may be justified; yet we must also realize those beliefs may lie beyond proof. MacIntyre, for example, argued that the Enlightenment notion of a universal human rationality could not be defended on the basis of the historical evidence: "There is no standing ground, no place for enquiry, no way to engage in the practices of advancing, evaluating, accepting, and rejecting reasoned argument apart from that which is provided by some particular tradition or other."

MacIntyre's view has been influential, and has secured widespread acceptance in academic circles. The Enlightenment, on his analysis, is simply a specific tradition of thinking that falsely believed that it was universally valid. MacIntyre's historical and philosophical analysis has made it clear that the sheer diversity of "rational" approaches to justice and ethics leads inevitably to the conclusion that "the legacy of the Enlightenment has been the provision of an ideal of rational justification which it has proved impossible to attain."

This is highly important apologetically. There is no universal standard of rationality by which Christianity can be judged. What really matters is to show that Christianity is internally coherent, that it can make sense of what we experience within us and observe around us, and that it can connect up with things that really matter to people – such as their longing for meaning and significance. These themes are clearly present in earlier periods of Christian apologetics, especially in early Christianity and during the Middle Ages. It is time to retrieve these approaches, and put them to new use, now that the hard rationalism of the Enlightenment is receding.

The limits of a rationalist approach to apologetics were emphasized by the great eighteenth-century American Puritan theologian Jonathan Edwards (1703–1758), who remains one of the most significant critics of a purely rationalist approach to apologetics. Edwards, one of the leading figures in the "Great Awakening" (a major religious revival that took place in New England during the 1730s and 1740s), believed that while rational argument had a valuable and important place in Christian apologetics, it was not the sole, and perhaps not even the most important, resource for the apologist. For Edwards, apologetics engages not only the mind but also the heart and the imagination, and we impoverish the gospel if we neglect the impact it has on all of our God-given faculties.

Great use may be made of external arguments, they are not to be neglected, but highly prized and valued; for they may be greatly serviceable to awaken unbelievers, and bring them to serious consideration, and to confirm the faith of true saints ... [Yet] there is no spiritual conviction of the judgment, but what arises from an apprehension of the spiritual beauty and glory of divine things.

Edwards's insight is that rational arguments do not *convert*, although they may change people's minds and make them more receptive to faith. Arguments may remove obstacles to conversion and support the faith of believers, but in and of themselves they do not possess the capacity to transform humanity. For Edwards, true conversion rests on an encounter with a glorious and gracious God, not being persuaded by an argument. This insight is liberating, in that it reaffirms that apologetics is not about developing manipulative human techniques, but about recognizing and coming to rely upon the grace and glory of God. It is about helping people to discover the Christian vision of God, which cannot be communicated or expressed adequately in words.

So can the Christian faith be shown to be reasonable? Or is it, as some of its more severe critics suggest, incapable of rational justification? For New Atheist writers such as Richard Dawkins and Christopher Hitchens, rational human beings just *think*, whereas religious people think *in the light of their religious commitments* – and so are locked inside a religious worldview that is impervious to criticism. The New Atheist philosopher A. C. Grayling echoes this concern, arguing that theological reasoning was unacceptable to a rational person because it was undertaken within "the premises and parameters" of a system. Yet Grayling seems to overlook the important fact that *all* human thinking – including scientific thinking – takes place within "the premises and parameters" of some system or other, including mathematics and logic.

With the passing of a dominant rationalist worldview in western Europe and North America, it is now possible to recover a broader approach to apologetics as a means of depicting Christianity's concern for beauty, goodness, and truth faithfully and vividly, so that people can be drawn by the richness and depth of its vision of reality.

In this chapter, we shall consider some major themes linked with the rationality of faith. Perhaps the best starting point is to consider the Christian idea of faith, and how this can be considered to be "reasonable." Apologetics is both about justifying the idea of trusting certain things that cannot be proved to be right, as well as offering justifications of what it is that is believed.

Faith as Justified Belief

What does "faith" mean? Christian writers down the ages have distinguished two senses of the word "faith." First, there is "a faith by which we believe" – that is to say, the act of trust and assent that says "yes" to God, and reaches out to grasp and hold fast to God as the secure ground of our life and thought. Second, there is a "faith which we believe" – in other words, a set of beliefs, such as those set out in the Creeds. In this sense of the word, faith refers to the *content* of what Christians believe, rather than the *act* of believing and trusting. In this chapter, our concern focusses primarily on the intellectual motivations for the *act* of believing. How are we to understand this?

Most people outside Christianity regard faith merely as some kind of belief or intellectual assent. To believe in God is to believe that God exists. Faith is a lower form of knowledge, dealing with matters or opinion or judgement, rather than matters that can be proved to be true. Yet, as Ludwig Wittgenstein pointed out, it is important to listen to how a community uses its language. If you want to understand what a person or group of people mean by a word, you have to listen to them, and see how they actually use that word. The Apostles' Creed, for example, opens with the Latin word *credo*, which is almost always translated as "I believe." Yet the meaning of this Latin word when the Creeds were written was "to trust or confide in a person or thing; to have confidence in; to trust." Recent scholarship suggests that the predominant sense of "faith" in the cultural world of the New Testament is best described as "relational trust."

The early Christian historian Teresa Morgan, for example, makes the point that "the operation of trust in the relationship between God, Christ, and humanity is, for Christians, historically and theologically foundational, and that by exploring it we do better justice to our understanding of Christian faith." While many today think of faith in terms of an *intellectual judgement*, the creeds see faith also as a *personal commitment*. The fifth-century theologian Faustus of Riez thus explained to his readers that to believe (*credere*) in God means to "respond to God in worship and adoration, by giving ourselves and our affections completely over to God." Faith thus involves the mind, the heart, and the will; it is relational, not just rational.

Faith is thus a venture, a relational journey in which believers entrust themselves to the one on whom they rely – not blindly, but on account of insights, intuitions, and reflections that lead them to conclude that this is a reasonable step to take. Faith is not merely *cognitive* ("I believe this statement is true"), but also *relational* and *existential* ("I trust this person"). As C. S. Lewis once remarked, you are not faced "with an argument which demands your assent, but with a Person who demands your confidence." Faith is about entrusting ourselves to God. Yet this act of trust or belief is held to be *warranted*, in that there are good reasons for trusting this. This point is emphasized by the US philosopher Alvin Plantinga, who argues that the "foundationalism" inherited from the "Age of Reason" creates false expectations about both the *nature of belief,* and the *reasons for belief.*

The Anglican theologian W. H. Griffith-Thomas offered a definition that integrates many of the key aspects of the Christian understanding of faith:

> [Faith] commences with the conviction of the mind based on adequate evidence; it continues in the confidence of the heart or emotions based on conviction, and it is crowned in the consent of the will, by means of which the conviction and confidence are expressed in conduct.

This useful definition weaves together the core elements of the characteristic Christian understanding of faith, and making it clear that faith involves the mind, the heart, and the will. The Genevan Protestant John Calvin made some similar points in his often-cited definition of faith in his *Institutes of the Christian Religion* (Figure 3.2):

INSTITVTIO CHRI-
ſtianæ religionis, in libros qua-
tuor nunc primùm digeſta, certiſque diſtincta capitibus, ad aptiſſimam
methodum : aucta etiam tam magna acceſſione vt propemodum opus
nouum haberi poſſit.

IOHANNE CALVINO AVTHORE.

Oliua Roberti Stephani.

GENEVAE.
M. D. LIX.

Figure 3.2   The front cover of the 1559 edition of John Calvin's *Institutes of the Christian Religion*, one of the most influential theological works of the sixteenth century. Alamy Image 2AG1128.

> [Faith] is a steady and certain knowledge of the divine benevolence towards us which is founded upon the truth of the gracious promise of God in Christ, and is both revealed to our minds and sealed in our hearts by the Holy Spirit.

Let's try to weave these themes together. In very general terms, Christianity uses the term "faith" to designate an attitude of warranted intellectual and relational trust, with three core elements.

1. Faith is about believing in a "state of affairs" in which certain things are true. When I say that I "believe in God," I mean that I think (and trust) that God exists. Faith is thus assent to a set of beliefs about the nature of reality. "I believe in God" means something like "I believe that there is a God," or "I think that God exists." This is a good starting point for an apologetic discussion. Before we can begin to say anything about what God is like, or the difference that belief in God can make to human existence, we need to start from the belief that there is a God in the first place.

2. Faith is trust. When I say that I believe in the promises of God, I am declaring that I *trust* them. Faith is thus more than a recognition that these promises exist; it is an awareness that they can be – and are *meant* to be – trusted and relied upon. As Martin Luther constantly emphasized, faith trusts in a God who makes promises: "For where there is the word of the promising God, there must also be the faith of the accepting person, so that the beginning of our salvation is a faith which clings to the Word of the promising God."

3. Faith is entry into the promises of God, receiving what they have to offer. Having recognized that the promises exist, and that they can be trusted, it is necessary to act upon them – to enter into them, and benefit from them by receiving what is promised. The first two stages of faith prepare the way for the third; without it, they are incomplete.

Faith, Evidence, and Uncertainty: From Clifford to Dawkins

The idea of trusting certain beliefs that cannot be proved to be true has been subjected to much criticism. Many rationalist writers, such as Richard Dawkins, follow the English mathematician William K. Clifford's 1877 declaration that "it is wrong always, everywhere, and for anyone, to believe anything upon insufficient evidence." Nobody should be allowed to believe something that was argumentatively or evidentially underdetermined. This, Clifford argued, is not simply an intellectual responsibility; it is a fundamental *moral* duty. Dawkins takes a similar view, arguing that faith refuses to engage evidence. For Dawkins, faith "means blind trust, in the absence of evidence, even in the teeth of evidence." While this is an interesting and influential assertion, the situation is really much more complicated than either Clifford or Dawkins seems to realize.

To appreciate this point, let us consider the major scientific debate about whether our universe is singular, or one among many universes (a hypothesis known as the "multiverse"). The evidence is inconclusive, and both possibilities have their supporters within the scientific community. But if Clifford is right, scientists should not support *either* option, in that there is "insufficient evidence" for each. No verdict can be reached on the basis of the evidence available, which is not compelling in either case. Happily, scientists are now much more aware of the problems of evidential underdetermination and theoretical provisionality than Clifford was. Even Richard Dawkins has come down in support of the rather speculative multiverse theory – for *theological* reasons. The cosmologist Bernard Carr famously remarked that "if you don't want God, you'd better have a multiverse." To his critics, Dawkins seems to have come down in favor of this under-evidenced option simply because it suits his own atheist beliefs.

Today, Clifford's statement is generally regarded as a rhetorical flourish, an attention-seeking overstatement by someone who wanted to impose mathematical conceptions of proof on everyone else. It is widely agreed that, by Clifford's own criteria, he could not be an "atheist," in the sense of someone who had *proved* that there was no God, and even in the weaker sense of someone who believes there is no God. A generation later, the philosopher and psychologist William James criticized Clifford, arguing that there are other proper grounds for belief than "sufficient evidence." In a powerful critique of the Enlightenment's aspiration to a certainty of knowledge that could not be achieved in practice outside the specific fields of mathematics and logic, James argued that in most cases a degree of uncertainty had to be acknowledged – and that this is something that most people accommodate without difficulty. Situations arise in which the evidence is equivocal but a decision is required. James and other writers in the pragmatist tradition argued that we may legitimately accept beliefs on nonevidential grounds, and live with a degree of uncertainty concerning their evidential basis. As the literary critic Terry Eagleton points out in response to Dawkins' refusal to entertain beliefs that cannot be proved, "we hold many beliefs that have no unimpeachably rational justification, but are nonetheless reasonable to entertain."

This view is also expressed in Bertrand Russell's significant assessment of the tasks of philosophy: "To teach how to live without certainty, and yet without being paralyzed by hesitation, is perhaps the chief thing that philosophy, in our age, can still do for those who study it." The intellectual historian and philosopher Sir Isaiah Berlin expressed this point more forcibly in his famous lecture "The Pursuit of the Ideal," in which he offered a philosophical demolition of those who have, by their own methods, arrived at "clear and unshakeable convictions about what to do and what to be that brook no possible doubt." Berlin was scathing about the foundations and implications of such epistemic arrogance, which amounted to little more than wish-fulfilment: "I can only say that those who rest on such comfortable beds of dogma are victims of forms of self-induced myopia, blinkers that make for contentment, but not for understanding of what it is to be human."

Russell and Berlin clearly call into question the shallow philosophical grounds of Clifford's atheism. Yet there is another point to be considered here. While Russell is often referenced as an "atheist" philosopher, Russell explicitly identified himself as an *agnostic*, in that he regarded the question of God as lying beyond proof. Russell took the *pragmatic* view that he could live *as if* there were no God, despite being unable to *prove* that this was the case. As the philosopher John Gray points out, an atheist is better defined as someone who has no use for God, not someone who has *proved* there is no God – for this intellectual demonstration simply lies beyond the reach of reason and evidence. Happily, some apologists have taken on board the implications of this chastened approach to the capacity and limits of human reason.

The Canadian philosopher and apologist John Stackhouse argues for "finding a middle course between unjustifiable certainty and cynical despair." No philosophy or theology can offer us a "perfect knowledge that answers all our questions to our complete satisfaction"; there are always going to be gaps, anomalies, and tensions in any attempt to make sense of life, reflecting the complexity of our world on the one hand, and the cultural embeddedness and limits of human reasoning on the other.

Charles Darwin.

Figure 3.3   The English naturalist Charles Darwin (1809–1882), author of *The Origin of Species* (1859). Adobe Stock Image 37313232.

Perhaps more interestingly, others pointed out that David Hume's critique of inductive generalizations meant that Clifford's overstatement undermined much of the work of the natural sciences. Charles Darwin (Figure 3.3), for example, was adamant that his 1859 "theory of natural selection" could not be proved to be true, and was evidentially underdetermined. Yet Darwin was quite clear that his theory of natural selection could still be trusted on account of its capacity to accommodate the evidence. In a letter praising the perspicuity of the naturalist F. W. Hutton, Darwin declared that "he is one of the very few who see that the change of species cannot be directly proved, and that the doctrine must sink or swim according as it groups and explains phenomena."

Yet even though Darwin did not believe that he had adequately dealt with all the philosophical problems that required resolution, he was confident that his explanation was the best available. A comment added to the sixth (and final) edition of *The Origin of Species* makes this point clear.

> It can hardly be supposed that a false theory would explain, in so satisfactory a manner as does the theory of natural selection, the several large classes of facts above specified. It has recently been objected that this is an unsafe method of arguing; but it is a method used in judging the common events of life, and has often been used by the greatest natural philosophers.

While recognizing that his theory could not be proved with total certainty, Darwin clearly believed that it could be defended on the basis of criteria of acceptance and justification that were already widely used in the natural sciences, and that its explanatory capacity was itself a reliable guide to its truth. If Darwin had adopted Clifford's criteria of rationality, he could not have been confident about the basis of his theory of natural selection.

Darwin's point needs to be taken seriously. In the philosophy of science, theories are often proposed because they appear to offer the best conceptual framework to hold together a wide range of observations. It is not so much that the observations *prove* those theories, but that the theories appear to offer the best framework to coordinate those observations. As we noted earlier in this chapter (pp. 38–40), this underlies what has become the dominant philosophy of science, now generally known as "inference to the best explanation." As Richard Swinburne and others have noted (pp. 51–4) this offers some important intellectual tools for Christian apologists.

Against those who demand proof for all beliefs and certainty in all intellectual commitments, the quantum theorist and theologian John Polkinghorne points out that no form of human truth-seeking enquiry – whether science or Christian faith – can attain absolute certainty about its conclusions. Faith is "a coherent and rationally motivated view of the way the world is." For Polkinghorne, neither science nor theology can ever hope to establish or attain a "logically coercive proof of the kind that only a fool could deny." Both enterprises necessarily involve "some degree of intellectual precariousness." The "unavoidable epistemic condition of humanity" is that we commit ourselves to beliefs that we have good reason to accept as true, but cannot prove to be true. We believe what we trust to be true, but cannot prove to be true – but believe there are good reasons for trusting this. Faith is thus a form of justified belief.

Arguments for the Existence of God: Three Approaches

Although we have already begun to consider some of the argumentative pathways used by Christian apologists in this chapter, we shall now focus on three broad families of approaches that are often discussed in philosophical textbooks. We begin by considering Thomas Aquinas's celebrated "Five Ways" – a set of classic "arguments" for the existence of God that are widely discussed in the literature, and can be developed in a variety of ways in an apologetic context.

Thomas Aquinas: The Five Ways

Thomas Aquinas (Figure 3.4), probably the most famous and influential theologian of the Middle Ages, is best known for his *Summa Theologiae*, composed towards the end of his life and not totally finished at the time of his death. However, he also wrote many other significant works, particularly the *Summa contra Gentiles*, which represents a classic statement of the rationality of the Christian faith, and especially the existence of God.

Figure 3.4   Thomas Aquinas (1225–1274), fresco by Andrea di Buonaiuto, Spanish Chapel in Santa Maria Novella church in Florence, Italy. Adobe Stock Image 255396860.

Aquinas believed that it was entirely proper to identify pointers towards the existence of God, based on general human experience of the world. His "Five Ways" represent five lines of argument in support of the existence of God, each of which draws on some aspect of the world that "points" to the existence of its creator.

So what kind of pointers does Aquinas have in mind? The basic line of thought guiding Aquinas is that the world mirrors God, as its creator – an idea which is given more formal expression in his doctrine of the "analogy of being." Just as an artist might sign a painting to identify it as his handiwork, so God has stamped a divine "signature" upon the creation. What we observe in the world – for example, its signs of ordering – can be explained if God was its creator. If God both brought the world into existence, and impressed the divine image and likeness upon it, then something of God's nature can be known from the creation.

So where might we look in creation to find evidence for the existence of God? Aquinas argues that the ordering of the world is the most convincing evidence of God's existence and wisdom. This basic assumption underlies each of the "Five Ways," although it is of particular importance in the case of the argument often referred to as the "argument from design" or the "teleological argument."

The first way begins from the observation that things in the world are in motion or change. The world is not static, but is dynamic. Examples of this are easy to list. Rain falls from the sky. Stones roll down valleys. This is normally referred to as the "argument from motion"; however, it is clear that the "movement" in question is actually understood in more general terms, so that the term "change" is more appropriate as a translation at points.

So how did nature come to be in motion? Why is it changing? Aquinas argues that everything that moves is moved by something else. For every motion, there is a cause. Things don't just move; they are moved by something else. Now each cause of motion must itself have a cause. And that cause must have a cause as well. And so Aquinas argues that there is a whole series of causes of motion lying behind the world as we know it. Now unless there is an infinite number of these causes, Aquinas argues, there must be a single cause right at the origin of the series. From this original cause of motion, all other motion is ultimately derived. This is the origin of the great chain of causality, which we see reflected in the way the world behaves. From the fact that things are in motion, Aquinas thus argues for the existence of a single original cause of all this motion. This, Aquinas insists, can only be God.

In more recent times, this argument has been restated in terms of God as the one who brought the universe into existence. For this reason, it is often referred to as the "cosmological" argument (from the Greek word *kosmos*, meaning "universe"). The most commonly encountered statement of the argument runs along the following lines:

1. Everything within the universe depends on something else for its existence;
2. What is true of its individual parts is also true of the universe itself;
3. The universe thus depends on something else for its existence for as long as it has existed or will exist;
4. The universe thus depends on God for its existence.

The argument basically assumes that the existence of the universe is something that requires explanation. It will be clear that this type of argument relates directly to modern cosmological research, particularly the "big-bang" theory of the origins of the cosmos.

The second way begins from the idea of causation. One event (the effect) is explained by the influence of another (the cause). Using a line of reasoning similar to that discussed earlier, Aquinas argues that all effects may be traced back to a single original cause – which is God.

The third way concerns the existence of contingent beings – in other words, beings that are not there as a matter of necessity. Aquinas contrasts this type of being with a necessary being (one who is there as a matter of necessity). While God is a necessary being, Aquinas argues that humans are contingent beings. The fact that we are here needs explanation. Why are we here? What happened to bring us into existence? Aquinas argues that a being comes into existence because something, which already exists, brought it into being. In other words, our existence is caused by another being. We are the effects of a series of causation. Tracing this series back to its origin, Aquinas declares that this original cause of being can only be someone whose existence is necessary – in other words, God.

The fourth way begins from human values, such as truth, goodness, and nobility. Where do these values come from? What causes them? Aquinas argues that there must be something which is in itself true, good, and noble, and that this brings into being our ideas of truth, goodness, and nobility. The origin of these ideas, Aquinas suggests, is God, who is their original cause.

The fifth and final way is known as the teleological argument, which derives its name from the Greek word *telos*, meaning "purpose" or "goal." Aquinas notes that the world shows obvious traces of intelligent design. Natural processes and objects seem to be adapted with certain definite objectives in mind. They seem to have a purpose. They seem to have been designed. But things don't design themselves: they are caused and designed by someone or something else. Arguing from this observation, Aquinas concludes that the source of this natural ordering must be conceded to be God.

Aquinas did not see his five "ways" as *proving* God's existence, making it clear that these were each to be seen as ways of demonstrating the internal rationality of the Christian faith. Aquinas thus uses the Latin term *ratio* ("reason") to refer to his approaches, rather than the stronger term *demonstratio* ("proof"). They remain important for modern Christian apologists, particularly in developing "big-picture" approaches to Christianity that aim to show how effectively Christianity can fit in or "accommodate" multiple aspects of the world.

Aquinas's fifth argument has been taken up extensively by later apologists. Although William Paley does not reference Aquinas as a source for this thinking, Paley's own argument for God in his famous *Natural Theology* (1802) echoes some of his themes. The biological world is too complex to have happened accidentally. Furthermore, the natural world seems to have an inbuilt teleology, in that they appear to be directed towards the production of certain ends or goals. The observation of design suggests the existence of a designer. Paley's point is important, but it is open to criticism. John Henry Newman, for example, took the view that the natural world could reinforce a Christian's belief in God as creator; it could not, however, give rise to that belief in the first place. "I believe in design because I believe in God, not in a God because I believe in design."

Anselm of Canterbury: The Ontological Argument

Anselm of Canterbury (c. 1033–1109) is noted for his strong defense of the intellectual foundations of Christianity, and especially for his "ontological argument" for the existence of God, first set out in his *Proslogion*, a work of spiritual meditation that dates from 1079. In the course of this work, Anselm reflects on how self-evident the idea of God has become to him, and what the implications of this might be. Anselm does not refer to his discussion of the plausibility of God either as "ontological" (a term that refers to the branch of philosophy that deals with the notion of "being") or an "argument." It was, as far as Anselm was concerned, simply an extended meditation on the internal coherence of faith. Later philosophers of religion have, however, isolated Anselm's line of thought from its informing context, which makes it seem strange and unconvincing for those unaware of its original setting.

In the *Proslogion*, Anselm suggests that we think of God as "that than which no greater thing can be conceived." In other words, God is something that exceeds any production of the human mind or imagination. If this way of thinking about God is correct, Anselm points out, it necessarily implies the existence of God. Why? Well, if God does not exist, then only the *idea* of God remains in the human mind, even though there is no God that it corresponds to. Yet, Anselm points out, the *reality* of God must greater than the *idea* of God. Therefore, if God is "that than which no greater thing can be conceived," this specific definition of God must lead to accepting the *reality* of God, in that otherwise the mere *idea* of God is the greatest thing that can be conceived. Therefore, given the existence of the idea of God, and the acceptance of the definition of God as "that than which no greater thing can be thought," the reality of this God necessarily follows. Anselm expresses this point as follows:

> There exists something than which nothing greater can be thought, that it cannot be thought of as not existing. And you are this thing, O Lord our God! So truly therefore do you exist, O Lord my God, that you cannot be thought of as not existing, and with good reason; for if a human mind could think of anything greater than you, the creature would rise above the Creator and judge you; which is obviously absurd.

This argument did not persuade one of Anselm's earliest critics, the Benedictine monk Gaunilo of Marmoutiers, who wrote a response known as "A Reply on Behalf of the Fool" (the reference being to Psalm 14:1, cited by Anselm, "The fool says in his heart that there is no God"). There is, according to Gaunilo, an obvious logical weakness in Anselm's "argument" (although it must be stressed than Anselm does not really regard it as an argument in the first place). Imagine, Gaunilo suggests, an island, so lovely that a more perfect island cannot be conceived. By the same argument, Gaunilo suggested, that island must exist, in that the reality of the island is necessarily more perfect that the mere idea. Yet this might be nothing more than an imagined island, a fantasy of the human mind.

Many consider that Gaunilo exposed a serious weakness in Anselm's argument. It may, however, be pointed out that Anselm is not so easily dismissed. Part of his argument is that it is an essential part of the definition of God that he is "that than which nothing greater can be conceived." God therefore belongs to a totally different category than islands. It is part of the nature of God to transcend everything else. Furthermore, Anselm argued that Gaunilo had not entirely understood him. The argument that he set out in the *Proslogion* did not involve the idea that there is a being that is, as a matter of fact, greater than any other being; rather, Anselm had argued for a being so great that a greater one could not even be *conceived*. The argument continues, and it remains a disputed question to this day as to whether Anselm's argument has a genuine basis.

So what use is this argument? While the argument has attracted much interest in recent years among philosophers – such as Alvin Plantinga – relatively few apologists now use it. In the first place, the argument is abstract and theoretical, and many find it difficult to understand (even in the condensed and simplified version I have set out in this section). It is difficult to see how this could be used in an apologetic talk or sermon. In the second place, it also seems implausible. Many would sympathize with Thomas Aquinas's view that a concept may exist in the human mind without any corresponding existence in reality. Anselm's argument requires that the inference of reality from mental concepts is only valid in one specific case, namely God, and does not apply to Gaunilo's island. Yet whatever its philosophical merits, this point is difficult to *communicate* simply and effectively in most apologetic contexts.

However, Anselm's approach has been reworked and reframed in an apologetically useful way in C. S. Lewis's first published book, *The Pilgrim's Regress* (1933). Lewis wrote this book in a burst of sustained literary activity between 15 and 29 August 1932 in Belfast. Its central character is the pilgrim – "John" – who has visions of an Island that evokes a sense of intense yet transitory longing on his part. At times, John is overwhelmed by this sense of yearning, as he struggles to make sense of it. Where does it come from? What is he yearning for?

So what is the ultimate object of this "intense longing"? Lewis sets out an early form of his "argument from desire," exploring a line of thought originally developed by Pascal – namely, that there is an "abyss" within the human soul, which is so great that only God can fill it. Or, to change the imagery, there is a "chair" in the human soul, awaiting some guest who has yet to arrive. "If nature makes nothing in vain, the One who can sit in this chair must exist."

We initially understand this desire as a yearning for something tangible within the world; then we realize that nothing within the world is able to satisfy our Desire. John, the pilgrim, initially desires the Island. Yet he gradually comes to realize that his true longing is actually for the "Landlord" – Lewis's way of referring to God. All other explanations and proposed goals for this sense of yearning fail to satisfy, intellectually or existentially. They are "false objects" of Desire, whose falsity is ultimately exposed by their failure to satisfy the deepest yearnings of humanity.

> If a man diligently followed this desire, pursuing the false objects until their falsity appeared and then resolutely abandoning them, he must at last come into the clear knowledge that the human soul was made to enjoy some object that is never fully given – nay, cannot even be imagined as given – in our present mode of subjective and spatio-temporal experience.

There is indeed a chair in the human soul, Lewis declares, and its intended occupant is God. Where Anselm argues from our *mental concepts* to the ontological reality of God, Lewis argues that our *desires* disclose God as an ontological reality, who alone can satisfy human longings precisely because this God is both the ground and goal of our longings. Our experience of this "Desire" both discloses our true identity, and points to our true goal.

Lewis's reformulation of the ontological argument is apologetically more helpful than Anselm's original approach. In the first place, it connects up with the common human experience of desire or longing; in the second, it makes the more plausible claim that for every human desire there is a corresponding reality that this desire points to, and which can satisfy it. Lewis later reworked this into his "argument from desire" (pp. 49–51), which is widely used in contemporary Christian apologetics.

William Lane Craig: The Kalām Argument

What is now generally known as the "Kalām" argument derives its name from an Islamic school of philosophy that flourished in the early Middle Ages. One of its most significant representatives is Al-Ghazālī (c. 1056–1111), a twelfth-century Islamic theologian whose book *The Incoherence of the Philosophers* set out a critique of the Aristotelian view of a "beginningless" universe. Al-Ghazālī was a prominent representative of the Sunni form of Islam, and was involved in major debates with theologians of the rival Shiite approach to Islam, as well as the Arabic tradition of Aristotelian philosophy. For Al-Ghazālī, the universe must have a beginning, and since nothing comes into existence without a cause, it follows that there must be a transcendent Creator of the universe. The basic structure of his argument can be set out as four propositions:

1. Everything which has a beginning must have a cause;
2. The universe began to exist;
3. Therefore the beginning of the existence of the universe must have been caused by something;
4. The only such cause can be God.

This form of the Kalām argument has been widely debated in recent years, having been given a new lease of life by the "big-bang" theory of the origins of the universe, which has gained wide acceptance since the 1950s. Modern cosmology strongly suggests that the universe had a beginning. If the universe began to exist at a certain time, it must have had a cause. And what cause could there be other than God? One of its most significant recent defenders has been the US philosopher of religion William Lane Craig (born 1949), who is widely credited with reintroducing this approach into scholarly debate and discussion. Craig sets out its main features as follows:

> Since everything that begins to exist has a cause of its existence, and since the universe began to exist, we conclude, therefore, the universe has a cause of its existence ... Transcending the entire universe there exists a cause which has brought the universe into being.

Debate over the Kalām argument has centered on two main questions. First, can something have a *beginning* without being *caused*? In one of his dialogues, David Hume argues that it is possible to conceive of something that comes into being, without necessarily pointing to some definite cause of that existence. Nevertheless, this suggestion raises considerable difficulties, partly because it is deeply counterintuitive. And second, if the universe can be considered to have been "caused," can this cause be directly identified with God? While some argue that this question cannot be meaningfully answered, others point out that a cause must be prior to the event that it causes. To speak of a cause for the beginning of the existence of the universe is thus to speak of something that existed before the universe. And if this is not God, what is it?

What is the Point of Arguments for the Existence of God?

So what use are such arguments for the existence of God? Some would argue that their primary role is to reinforce the faith of those who already believe in God, rather than persuade those who have yet to take this position. This was the view of the Austrian philosopher Ludwig Wittgenstein, who suggested that the so-called "proofs of God's existence" are generally developed by people who already believe in God for other reasons, but hold that it is important to provide a reasoned defense of their faith.

A proof of God's existence ought really to be something by means of which one could convince oneself that God exists. But I think that what *believers* who have furnished such proofs have wanted to do is to give their "belief" an intellectual analysis and foundation, although they themselves would never have come to believe as a result of such proofs.

Although Wittgenstein refers to these arguments as "proofs," it is important to appreciate that these are not strictly *proofs*, as this term would be understood in mathematics or logic. In my view, these are really arguments for the rational consistency and coherence of belief in God – which is an important issue for apologetics, even though it falls short of a "proof" in the strict sense of the term. Many apologists – such as the philosopher of religion Richard Swinburne – argue that the evidential case for God is cumulative, resting on a number of considerations, none of which is decisive in itself, but which when taken together have significant force. In his work *The Existence of God*, Swinburne argues that religious experience can be integrated into a cumulative argument. On its own, religious experience does not offer a secure justification of belief in God; nevertheless, it can play a significant role in a cumulative argument for the existence of God. The philosopher of religion Basil Mitchell earlier suggested that a "cumulative case" approach to apologetics is like a trial in a court of law. The case does not rest on a single argument or piece of evidence, but a body of evidence, which needs to be weighed up and assessed. What is the most satisfying "Big Picture"? What theoretical framework holds the individual pieces of evidence together most convincingly and naturally?

The French mathematician and philosopher Blaise Pascal had two major concerns about the kind of rational arguments used by Aquinas. First, there seemed to be a significant gap between the rather abstract philosophical "god" that resulted from such arguments and the living God of the Old and New Testaments. In his *Pensées*, Pascal suggested that "metaphysical proofs for the existence of God are so remote from human reasoning, and so complex, that they have little impact."

And second, Pascal argued that these "proofs" assumed that God was known primarily through *reason*. But what about human *affections*? For Pascal, the human heart also had its reasons for believing (or not believing!) in God. "We know the truth, not only through our reason, but also through our heart." The appeal of God to the human condition goes far beyond any resonance between the world as we know it and the ideas of the Christian faith. It extends to include a deep-seated longing for God, which Pascal held to be of major importance in the long, unended human quest for God and final meaning. In the end, according to Pascal, the existence of God is not something that can be proved or disproved.

G. K. Chesterton made a further point of interest in his famous essay "The Return of the Angels," when he pointed out that it was not any individual aspect of Christianity that was persuasive, but the overall big picture of reality that it offered. This larger vision of reality could not be *proved* to be true; it was, however, credible because of its capacity to render the world *intelligible*. After his initial agnosticism, Chesterton found himself returning to Christianity because it seemed to make sense of a complex and otherwise puzzling world. Individual observations of nature do not "prove" Christianity to be true; rather, Christianity validates itself by its ability to make sense of those observations. "The phenomenon does not prove religion, but religion explains the phenomenon". Chesterton invites his readers to step into the Christian mindset, and grasp and experience the quality of its intellectual rendering of reality. "The best way to see if a coat fits a man is not to measure both of them, but to try it on."

We now turn to consider C. S. Lewis's discussion of the apologetic importance of "clues" in making sense of reality.

Connecting up the Clues: C. S. Lewis and the Argument from Desire

C. S. Lewis is one of the best-known apologists of the twentieth century, whose reputation rests on his lucid prose, his clarity of expression, and his appeal to the imagination and reason in the exploration of faith. Lewis's most influential works of apologetics were written at Oxford during the period 1939–1954, and are richly textured by his love and deep knowledge of Renaissance literature. As a former atheist who discovered Christianity at Oxford, Lewis felt that he could speak to those who had difficulties with Christianity as one who had once shared those concerns, but had now resolved them.

For Lewis, belief in God provided an *explanatory and imaginative* framework for both what he observed around him and experienced within him. I have argued that Lewis offers an "enhanced vision of rationality," which recognizes that the Christian faith is capable of being grasped by reason and visualized by the imagination. Lewis helps us see that apologetics need not take the form of a purely deductive argument, but can be understood and presented as an invitation to step into the Christian way of seeing things, and explore how things look when seen from its standpoint. "Try seeing things *this* way!" If worldviews or metanarratives can be compared to lenses, which of them brings things into sharpest focus? For Lewis, apologetics is about discovering the quality of the Christian account of our observations and experiences, and choosing to live within this transformed vision of ourselves and the world.

While individual elements of the Christian faith could be defended, Lewis followed Chesterton in seeing that the apologetic strength of Christianity lay in the "big picture" of reality which it generated, which was capable of fitting in so many aspects of the world and human existence. Lewis's overall approach is captured in the final sentence of an Oxford lecture: "I believe in Christianity as I believe that the Sun has risen, not only because I see it, but because by it I see everything else." Lewis holds that the Christian faith makes sense of what we observe and experience, even if it cannot offer unassailable and incorrigible proof of its truths. Its capacity to explain is, for Lewis, an indicator of its truthfulness.

Lewis's most significant work of apologetics is *Mere Christianity*, now widely regarded as one of the most important and influential works on Christianity to have been published in the twentieth century. Although the work affirms the fundamental rationality of the Christian faith, Lewis's approach appeals primarily to the shared experience of ordinary people – such as a sense of moral obligation, or a feeling of longing for something that is deeply satisfying, yet is not delivered in or through anything that is finite or created. This is clearly seen from his famous popular statement of the "argument from morality" in the opening chapter of *Mere Christianity*.

Lewis here invites us to reflect on two people having an argument. Any attempt to determine who is right and who is wrong depends on recognition of some norm or standard that stands over and above both parties to the dispute, and which both implicitly recognize as binding and authoritative. Lewis suggests that everyone has some sense of there being something "higher" than us – an objective norm to which people appeal, and which they expect others to observe; a "real law which we did not invent, and which we know we ought to obey." This, Lewis argues, is one of many "clues" to the meaning of the universe.

Yet although everyone knows about this law, everyone still fails to live up to it. Lewis thus suggests that "the foundation of all clear thinking about ourselves and the universe we live in" consists in our knowledge of a moral law, and an awareness of our failure to observe it. This awareness ought to "arouse our suspicions" that there "is Something which is directing the universe, and which appears in me as a law urging me to do right and making me feel responsible and uncomfortable when I do wrong." Lewis suggests that this clue points to an ordering mind governing the universe – which resonates with the Christian idea of God.

Right and wrong are thus treated as "clues to the meaning of the universe." Clues, taken by themselves, prove nothing; their importance lies rather in their cumulative and contextual force. In other words, the greater the number of clues that can be satisfactorily accommodated by a given view of reality, the more reliable that view of reality. Lewis uses many other such "clues" throughout his writings, including a deep and intense feeling of longing within human beings, which no earthly object or experience proves able to satisfy. There is a "divine dissatisfaction" within human experience, which prompts us to ask whether there is anything that may satisfy the human quest to fulfil the desires of the human heart. Lewis refers to this experience as "joy," and argues that it points to God as its source and goal (hence the title of his autobiography, *Surprised by Joy*).

In *Mere Christianity*, Lewis argues that any authentic human longing points to a genuine human need, which in turn points to a real object corresponding to that need. Hunger, he suggests, is an excellent example of a human feeling that corresponds to a genuine physical need. This need points to the existence of food by which it may be met. Thirst is a further example of a human longing pointing to a human need, which in turn points to its fulfilment in drinking. Lewis thus suggests that it is reasonable to argue that the deep human sense of infinite longing, which cannot be satisfied by any physical or finite object or person, must point to a real human need that has both its origin and its fulfilment in God. In this, Lewis echoes a great theme of traditional Christian thinking about the origin and goal of human nature. "You have made us for yourself, and our hearts are restless until they find their rest in you" (Augustine of Hippo).

Lewis's "argument from desire" is based on his core belief that God is able to satisfy the deepest desires of the human heart. Humanity has been created to relate to God; God creates a sense of dissatisfaction as a way of helping us to find our way home. For example, in *Mere Christianity*, Lewis explores how the human experience of an unfulfilled desire can be interpreted, and what the best explanation might be: "If I find in myself a desire which no experience in this world can satisfy, the most probable explanation is that I was made for another world." This is not about "proving" anything; it is about trying to identify which is the best explanation of our experience of unfulfilled desire.

Lewis identifies three such explanations, and subjects them to a critical comparative analysis. Some suggest that this frustration arises from looking for the true object or goal of desire in the wrong places; the solution is thus to keep on searching. Others hold that, since further searching will only result in repeated disappointment, there is simply no point trying to find something better than the present world; the solution is thus to give up hope of ever finding the true object of our desire. Lewis, however, notes that there is a third approach, which recognizes that these earthly longings are "only a kind of copy, or echo, or mirage" of our true homeland. Nature cannot, and is not meant to, satisfy our deepest desires. Lewis's solution is thus to propose God as both the origin and goal of our heart's desire. Lewis does not overstate his case by suggesting that this is the only possible explanation of human desire; it is rather "the most probable explanation."

Lewis's "argument from desire" is not a deductive argument leading to a proven conclusion. Lewis's argument is *suppositional*. It is like a mental experiment. Suppose that there really is a God. Does not this fit in well with what we actually experience of reality? And is not this resonance of supposal and experience an indication of the truth of the supposal? Lewis invites his readers to imagine themselves inside the Christian way of thinking and envisaging the world, and to try to grasp how the world is seen and experienced from this standpoint. How well does this theoretical lens bring things into focus?

Lewis's approach here amounts to a kind of intellectual or imaginative empathy, in which outsiders are invited to see the world through a Christian lens, and see and feel what it might be like. Lewis is not asking his audience to accept the truth of Christianity; he is rather asking them to appreciate the quality of the vision of reality that it offers, and the difference that it makes to life. And once these are appreciated, this line of approach naturally leads into the question: is this true? Can it be trusted? Yet the context of this question is no longer mild curiosity; it is an awareness that this might be a viable answer to life's great questions.

Although Lewis does not use this language, his approach is very similar to the notion of "inference to the best explanation," now widely regarded as the dominant philosophy of the natural sciences. What "big picture" makes the most sense of observation? What metanarrative offers the best map of reality, positioning observations in the most comprehensive and plausible manner? For Lewis, the kind of "sense-making" offered by the Christian vision of reality is about discerning a resonance between its theory and the way the world seems to be. Its theoretical spectacles seem to bring reality into sharp focus, just as a false theory prevents us from seeing what is really there.

In the next section, we shall consider how the British philosopher and apologist Richard Swinburne applies this method of "inference to the best explanation" in his apologetic writings, and then turn to reflect further how Lewis uses something very similar to this approach. Both are very helpful apologetically.

Inference to the Best Explanation: Richard Swinburne

Recent years have seen a growing interest within the philosophy of science in the idea of "inference to the best explanation." This represents a decisive move away from older positivist understandings of the scientific method, still occasionally encountered in popular accounts of the relation of science and religion, which holds that science is able to – and therefore ought to – offer evidentially and inferentially infallible evidence for its theories. This approach, found at many points in the writings of Richard Dawkins, is now realized to be deeply problematic. It is particularly important to note that scientific data are capable of being interpreted in many ways, each of which has some evidential support. In contrast, positivism tended to argue that there was a single unambiguous interpretation of the evidence, which any right-minded observer would discover. Since there are many explanations of the question, how can we work out which of these explanations is the best?

The approach now generally known as "inference to the best explanation" recognizes that multiple explanations might be offered for any given set of observations and sets out to identify criteria by which the best such explanation might be identified and justified. Yet the best theory may not be a true theory – it may simply be the best approach available at this specific moment in history. So what are these criteria? A number of ways of evaluating theories or explanations have been put forward by philosophers of science. In what follows, we shall consider three widely used criteria.

1. *Simplicity.* In the later Middle Ages, the philosopher William of Ockham recommended avoiding unnecessary hypotheses. This principle – often known as "Ockham's Razor" or the "Principle of Parsimony" – is useful. The simplest theories are often the best – but not always. Copernicus' model of the solar system was elegantly simple, envisaging the planets revolving round the sun in circular orbits at constant speed. Yet as the astronomer Johann Kepler later demonstrated, the planets did not orbit around the sun in mathematically simple circles, but in the more complex curves of ellipses, requiring more complex mathematical representation. Furthermore, the planets moved at variable speeds as they rotated round the sun. Simplicity may be an *indicator* of truth, but it is not a *guarantor* of truth. There is also an unresolved debate about whether simplicity means mathematically uncomplicated, easy to understand, or explaining a wide variety of phenomena on the basis of a minimal set of laws.

2. *Elegance and Beauty.* Many have noted that successful theories are often elegant. In 1955, the physicist Paul Dirac set out his philosophy of physics by writing this statement on a blackboard: "physical laws should have mathematical beauty." Dirac pointed out that Newton's classical mechanics were simple; Einstein's relativistic mechanics were complex – yet mathematically elegant. What makes the theory of relativity so acceptable to physicists in spite of its going against the principle of simplicity, Dirac remarked, is its "great mathematical beauty." Yet it is not clear why such a subjective criterion of elegance or beauty should be an indicator of truth.

3. *A Capacity to Predict.* Many scientists argue that it is essential that a scientific theory ought to have a capacity to predict. There are some excellent examples of innovative theories – such as Einstein's theory of general relativity, noted above – which made unexpected predictions that were subsequently confirmed. Yet it remains unclear why a capacity to predict should be so important, apart from the psychological impact of the confirmation of a novel prediction. The critical question is whether evidence is supportive of a theory, and the rigor of the selection

procedure used to generate the evidence. Darwin was adamant that his theory of natural selection could not be proved to be true, and that it made no testable predictions – but he still believed it was right. Modern "String Theory" also makes no predictions, and is empirically unverifiable or unfalsifiable. Yet both theories are regarded as scientific, despite failing to meet this criterion.

Christian philosophers and apologists have become increasingly interested in inductive approaches to the rationality of faith, especially in relation to the question of the existence of God. In this section, we shall consider the approach of the philosopher Richard Swinburne, who argues that the existence of God is to be seen as the best explanation of what is observed within the world, when seen as part of a larger cumulative case. For Swinburne, the existence of the universe can be made comprehensible if we suppose that it is brought about by God.

Swinburne sets approach within a wider framework, grounded in the core belief that the existence of a universe needs explaining, rather than merely being accepted as a "brute fact" (Bertrand Russell). For Russell, there can be no further explanation for its existence or its fundamental features other than the statement "it is there." So what are the possible explanations, and which of them is the best? Swinburne suggests that there are basically two main rival theories which need to be considered as possible explanations: the view that science can provide a natural explanation for the existence of this universe, or the theistic view that the universe and its phenomena exist because of the intentional causal activity of a personal being, known as "God."

Swinburne thus sets out to identify possible explanations of the universe, and to determine which of these is "best." In making this decision, Swinburne does not see himself as having to prove the existence of God. His task is rather to show that the existence of God, however unlikely this might appear as an independent hypothesis, is better at explaining our nexus of observations and experiences than its alternatives – such as a materialist naturalism. *A priori*, theism might perhaps seem very unlikely; yet, Swinburne argues, it is far more likely than its explanatory rivals.

So what criteria does Swinburne use in evaluating rival explanations of the existence of the universe? In developing this kind of inductive cosmological argument, however, Swinburne appeals to the criterion of simplicity in deciding between competing hypotheses concerning the existence of the universe, arguing that "science requires us to postulate the simplest explanation of the data." The simpler a theory, the more likely it is to be right. His argument is open to challenge. However, Swinburne's approach to the rationality of theism is an important indication of the way in which scientific criteria of theory choice have found their way into recent apologetic discussions.

Earlier in this section, we noted the apparent correlation between beauty and truth in scientific theories. So might this also opening the way to some important lines of apologetic argument? Swinburne certainly thought so.

God has reason to create a beautiful inanimate world – that is, a beautiful physical universe. Whatever God creates will be a good product; and so any physical universe that he creates will be beautiful.... And maybe the kind of beauty that it exemplifies is different from that of finite beings, or of God himself. But I do not find it obvious that it exemplifies in respect of its beauty a kind of goodness not possessed by God himself.

Swinburne's analysis helps us to appreciate the apologetic potential of "inference to the best explanation." At its core, this approach recognizes that there are multiple plausible explanations of this world, and that none of these can be decisively *proved* to be true. It identifies a number of criteria by which the best such explanation might be identified and justified – such as simplicity, elegance, and coherence. Yet it also recognizes that what is presently the *best* explanation may not be the *right* theory – it is simply the best that we can offer at present, on the basis of the evidence and theoretical tools at our disposal at this specific moment in history. The best theory thus may not be a true theory.

The apologetic importance of this approach lies in its explicit recognition that scientific explanations need not be proved to be true to be considered acceptable and trustworthy. Rather, they need to be shown to be better than their rivals. The scientific positivism of the earlier twentieth century, which optimistically believed that it was possible to prove scientific theories, has been superseded by a more realistic approach that is more aware of the limitations of proof in such contexts. Many apologists – such C. S. Lewis – therefore aim, not to *prove* their Christian faith, but to show that it makes more sense than rival alternatives, such as materialism or scientism. For Lewis and Swinburne, Christianity offers a better explanation of our world than its secular or materialist alternatives.

The Use of Rational Arguments: A Theological Concern

Throughout this chapter, I have argued that part of the task of apologetics is to disclose and affirm the rationality of Christian belief. Yet we need to be aware of the danger of overestimating the capacity of human beings to make sense of a complex world. In his analysis of the emergence of a "secular age," Charles Taylor rightly notes that modernity led to the "eclipse of grace," in that divine assistance was no longer seen as a necessary requirement to achieve human goals, including achieving a full understanding our world.

> The order God designed was there for reason to see. By reason and discipline, humans could rise to the challenge and realize it. Now even those orthodox thinkers in the past who might have agreed with such a high view of the power of reason would have wanted to add at this point that the full measure of good will required for carrying out the programme of rational discipline, given our fallen condition, required God's grace.

Taylor's point is that an expectation emerged that human beings could, by exercise of purely natural powers, uncover the mystery of the universe, which were transparent to human reason. This led to an unrealistic expectation that human reason could penetrate every mystery and answer every question – and demonstrate the existence of God by unaided reason.

Drawing on Charles Taylor, the US philosopher and theologian James K. A. Smith uses the term "epistemic Pelagianism" to refer to the overconfidence of the "Age of Reason" in the capacity of human intellectual powers to fully comprehend reality. Smith here alludes to the fifth-century writer Pelagius, who regarded human nature as eminently perfectible, and was alarmed by Augustine of Hippo's suggestion that humanity was in some sense compromised or incapacitated by sin. Pelagius's ideas can be developed with reference to the idea of *revelation* (human beings can grasp everything about God by reason) and *salvation* (human beings can do whatever is required to secure redemption).

Yet early and medieval Christian writers held that a reliable knowledge of God came about only by the grace of revelation, in which God self-disclosed in a manner that was adapted to human frailty and weakness. While Anselm and Aquinas were clear that neither the existence nor the character of God could be "proved," it was possible to develop rational pathways that pointed towards the divine imprint on the created order or the human mind, thus disclosing God's fingerprints within creation. This, however, did not amount to a *proof* of the existence of God, in that human reason did not have the capacity to achieve this. Writers in the Reformed tradition added an additional concern, noting that human rational capacities were not merely *limited* by our creaturely status; they were *distorted* by sin. The recognition of a noetic impact of sin called into question whether human reason could reliably disclose the Christian God; might it not point towards some distorted or disfigured account of God?

For these reasons and others, most Christian apologists have moved beyond the rationalism of some early modern forms of apologetics, which was based on the deeply problematic assumption that we can work out everything by ourselves. Yet we cannot prove or understand everything; we have to learn to live with a degree of uncertainty, without abandoning any fundamental belief in the rationality of human beings or the world in which we live. Rationalist demands that every aspect of our world – such as the existence of evil – must be "explained," or that every one of our beliefs must be "proved," is now seen as rationalist overreach, representing a failure to deal with the complexity of our world on the one hand, and an exaggerated view of the ability of the human mind to master that world on the other.

The classic Christian view is that human reason cannot prove the existence of God, but can show that believing in God makes sense – and thus lead people to reach beyond the limits of reason and discover a revealed God. Human reason and experience point beyond themselves to a world that they cannot grasp or disclose. For Aquinas, that's when revelation takes over – not contradicting reason, but taking us beyond its limits, and showing us what God is like.

The Demand for Proof: The Problem with the "New Atheism"

Many commentators have noted the curious rational asymmetry of the "New Atheist" writers Richard Dawkins and Christopher Hitchens, who both demand that Christians should prove their belief in God by reason and science, while assuming that their own atheism is so self-evidently correct that it needs no proof. This has puzzled many critics of this movement, for two reasons. First, it is widely agreed that the existence of God cannot be conclusively proved or disproved in these ways; and second, these writers use criteria of assessment to judge Christianity that they fail to apply to their own ideas.

Dawkins's evidential asymmetry has left many of his fellow travelers feeling deeply uneasy. If Dawkins demands that his opponents should prove their beliefs, surely he should be able to prove his own beliefs, rather than simply use his atheist belief system as a standpoint from which to criticize religious belief? Consider, for example, this argument (which is really an assertion), which is encountered at multiple points in Dawkins's writings.

Religious people believe in God.
But there is no God.
Therefore belief in God is a delusion.

This bold argument may have proved to be influential, but it is deeply flawed. An unprovable belief ("there is no God") is here treated as an unassailable truth, and used to ridicule a different belief. Dawkins's argument is simply this: when seen from an atheist perspective, religious belief makes no sense. *Assuming* (because it cannot be proved) that there is no God, it follows that those who believe there is a God are deluded. The atheist philosopher John Gray, recognizing the importance of this point, suggests that the discussion ought now to move on from a pointless discussion about whether God's existence can be proved or disproved to the more significant exploration of why some people find that they have "no use" for God, and are thus moved to search for "God-surrogates."

Christopher Hitchens, however, meets this challenge by arguing that New Atheism does not have any "beliefs," in that the movement only recognizes truths that are demonstrably true. It is a puzzling statement, given that the argumentative force of Hitchens's *God is Not Great* (2007) is dominated by the assertion that religion is evil – a moral judgement that is clearly an *opinion* that cannot be proved by reason or science.

Christian apologists need to learn from the "New Atheism." By presenting its ideas as self-evidently true, rational certainties that no right-thinking person could deny, Dawkins and Hitchens were using rhetorical techniques to dismiss their opponents, and conceal the fundamental evidential underdetermination of their own positions. The New Atheism's asserted certainties, though initially appealing to many, were soon deconstructed and exposed as transient cultural beliefs.

This point was picked up by Gary Wolf, the journalist who coined the term "New Atheism" in 2006 to designate the messianic atheism of Dawkins and his colleagues Daniel Dennett and Sam Harris, and to highlight the rhetorically aggressive means in which they asserted their beliefs. Wolf was struck by the trenchant certainties of these leading proponents of atheism, while noting that many people found these asserted certainties to be arrogant and improbable, amounting to a significant intellectual over-reach on the part of the "New Atheism." "People see a contradiction in its tone of certainty. Contemptuous of the faith of others, its proponents never doubt their own belief. They are fundamentalists."

Conclusion

In this chapter, we have considered some aspects of discussions of the rationality of faith. As we have seen, this can be expressed both in terms of exploring reasons for believing that Christianity is true on the one hand, and the capacity of Christianity to make sense of things on the other. In the former case, the question is how the historical evidence and rational reflection lead to Christianity; in the latter, the question is how accepting Christianity makes sense of the world in ways that other faith traditions or ideologies do not. Yet it is important to appreciate the different directions of intellectual travel. The first begins with evidence, and asks how this points to Christianity as the best explanation; the second, however, begins from the explanatory framework of Christianity, and asks how this lens brings reality into focus. Each has its distinct merits!

Yet there is a danger here of *rationalizing* Christianity, of relocating the significance of God from the realm of human *understanding* to the more intellectualized realm of *explanation*. To understand involves more than explanation; it is about grasping a bigger picture of reality, and appreciating our place and role within that. As the philosopher Linda Zagzebski points out, "understanding is not directed toward a discrete object, but involves seeing the relation of parts to other parts and perhaps even the relation of part to a whole." Where the philosopher Richard Swinburne treats God primarily as an "explanatory hypothesis" that aims to make sense of our experience of the world, rather than as one who enriches and transforms the life of the soul, C. S. Lewis sees God as enabling an *understanding* of our world, not simply an *explanation* of its forms. Christianity engages the significant questions of meaning and value, rather than merely offering rational explanations. In the next chapter, we shall follow through on this point, as we explore how apologetics aims to make significant connections with its audiences through correlating the core themes of the Christian gospel with multiple elements of the human situation.

Study Questions

1. If God cannot be proved to exist by argument, what is the point of using these arguments?
2. Summarize Aquinas's arguments for the existence of God in your own words. How might you be able to use these in an apologetic talk or article?
3. C. S. Lewis's "argument from desire" has proved very accessible and engaging. Set out its basic themes in your own words. Why does it have such an appeal? How might you use it?
4. Earlier in this work (p. 1), I noted Avery Dulles's remark that many people see an apologist as an "aggressive, opportunistic person who tries, by fair means or foul, to argue people into joining the church." How might this perception arise? And how can arguments be used wisely and graciously?

For Further Reading

Ahvio, Juha. *Theological Epistemology of Contemporary American Confessional Reformed Apologetics.* Helsinki: Luther-Agricola-Society, 2005.

Aliseda, Atocha. *Abductive Reasoning: Logical Investigations into Discovery and Explanation.* Dordrecht: Springer, 2006.

Azadegan, Ebrahim. "Divine Hiddenness and Human Sin: The Noetic Effect of Sin." *Journal of Reformed Theology* 7, no. 1 (2013): 69–90.

Baker, Keith M., and Peter H. Reill, eds. *What's Left of Enlightenment? A Postmodern Question.* Stanford, CA: Stanford University Press, 2001.

Boone, Mark J. "Augustine and William James on the Rationality of Faith." *Heythrop Journal* 61, no. 4 (2020): 648–59.

Brown, J. R. *The Laboratory of the Mind: Thought Experiments in the Natural Sciences.* 2nd ed. London: Routledge, 2011.

Carr, Bernard, ed. *Universe or Multiverse?* Cambridge: Cambridge University Press, 2007.

Collins, Robin. "The Teleological Argument: An Exploration of the Fine-tuning of the Cosmos." In *Blackwell Companion to Natural Theology*, edited by William Lane Craig and J. P. Moreland, 202–81. Oxford: Blackwell, 2009.

Copan, Paul, and William Lane Craig. *The Kalām Cosmological Argument: Scientific Evidence for the Beginning of the Universe.* New York, NY: Bloomsbury Academic, 2018.

Craig, William Lane. *The Kalām Cosmological Argument.* London: Macmillan, 1979.

Craig, William Lane. "The Existence of God and the Beginning of the Universe." *Truth: A Journal of Modern Thought* 3 (1991): 85–96.

De Cruz, Helen. "The Enduring Appeal of Natural Theological Arguments." *Philosophy Compass* 9, no. 2 (2014): 145–53.

Flórez, Jorge Alejandro. "Peirce's Theory of the Origin of Abduction in Aristotle." *Transactions of the Charles S. Peirce Society* 50, no. 2 (2014): 265–80.

Gendler, Tamar. *Thought Experiment: On the Powers and Limits of Imaginary Cases.* New York, NY: Garland, 2000.

Gschwandtner, Christina M. *Postmodern Apologetics? Arguments for God in Contemporary Philosophy.* New York, NY: Fordham University Press, 2013.

Hadot, Pierre. *What is Ancient Philosophy?* Cambridge, MA: Harvard University Press, 2002.

Harris, Peter. *The Rage against the Light: Why Christopher Hitchens is Wrong.* Eugene, OR: Wipf & Stock, 2018.

Holten, Wilko van. "Theism and Inference to the Best Explanation." *Ars Disputandi* 2, no. 1 (2002): 262–81.

Kenny, Anthony. *The Five Ways: St. Thomas Aquinas' Proofs of God's Existence.* London: Routledge & Kegan Paul, 2003.

Leftow, Brian. "The Ontological Argument." In *Oxford Handbook of Philosophy of Religion*, edited by William J. Wainwright, 80–115. Oxford: Oxford University Press, 2005.

Lipton, Peter. *Inference to the Best Explanation.* 2nd ed. London: Routledge, 2004.

Loke, Andrew Ter Ern. *God and Ultimate Origins: A Novel Cosmological Argument.* New York, NY: Palgrave Macmillan, 2017.

McGrath, Alister E. "An Enhanced Vision of Rationality: C. S. Lewis on the Reasonableness of Christian Faith." *Theology* 116, no. 6 (2013): 410–17.

McGrath, Alister E. *The Territories of Human Reason: Science and Theology in an Age of Multiple Rationalities.* Oxford: Oxford University Press, 2019.

Mongrain, Kevin. "The Eyes of Faith: Newman's Critique of Arguments from Design." *Newman Studies Journal* 6 (2009): 68–86.

Morgan, Teresa. *The New Testament and the Theology of Trust: "This Rich Trust."* Oxford: Oxford University Press, 2022.

Nottelmann, Nikolaj, and Patrick Fessenbecker. "Honesty and inquiry: W. K. Clifford's Ethics of Belief." *British Journal for the History of Philosophy* 28, no. 4 (2020): 797–818.

Peterfreund, Stuart. *Turning Points in Natural Theology from Bacon to Darwin: The Way of the Argument from Design.* New York, NY: Palgrave Macmillan, 2012.

Plantinga, Alvin. *Warranted Christian Belief.* Oxford: Oxford University Press, 2000.

Reichenbach, Bruce. "Explanation and the Cosmological Argument." In *Contemporary Debates in the Philosophy of Religion*, edited by Michael Peterson and Raymond van Arragon, 97–114. Oxford: Wiley-Blackwell, 2004.

Rodrigues, Cassiano Terra. "The Method of Scientific Discovery in Peirce's Philosophy: Deduction, Induction, and Abduction." *Logica Universalis* 5 (2011): 127–64.

Rothenberg, Albert. "Creative Cognitive Processes in Kekulé's Discovery of the Structure of the Benzene Molecule." *The American Journal of Psychology* 108, no. 3 (1995): 419–38.

Schumacher, Lydia. "The Lost Legacy of Anselm's Argument: Rethinking the Purpose of Proofs for the Existence of God." *Modern Theology* 27, no. 1 (2011): 87–101.

Sobel, Jordan Howard. *Logic and Theism: Arguments for and against Beliefs in God.* Cambridge: Cambridge University Press, 2004.

Swinburne, Richard. *The Existence of God.* 2nd ed. Oxford: Clarendon Press, 2004.

Swinburne, Richard. "God as the Simplest Explanation of the Universe." *European Journal for Philosophy of Religion* 2, no. 1 (2010): 1–24.

Winnicott, Donald W. *Playing and Reality.* London: Routledge, 2005.

Yancey, Philip. *Rumours of Another World.* Grand Rapids, MI: Zondervan, 2007.

Zagzebski, Linda. 2001. "Recovering Understanding." In *Knowledge, Truth, and Duty: Essays on Epistemic Justification, Responsibility, and Virtue*, edited by Matthias Steup, 235–52. Oxford: Oxford University Press.

4

Connecting the Christian Faith with the Human Situation

Apologetics, as we saw earlier in this work, can be seen as having three main elements. First, it needs to engage with cultural objections to religious belief, particularly those that dominate public discourse in post-Christian society. (The rise of the "New Atheism" is a useful case study in understanding these dominant controlling assumptions, and their apologetic implications.) Second, it needs to affirm and explore the various ways in which the Christian faith is able to connect up with the lives and concerns of ordinary people. And third, it needs to translate its ideas into the cultural vernacular of its audiences, so that Christian beliefs are presented in a way that makes intellectual, relational, and emotional sense to contemporary culture. Apologetics is not about *inventing* the rationality, imaginative depth, or moral vision of the Christian faith. It is rather about *showcasing* these features of faith, both *pointing them out* and *living them out* so that people can see them clearly and appreciate them for what they are.

This point is particularly important in dealing with the phenomenon of "deconstruction," in which individuals, for various reasons, feel themselves becoming disconnected from their Christian faith. One factor that is significant in this process is a growing sense that Christianity does not connect up with the realities of personal experience. The material presented in this and the following chapter aims to help lay the groundwork for a process of reconnection by bringing out some of the many ways in which Christianity engages with existential issues. While the material presented in these chapters will need to be particularized for specific audiences (discussed in Chapter 6), the basic themes can be used in a variety of apologetic contexts.

In the previous chapter, we considered some ways in which the rationality of the Christian faith could be affirmed and explored. Yet the lingering impact of the bygone "Age of Reason" often misleads apologists into assuming that demonstrating that a certain belief is "reasonable" is sufficient grounds for people to accept and embrace this

Christian Apologetics: An Introduction, First Edition. Alister E. McGrath.
© 2024 John Wiley & Sons Ltd. Published 2024 by John Wiley & Sons Ltd.

idea as relevant and transformative. If you show someone that a belief is rational, we are told, they will automatically embrace it. *This is simply not the case*. For example, there is excellent evidence that the planet Uranus has five major moons. I can also be certain of the mathematical truth that the square root of two is an irrational number. Yet while I can accept both these ideas *intellectually*, they make no difference to me, *practically* or *existentially*. They have no traction on real life. Yes, they are *true* – but so what? What do they have to do with the human quest for meaning, our attempts to live well, or our longing to make sense of our lives? Apologetics is about showing how Christianity *connects up* with its audiences, making a difference to how they see and inhabit the world.

The Christian way of seeing things makes cognitive and existential sense of reality, offering us a powerful, persuasive and attractive account of ourselves and our universe. Christianity does not simply make sense *to* us; it makes sense *of* us. It positions us in the great narrative of cosmic history, and locates us on a mental map of meaning. It offers us another way of seeing things and another way of living, and invites its audiences to discover and these.

This chapter deals with one of the most important themes in Christian apologetics: the need to connect the realities of the Christian faith with the lives, hopes, aspirations, and traumas of ordinary human beings. While some recent apologists have suggested that an "apologetic for Christianity based on the human predicament is an extremely recent phenomenon," the historical evidence clearly shows that this form of apologetic is at least 1,500 years old, going back to the early Christian period and being definitively exhibited in the writings of Augustine of Hippo (Figure 4.1).

Augustine offers a theological analysis of human desires, grounded in the doctrines of creation and redemption. Human beings have been created in order to relate to God; yet this relationship has been disrupted or damaged by sin. Despite this, we experience feelings of longing that point to our true goal lying in God. Augustine expressed this in a famous prayer: "You have created us for yourself, and our heart is restless until it finds its rest in you." The idea of humanity bearing the "image of God" speaks of some inbuilt drive within human nature that acts as a "homing instinct" for God as the creator and ultimate goal of humanity. Just as a compass needle is drawn towards the magnetic pole, so the human imagination is drawn, as much by intuition as by reason, towards its origin and goal in God.

Our intuitions, desires, and anxieties are all apologetically significant, in that they are clues to the true goal of human fulfilment. What rationalism once dismissed as dreams and delusions are now recognized, as they were in the Christian past, as vital clues to human identity and fulfilment. The philosopher Alvin Plantinga argues that God has created humanity with a natural faculty, a *sensus divinitatis* ("sense of divinity") similar to our other natural faculties (such as perception, memory, or reason), which can create belief within us without those beliefs resting on any external evidence.

The philosopher Hans-Georg Gadamer used the phrase "a fusion of horizons (*Horizontverschmelzung*)" to describe this kind of process of interpretation and connection. The concept of "horizon," he notes, "expresses the superior breadth of vision that the person who is trying to understand must have. To acquire a horizon means that one learns to look beyond what is close at hand – not in order to look away from it but to see it better." Gadamer's point is that discovering a new horizon – such as that of the Christian faith – allows us to see and understand ourselves in a new way.

Figure 4.1   The early Christian theologian Augustine of Hippo (354–430) in conversation with colleagues, as depicted in a French manuscript. Alamy Image D95YMN.

Although the importance of connecting Christianity with the experiential world of human beings was played down by many US rationalist apologists of the mid-twentieth century, such as Edward John Carnell, the subsequent disillusionment with rationalism in western culture has led twenty-first century apologetics to refocus on connecting the world of the Christian faith with the inner world of human beings. This does not mean reducing Christianity to its existential impact on individuals; it is rather acknowledging that Christianity already possesses such an existential, imaginative, and emotional appeal as part of its birthright, and invites us to discover and apply it *apologetically*. To illustrate this point, we may consider the case of the US attorney Charles Colson, who discovered the appeal of Christianity through reading C. S. Lewis.

Colson served as Special Counsel to President Richard Nixon from 1969 to 1970, and was later imprisoned for his role in the Watergate scandal. Colson had no interest in religion at this time; however, he changed his mind in August 1973, when he suddenly made a connection between his own situation and the Christian faith. This happened while a visitor was reading aloud to him the section of Lewis's *Mere Christianity* dealing with pride. Colson suddenly *recognized himself* in the text, feeling that Lewis was talking about *him*. And having made this connection, Colson realized that Lewis had both diagnosed his problem and pointed towards its cure. Lewis allowed Colson to make a life-changing link between his own situation and some key themes of the Christian faith.

Similarly, some apologists suggest it is simply enough to quote from the Bible to their audiences, who will understand its relevance and implications for their situation without explanation or guidance. The meaning of the text, they argue, is self-evident. Yet the New Testament scholar John Barclay rightly points out that texts need theological interpretation.

> Our task in each generation, and in each cultural and historical context, is not simply to preserve these words but to unfold them, to explicate them, to tease out their meaning, in a way that "masters" – that comes to grips with and persuasively communicates to – our constantly changing present.

Barclay's analysis highlights the role of both preachers and apologists in showing how biblical passages speak into the existential situations of their audiences. (We shall consider the importance of the specificity of audiences later in this work, pp. 122–40.)

In this chapter, we shall consider the apologetic importance of this theme of "connecting up" – of helping individuals grasp how Christianity makes sense of their own situations, and brings hope of their renewal and transformation. Two themes converge here: first, that Christianity *illuminates* the human situation; and second, that it can *transform* us. Or, to use medical language, Christianity both diagnoses our condition, and is able to heal us. In this chapter, we shall consider how some leading themes of the Christian faith connect with the realities of human existence, and reflect on how the apologist can develop these ideas effectively.

Why Facts aren't Enough: Apologetics and the Human Situation

A core theme of Christian apologetics is that the Christian faith is truthful. So what is to be understood by this central notion of "truth"? For some, the word "truth" simply means "factually correct." The evangelical apologist John Warwick Montgomery is best known for his work *History and Christianity* (1971). This work presents a "historical–legal" apologetic that sets out legal standards of evidential probability and criteria by which the reliability of the New Testament texts can be established. Montgomery develops the apologetic approach of Simon Greenleaf (1783–1853), an influential scholar during the early years of Harvard Law School, which focusses not on arguments for the existence of God, but on the reliability of the texts of the New Testament gospels. Christianity "declares that the truth of its absolute claims rests squarely on certain historical facts, open to ordinary investigation."

Montgomery's positive, fact-driven, evidentialist approach was particularly influential within North American evangelicalism in the second half of the twentieth century, serving the dual purpose of defending the reliability of certain New Testament texts, and the public truthfulness of the Christian faith in general. Yet apologetics has to go beyond the question of the "truthfulness" of the historical accounts of, for example, the resurrection of Christ. The issue here is that while facts are *important*, they are not *enough*; they need to be *interpreted and explained*, so that their significance for their audience becomes clear. Something can be *true* and *insignificant* at one and the same time.

Evidentialism offers an excellent foundation and starting point for apologetics; there is, however, much more that needs to be said. Facts are not enough; we need to grasp a "big picture" of reality that discloses the value and significance of life, and engages deep questions of meaning. Ludwig Wittgenstein made this point back in 1916, when he penned these words: "To believe in a God means to understand the question about the meaning of life. To believe in a God means to see that the facts of the world are not the end of the matter."

Albert Einstein is an important witness to the importance of going beyond facts to grasp their deeper significance. Einstein argued that "the scientific method can teach us nothing else beyond how facts are related to, and conditioned by, each other." Yet he insisted that human beings need more than what a "purely rational conception of our existence" is able to offer. We have to go beyond facts and offer an interpretation of our world, and our place within it. For Einstein, the fundamental beliefs that are "necessary and determinant for our conduct and judgments" cannot be developed or sustained in a "solid scientific way." We need more than science can provide us if we are to lead meaningful lives. Ludwig Wittgenstein confirms this point. "We feel that even if *all possible* scientific questions be answered, the problems of life have still not been touched at all."

Apologetics certainly aims to show that there are good historical and rational grounds for Christian belief. Yet this is not, in itself, enough to demonstrate that Christianity can change people's lives, giving them meaning and hope so that they can cope with a deeply puzzling and disturbing world. For example, consider these two statements:

1. Jesus Christ died on a cross.
2. Jesus Christ died on a cross for the sins of the world.

The first is an historical statement, making a statement that Christians would regard as factually correct. The second affirms this historical statement, but supplements this with a significant theological interpretation – namely, that the death of Christ in some way achieves the forgiveness of sins. This is the point made by Paul in his famous statement of the faith that was entrusted to him: "For I handed on to you as of first importance what I in turn had received: that Christ died for our sins in accordance with the scriptures" (1 Corinthians 15:3). What Paul is handing on to his readers is not simply the *factuality* of Christ's death on a cross, but the Christian interpretation of the meaning of that event – that it brings salvation. It is not enough to affirm the mere historical factuality of the crucifixion; its significance for individuals must be affirmed and explained.

The apologist thus needs to explain the relevance of, for example, Christ's resurrection to audiences who cannot see how this makes any difference to them. Apologetics needs to go beyond simply repeating the historical assertions of the New Testament; it seeks to explain what they mean in contemporary language, so that their potential significance can be appreciated. The great Dutch missiologist Hendrik Kraemer made this point forcefully in a major work laying the groundwork for the 1938 International Missionary Council meeting at Tambaram in India: "There is an obligation to strive for the presentation of the Christian faith in terms and modes of expression that make its challenge intelligible and related to the peculiar quality of reality in which they live." Apologetics aims to communicate what the biblical text means to today's readers, rather than simply repeat its words without explaining them in terms that are transparent to the present.

C. S. Lewis suggests that apologetics takes the form of a continuous translation of the realities of biblical faith into language and concepts that connect with today's audiences. Lewis's famous lecture on "Christian Apologetics" of Easter 1945 both emphasizes the importance of the truthfulness of the Christian faith on the one hand, and the need to translate this into terms that the audience can understand on the other. "Our business is to present that which is timeless (the same yesterday, today and tomorrow – Hebrews 8:8) in the particular language of our own age. … You must translate every bit of your Theology into the vernacular."

One of the questions that has not been given sufficient attention within apologetics is this: if any given Christian belief – such as the doctrine of the incarnation – is *true*, what difference does it make to individuals and communities of faith? How, for example, does it help people cope with uncertainty? How does it help us to live meaningfully? Is this something that can be lived out? How does it help us become wise? How can it help us to flourish? Apologists need to help their audiences to make these connections – and the best way of achieving this is to have seen these connections for yourself, appreciate the difference that faith makes to life, and be able to explain these to others.

This chapter explores how the core themes of Christianity connect up with important aspects of real life – such as the human quest for meaning, and the deep concerns many have about human significance in a vast universe. In particular, we shall consider the transformative aspects of Christianity, set out in its rich understanding of the nature of salvation, and its apologetic appeal. We begin, however, by exploring how the Christian faith can be seen as a *complex unity* – a reality that has many aspects and facets, all of which have both theological and apologetic importance, which are to be seen as a unified whole rather than as a set of disconnected ideas.

Why is this point important? Because some apologists limit themselves to a narrow range of aspects and facets of the Christian faith, failing to appreciate or deploy the full range of possibilities open to them. Some reduce Christianity to a small set of basic themes, and are unwilling to expand these, despite the New Testament's rich witness to the vitality of faith. This chapter aims to expand and enrich the apologist's range of options, opening up some potentially productive and helpful ways of connecting the "two horizons" – the New Testament on the one hand, and contemporary individuals on the other. This includes considering how the identity of our audience shapes the way in which we present Christianity, and how we develop links between the gospel and individual. Apologetics is about respecting the complexity and richness of Christianity on the one hand, and trying to identify and appreciate the apologetic importance of its many elements on the other.

Communicating Christian Complexity: Isaac Newton and Mary Midgley

In his famous work *The Mastery and his Emissary*, the philosopher Iain McGilchrist remarks that "our talent for division, for seeing the parts, is of staggering importance – second only to our capacity to transcend it, in order to see the whole." McGilchrist helpfully highlights the interplay of the whole and the parts, which is so important apologetically. Christianity is like an intellectual and spiritual ecosystem, with many interconnecting aspects and elements. While these are all part of a greater whole, each has its own distinct theological identity and apologetic significance. The one Christian gospel has many interconnected elements, each of which can connect up with human concerns, desires, and needs. One of the tasks of apologetics is to identify and appreciate the apologetic potential of these many aspects of Christianity. So how can we visualize this idea of a complex unity? In this section, we shall consider two models, which many find helpful in thinking this through.

The first of these dates from the seventeenth century. In 1672, the great English scientist Isaac Newton published a paper reporting on some experiments that he conducted in his rooms at Trinity College, Cambridge (Figure 4.2). These involved passing beams of sunlight through glass prisms, which split this white light up into a continuous spectrum of seven main colors: red, orange, yellow, green, blue, indigo and violet. Technically, this process of separating light into its spectral components, which occurs naturally in rainbows, is known as "dispersion." (Medieval descriptions of the rainbow recognized only five colors: red, yellow, green, blue and violet. Newton added orange and indigo, for reasons that remain unclear.) The important point here is that Newton's experiment showed that these colors were not *added* to the beam of white light by the prism. The colors were originally present in the sunbeams; they were not *created* by the prism but were rather *dispersed* (to use Newton's own term) or "separated out" and made individually visible.

So how does this well-known experiment help us think about a complex unity, such as the Christian faith? Newton's experiment offers us a visual model of how the multiple

Figure 4.2 Isaac Newton breaking down a beam of white light into its constituent colors in his rooms at Trinity College Cambridge. Adobe Stock Image 162450870.

aspects or elements of a complex single reality (sunlight) can be identified and studied individually, without losing sight of the fact that they are elements of this greater whole. There is a clear counterpart to this process of "dispersion" in theology, which aims to respect the fundamental unity of the Christian gospel, while at the same time identifying and appreciating the apologetic potential of each of its components. As we shall see in the next section, theological analysis of the New Testament's rich understanding of the nature of salvation enfolds a number of "images" or "models" of the transformation of human existence that results from the life, death, and resurrection of Christ. While each is part of the overall Christian understanding of salvation, each has its own distinct identity and apologetic appeal.

A second way of approaching this issue is due to the British public philosopher Mary Midgley, who affirms the unity of our world on the one hand, and its richness on the other. Midgley was a vigorous critic of reductionist approaches to the world, which she believed impoverished and distorted its complexity. To do justice to our world, we have to respect its complexity and attempt to capture and represent it as best we can.

> On the one hand, I want to emphasize that there really *is* only one world, but also – on the other – that this world is so complex, so various that we need dozens of distinct thought-patterns to understand it. We can't reduce all these ways of thinking to any single model. Instead, we have to use all our philosophical tools to bring these distinct kinds of thought together.

Midgley's point is that we are tempted to reduce our world to its most simple forms, and in doing so, lose sight of its many different aspects, each of which is important in its own right.

Midgley suggests that we think of a set of maps of our world, each of which is very effective at identifying some of its features, but none of which are good enough in themselves to represent our world in its totality. We need "a collection of maps, all of them incomplete, which together gradually shape our understanding of a new piece of country. By bringing those maps together … we build up a composite picture which brings us closer and closer to what the outside world is actually telling us." Similarly, theology aims to uncover the richness and fine detail of the Christian vision of reality, as well as celebrating its unity. And each theological map – to use Midgley's image – turns out to be helpful apologetically.

In what follows, we shall explore how the rich understanding of human transformation through Christ that is usually referred to as "salvation" can be dispersed into a series of individual elements, each with its own distinct theological identity and apologetic significance.

Apologetic Aspects of Salvation

In 1521, the German Lutheran theologian Philip Melanchthon published his *Loci Communes* (Latin: "Common Places"), a theological textbook that organized its discussion around central topics such as the identity and significance of Christ. One short phrase in that work is very significant apologetically: "to know Christ is to know his benefits." To understand who Christ is, Melanchthon declares, we need to understand what he has done for us. The Christian understanding of salvation – often referred to as "soteriology" – involves identifying these many "benefits of Christ," so that we can map the multiple ways in which the New Testament understands Christ to have transformed human existence. And each of these ways connects up with human concerns, needs, and our deepest aspirations – but in different ways.

The New Testament makes it clear that something new has happened through the life, death, and resurrection of Christ, with the capacity to transform human life and thought. A number of images are used to express the transformation of the human situation that is possible through Christ. New Testament writers drew on a series of metaphors and analogies that connected with the experiential world of their readers, enabling them to imagine or envisage what had happened to them in embracing Christ. Some were drawn from the rich heritage of Judaism, from which Christianity had emerged; others had their origins in first-century Greco-Roman commercial, legal and social worlds, familiar to so many readers of the New Testament letters. As Jan G. van der Watt points out, the New Testament uses images that were accessible to its readers, drawing on familiar religious or cultural practices to help them grasp the nature of salvation.

> The Christian message of salvation was contextualized in language that was accessible to ordinary people. Imagery, metaphors and comparisons that these early Christians could understand and relate to became an important tool in the hands of the evangelists for explaining to these new converts what had happened to them when they ventured onto this new road with God.

These images became the basis of teaching within the church and outreach beyond the church. In this chapter, we shall reflect on the New Testament's images of salvation, and how they can be used apologetically.

Many Christians tend to think of salvation simply in terms of deliverance *from* something – such as bondage to sin or the fear of death, or the guilt of sin. Yet this fails to take account of the fact that salvation also involves a transition *from* something *to* something else. Salvation is about the transformation of the human situation, whether this is understood as a change in legal or personal status, extrication from a place of danger to a place of safety, or healing of an illness (to mention some familiar ways of thinking about salvation).

Yet each of these specific images or models of salvation represents only one aspect of a greater whole. Though each of these models is thus incomplete (in that there is more to the Christian vision of salvation than any of them), they each helpfully illuminate individual aspects of this vision – and thus allow the apologist to use them to communicate and connect with an audience, exploring different angles of approach to the Christian gospel. This process of focusing on individual images of salvation is not reductionist, in that every such image is valued, respected, and explored. The point is that the apologetic impact of each individual image needs to be grasped.

The apologist can focus on each of these individual New Testament accounts or models of salvation, asking two specific questions about them. First, what is distinct about the way they depict the status of humanity, and the manner in which this may be transformed? For example, if salvation is understood in terms of reconciliation to God, this implies that the natural human state is that of alienation from God. Second, how might this way of envisaging or understanding salvation shape our apologetic use of this image? Is there some specific human situation or type of person who might find this particularly illuminating or helpful?

Truth and Desire in Apologetics

Some might express a concern at this point, in that this might seem to reduce Christianity to a need-based form of therapy. Yet a theologically informed account of human nature suggests that "need" and "desire" are created by God within us as a means of disclosing to us that we are unfulfilled and incomplete without God. A prayer by the eleventh-century theologian and spiritual writer Anselm of Canterbury makes this point very clearly: "Lord, give me what you have made me want; I praise and thank you for the desire that you have inspired; perfect what you have begun, and grant me what you have made me long for."

Note that Anselm begins this prayer by identifying a need; a desire; something that we want. But notice that he immediately offers a theological interpretation of this need: *God has created this need, in order to draw us home.* This is not a human construction; it is a human perception of a stimulus that originates from God, and is intended to lead to God. It is therefore important to acknowledge – not suppress – this desire, and ask what it points towards. It is true that we often attach ourselves to lesser goods, rather than to the supreme good for which we were created. Anselm's point is that our sense of longing is not something we should deny or ignore; it is a homing instinct implanted within us by our Creator, a clue to who and what we are meant to be – and this is achieved by coming home to God.

Christianity thus provides an interpretative framework – a "big picture" – which allows an experience (in this case, a human desire for something of ultimate significance) to be understood as a God-given longing for God. Within the context of this Christian framework, this experience is a clue to *who* we really *are*, and *what* we really *desire*. The uninterpreted experience on its own is of little apologetic value, until it is seen in the right way as a "signal of transcendence," a reminder that humanity's ultimate goal lies in relating to God. This is the point Anselm makes in his prayer.

We find a similar theme in the writings of apologists down the ages – such as Augustine of Hippo, Blaise Pascal, and C. S. Lewis. God creates this sense of emptiness within us, in order to help us grasp that only God can satisfy our deepest longings. Lewis, for example, speaks about this longing in terms of "Joy," and sees God as both its source and its goal. In his spiritual autobiography *Surprised by Joy*, Lewis describes the events that led to his conversion. "I was now approaching the source from which those arrows of Joy had been shot at me ever since childhood. … I had hoped that the heart of reality might be of such a kind that we can best symbolize it as a place; instead, I found it to be a Person."

The Christian faith thus gives us a truthful framework through which we can see ourselves. It helps us realize that we have been created by God in order to relate to God, and explains or interprets our sense of need as a disclosure of our need for God, and the "benefits of Christ." And this truth has experiential implications – that we shall never be satisfied until we relate to God. Christianity thus offers us a way of seeing human nature that helps us to understand what the human problem really is, what can be done about it, and the difference that this makes. It illuminates our situation, stripping away delusions and misunderstandings; it helps us grasp the significance of the saving work of Christ in dealing with this problem; and it unfolds the consequences of this for the lives of human beings. To use Melanchthon's phrase that we noted earlier in this chapter (p. 67), while theology helps us to *understand* the "benefits of Christ," apologetics helps us to *connect* each of these benefits with individual human situations. In doing this, the apologist is not *inventing* such connections, but is rather drawing them out, and showing their significance.

Christianity meets our deepest needs, and calms our deepest fears. To pick up some themes from John's gospel, Christ is the living water who quenches our thirst (John 4:5–30), and the bread of life who satisfies our hunger (John 6:30–5). The gospel thus provides both a diagnosis of the human situation and how it may be transformed. Christ is the physician who holds up a mirror to our souls, so that we can grasp our predicament, before offering to heal our wounds.

In what follows, I will reflect briefly on the ways in which a number of New Testament images of salvation helps us develop a theologically informed apologetics. They help us to explain and communicate the identity of Christ, and the nature of sin and salvation. Each image casts its own distinct light on the human predicament, and how it is transformed through Christ, making the complex notion of salvation accessible both to those within and beyond the church. Readers can easily extend this list of biblical images, and develop further possible connections with their audiences.

Christ the Physician: Healing a Wounded and Broken Humanity

One of the central themes of the Old Testament is that God heals a broken world, and restores damaged people. The "suffering servant," which is such a significant element of the prophecy of Isaiah, explicitly sets out a narrative of divine healing of a wounded humanity.

> Surely he has borne our infirmities and carried our diseases; yet we accounted him stricken, struck down by God, and afflicted. But he was wounded for our transgressions, crushed for our iniquities; upon him was the punishment that made us whole, and by his bruises we are healed (Isaiah 53:4–5).

Other Old Testament prophets emphasized this hope of healing, comparing God to a physician, or to a "sun of righteousness" that would rise "with healing in its rays" (Malachi 4:2). For Christianity, Christ's healing ministry can be seen as an extension of this theme of the divine healing of humanity.

This theme is intensified through the intense focus on the cross in the New Testament. The crucified Christ's wounds and suffering are here seen as transforming the lives of believers. In some way, Christ bore this pain and suffering for others, in order that they might be healed. Early Christian writers were aware of the apologetic importance of this theme. In the late first century, Ignatius of Antioch spoke of the "medicine of immortality" – in other words, comparing the gospel to a drug that was able to heal humanity's fatal illness, so that death need no longer be feared.

In the fifth century, Augustine of Hippo suggested that the church was like a field hospital – full of wounded and ill people, who were recovering under the care of Christ the physician and the medicine that he provides. For Augustine, human beings were damaged and trapped by sin, which was like a hereditary disease, passed down from one generation to another, which weakens humanity, and cannot be cured by human agency. Christ is the divine physician, who diagnoses our situation, and by whose "wounds we are healed" (Isaiah 53:5). We are thus healed by the grace of God, so that our minds may recognize God and our wills may respond to the divine offer of grace.

So how can this theme be used apologetically? How does it connect up with the cultural mood, and with the aspirations and concerns of ordinary people? The US theologian H. Richard Niebuhr distinguishes two different kinds of narratives of healing – a "scientific case history" of someone who had been blind, and who can now see, which focusses on changes in his optic nerve; and an "inner history" of someone who "had lived in darkness and now saw again trees and the sunrise, children's faces and the eyes of a friend." The second narrative is about personal transformation, and a renewal of the capacity to live fully and properly – rather than an essentially mechanical narrative of fixing the optic nerve. The "inner history" explains how the subjective world of the healed individual was transformed by an objective correction of a physical defect. The "scientific case history," however, fails to bring out the subjective and existential significance of this healing.

The human situation is that we are wounded or damaged, and need putting back together again. Yet we need a healing that goes deeper than merely fixing our physical damage. In a recent reflection on the nature of divine healing, the Australian surgeon James McTavish tells of a distressed young man who slashed his wrists, hoping to end his life. McTavish and his team operated on him, and they were able to reconstitute the damaged wrists.

> I told the boy that we had fixed his hand. He started to cry. I asked him "Why are you crying? The worst part is over. We fixed your hand." He replied "You fixed my hand but who is going to fix my life?"

There may indeed be an important correlation between "health" and "salvation." Yet, as McTavish noted, salvation is about more than health: is it about a new quality and vitality of life, characterized by *significance* and *meaning*.

The soteriological metaphor of healing can also be used to explore the question of what needs to be done if we are to benefit from Christ. Any discussion of the nature of what Melanchthon termed the "benefits of Christ" must lead into reflection on how we can connect up with these benefits. Melanchthon himself answered this question as follows:

> Therefore when we say that faith lays hold of the benefits of Christ, it is necessary to understand that people lay hold of them because of Christ, and they must assent to the divine promise and believe that the promises are truly given for us. Faith does not signify merely a knowledge of history, but trust in the promised mercy because of Christ, giving assent to the divine promise.

For Melanchthon, faith is the means or channel by which the believer is connected to Christ, and thus shares in the benefits that Christ has secured through his life, death, and resurrection.

So how can Melanchthon's idea of taking hold of the benefits of Christ through faith be visualized or modelled? Here's an example, which will give you a sense of how you might approach this. I am based in the Humanities Division at Oxford University, which is located in what was formerly the Radcliffe Infirmary, a hospital built in 1770 near the center of Oxford. In February 1941, Professor Howard Florey carried out the first clinical trials of the new drug penicillin on a human being – Albert Alexander, a 43-year-old policeman – at the Radcliffe Infirmary, demonstrating that this antibiotic was both safe and effective.

So imagine that you, like Albert Alexander, have a potentially fatal infection. You know you need to be healed. And you further know that penicillin has the capacity to heal your infection. *Yet this knowledge in itself does not heal you.* This requires action on your part – namely, to take this medicine, in order that it can fight your infection. Faith, for Melanchthon, is about taking hold of Christ, in order that his benefits become part of us, rather than keeping him at a distance. Faith is about the internal appropriation of Christ through faith. If Christ is our physician, we need to follow his instructions, and use the medicine that he supplies.

Other analogies could easily be developed. Part of the art of apologetics is crafting images, analogies, or stories that connect up with your audience, and help them appreciate the importance of the personal appropriation of the benefits of Christ.

Christ the Sacrifice: Entering the Presence of God

In its first phase, Christianity gave careful thought to clarifying its relation to the history of Israel, presenting itself as the simultaneous fulfilment and reframing of the hopes and mission of the people of God. Christ's declaration in the Sermon on the Mount was widely cited in support of this view: "Do not think that I have come to abolish the Law or the Prophets. I have come not to abolish them, but to fulfil them" (Matthew 5:17). The Letter to the Hebrews developed an approach that was particularly influential, portraying Christ as having fulfilled the religious cult of ancient Israel – and in doing so, made redundant the practice of sacrifice, and the institution and instruments of the cult itself. Christ is presented in this analysis as both a purified high priest and a perfect sacrifice, framed by the context of the traditional "Day of Atonement" cultic ritual (Leviticus 16:6; 15–19; 32–33). The fact that this ritual had to be repeated annually is interpreted as indicative of the failure of this cultic means for purging sin, partly on account of defects or impurities on the part of both the High Priest who offers the sacrifice and the sacrifice which is offered. The problem is *affirmed*; it is not possible to draw close to God without an effective sacrifice; the Jewish cultic solution to this problem, however, is declared to have been *superseded*.

The letter to the Hebrews portrays Christ as the High Priest whose "once and for all" sacrifice has finally dealt with the problem of sin. The human situation is here understood as a loss of access to the presence of God. Humanity is contaminated or tainted by impurity, and is thus unable to draw close to God. Christ is the one who, by making a sacrifice on behalf of humanity, is able to secure renewed access to God through the removal of the taint of impurity.

So what is the apologetic payload of this aspect of the Christian understanding of salvation? A key point to emphasize is that many people have a sense of inadequacy or guilt that makes them feel that they cannot enter into the presence of a holy God. While they may not articulate this in terms of sin, their basic sense is that they are not entitled to draw close to God; they are not worthy of entering God's presence; or that they are so insignificant that God would have no interest in them. We shall reflect on the importance of the incarnation for self-worth later in this chapter (pp. 77–81). The apologetic point is that Christ compensates for our inadequacies and purges our guilt, thus enabling us to draw close to God.

Adoption: Believing and Belonging

Many of the images of salvation used in the New Testament have clear links to the history of Israel – such as Christ as a High Priest who makes a sacrifice that enables believers to stand in the presence of a holy God, discussed in the previous section. Yet some other images of salvation are located within a cultural framework that might have been unfamiliar and unintelligible to Jewish readers. A good example of this is the image of "adoption," which Paul uses at several points in his letters to express the distinction between believers as "sons of God" and Jesus Christ as "the Son of God" (Romans 8:15; 23; 9:4; Galatians 4:5). Under Roman adoption law, the head of a family (*paterfamilias*) was free to adopt individuals – always males – from outside his natural family, and give them the legal status of adoption. This had three consequences for those who were adopted. First, it meant that all their existing debts would be cancelled; second, they would be granted the same inheritance rights as the natural children of the *paterfamilias*; and third, they would take on the name of the adopting family and have the same social status as its other members.

This metaphor provides a cultural analogy, drawn from Roman cultural practice, for the process of the legal and social translocation of the believer from *outside* the people to God to *within* this privileged community. It establishes an intellectual and imaginative bridge between Christ and believers, exploring the consequences of believers being accepted by God for their social status, inheritance rights, and self-esteem. The metaphor offers a clarification of the legal aspects of this act of social reallocation and redesignation, while also allowing us to appreciate its emotional impact on those who are adopted. The *outsiders* become *insiders*, gaining a status and new identity, which results in relational transformation and personal and social transvaluation. They *feel* accepted and valued, and potentially empowered.

This rich biblical image connects up with one of the most profound human emotions and aspirations – the desire to *belong* somewhere. Adoption is about being wanted. It is a compelling affirmation of belonging. In adoption, someone is transferred from a relational wasteland, and welcomed into a family. The person enters the family home by invitation of the head of the family, because they have been chosen. They are wanted, valued, and significant. They are not gate crashers or interlopers, who must constantly fear the threats of discovery, exposure, and expulsion, which are often described as an "imposter syndrome." They are not unwanted intruders in the kingdom of God, but are rather welcome guests, who can luxuriate in the security and warmth of the family home, knowing that they have the right to be there. And having received this legal status of being adopted, we can call God "Abba" – Father! – because that is what God has now become to us (Romans 8:15).

The image of adoption thus provides a plausible analogy, drawn from Roman cultural practice, for the process of the legal and social translocation of the believer from outside the people of God to within this family. The important point to appreciate here is not primarily the legal aspects of this act of social reallocation and legal redesignation, but its emotional impact on those who are adopted – the outsiders who become insiders, gaining a status and new identity, which results in relational transformation and personal and social transvaluation. They *feel* accepted and valued, and potentially empowered. It is also important to note how this soteriological metaphor gives a significant role to the Christian community – the church – as the family of God, which welcomes, affirms, and enfolds an outsider who has now become a family member.

Liberation: Salvation as Deliverance from Bondage

In explaining the difference that the death and resurrection of Christ makes, the New Testament often uses the language of "redemption" – the idea of being set free from some form of bondage or slavery. The social world of early Christianity had little difficulty in making sense of the ideas of bondage and enslavement, in that both were familiar everyday social realities. The Pauline notion of "redemption" is located within a specific context in which as many as one in three inhabitants of first-century cities were slaves, perhaps having sold themselves into slavery to pay off a debt. These slaves could be "redeemed" through a commercial transaction in which their freedom was purchased by a benefactor. For Paul, the freedom of Christians has been purchased, in that Christians have been "bought with a price" (1 Corinthians 6:20; 7:23). God has set Christians free from the bondage of sin by means of Christ, in order that we might be "adopted" as God's sons (Galatians 4:4–5).

Taken on its own, this way of thinking about Christ's role as "paying a price" in securing the salvation of humanity may seem impersonally transactionalist. Yet the important point to note is that the New Testament sees Christ as a liberator, someone who is prepared to do whatever it takes to secure the release of captives and those in bondage, whether this includes paying a price for their redemption, or overwhelming those who held them captive (a point made particularly in the "Christus Victor" approach to the work of Christ). Christian theologians subsequently explored the question of what it was about Christ that enabled the purchase of the liberation of those in bondage. Two main lines of argument were developed: that Christ's capacity to purchase freedom for captives rested on his status as God incarnate; and that it was grounded in his obedience to God. This image of salvation thus asks us to imagine the human condition as bondage or imprisonment, and to think of the transformative impact of Christ in terms of liberation, understood both in terms of a changed social or legal status, and the benefits that this brings.

The image of liberation is also significant apologetically in terms of being set free from sin. From a Christian perspective, human nature is damaged and wounded by sin, and not able to achieve its full potential unaided. This theme was developed particularly by Augustine of Hippo, who was exquisitely sensitive to human weakness, fragility, and brokenness. Augustine argues that sin is like a power that holds us captive, and from whose grip we are unable to break free by ourselves. The human free will is held captive by sin, and may only be liberated by grace. Christ is thus seen as the liberator, the source of the grace which breaks the power of sin. Or again, sin is a type of guilt or moral impurity which is passed down from one generation to another. Christ thus comes to bring forgiveness and pardon. Using such images, Augustine builds up a powerful account of human nature being weakened, impoverished, and trapped by sin – but healed and liberated by grace. Yet that word "sin" needs further exploration and explanation.

Explaining the Nature of Sin

The term "sin" is one of the most difficult Christian terms to explain to a secular audience, partly because many resist any suggestion that humanity is imperfect or flawed, seeing this as insulting or demeaning. It is helpful here to turn again to Augustine of Hippo, who helps us set these concerns in perspective. Augustine regularly used the image of *Christus Medicus* ("Christ the Physician") in his sermons, drawing on the gospel accounts of Christ's healing ministry. Early in that ministry, Christ declares that "it is not the healthy who need a doctor, but the sick" (Mark 2:17). Christ thus insists that he has "not come to call the righteous, but sinners." Especially when set in the context of Christ's healing ministry, the analogy between sin and illness is compelling. Christ's words to those who have been healed are important here: "Your faith has healed you" (e.g., Luke 18:42). The Greek verb *sōzein*, here translated as "healed," can also be translated as "saved" or "made whole." Salvation is about the restoration of humanity, a process of healing that purges us of guilt and sin.

Augustine developed a rich conception of sin, drawing on the biblical witness to identify a number of its core elements. Sin, for Augustine, is a condition that predisposes us to self-centeredness, blindsiding us to our flaws and weaknesses. There is something that is wrong with us, inclining us to mess up things and become locked into self-deceptive patterns of thought and destructive patterns of behavior. Sin is primarily a state of alienation from God leading to sinful actions. As the noted evangelist Billy Graham repeatedly stated: "S-I-N causes S-I-N-S." Sin is like a spiritual disease that resides deep within us, preventing us from recognizing who we really are and what we ought to be doing.

This idea of sin as entrapment or imprisonment is brilliantly captured in Paul's reflections on his failure to do what he knows to be right.

> Although I want to do good, evil is right there with me. For in my inner being I delight in God's law; but I see another law at work in me, waging war against the law of my mind and making me a prisoner of the law of sin at work within me. What a wretched man I am! Who will rescue me from this body that is subject to death? Thanks be to God, who delivers me through Jesus Christ our Lord! So then, I myself in my mind am a slave to God's law, but in my flesh a slave to the law of sin (Romans 7:21–5).

Sin is here understood as a force or presence within us, making us unable to master or control use of our own resources, and locking us into patterns of rebellion, failure, guilt, and dissatisfaction. The problem is our inbuilt state of sin – what Augustine terms "original sin," to make the point that this is not an option that we choose, but is something that is intrinsic to human identity. This is not an outdated premodern worldview that should be abandoned, but a perennial truth about human nature which, as G. K. Chesterton points out, history keeps on reaffirming, and is essential to a proper understanding of the human situation. Even in the classical age, Stoic philosophers warned against being trapped by *epithymia* – an irrational emotion based on a mistaken opinion about the true value of things, which prevents a proper understanding of life.

Many recent secular writers, reacting against the naïve optimism of the "Age of Reason," have recognized this problem of human entrapment, and reflected on how human beings might be able to break free from this captivity. In her *Prisons We Choose to Live Inside*, Doris Lessing explored how we create prisons of the mind, setting out deficient and destructive worldviews that first seduce us and then imprison us. In his *Symphonie Pastorale*, André Gide wrote of a girl, blind from birth, who simply could not see the beauty of the mountains and lakes around her. It was only when her sight was healed by a surgeon in Lausanne that she was liberated from her entrapment within a deficient view of reality, and could see the world as it really is. Ludwig Wittgenstein remarked that we are "held captive by a picture," which distorts our view of the world, and traps us within its falsities. Sigmund Freud wrote of humanity being trapped by illusions, which imprisoned and impoverished them psychologically. Perhaps one of the most effective, if disturbing, cultural analogies that captures some of the core themes of the Christian understanding of sin is addiction. Alcohol and opiates so easily capture and entrap individuals, leading to them being driven by a desire that overwhelms their moral instincts, dominating their lives without delivering satisfaction. Everything becomes secondary to finding the next fix.

All these approaches recognize some aspects of the human predicament. Yet Christianity offers a diagnosis of the human situation, in order that humanity might find healing. Sin is about being spiritually overwhelmed and locking God out – and by doing so, preventing us from being healed. Sin is like an illness that prevents us from admitting that we are ill and need to be cured. Apologetically, it is helpful to compare sin to an illness, which causes certain symptoms. You cannot heal someone by addressing their symptoms; you have to deal with the root cause of those symptoms. Sinners need to be healed.

One of the reasons that Christians place so much emphasis on the acknowledgement or "confession" of sin (for example, in public worship) is that this breaks delusional patterns of thinking that we are good and self-sufficient, and reorientates us towards God as the source of healing, transformation, and joy. We acknowledge both that we are ill and that we are unable to heal ourselves; as a result, we seek the help of a competent physician, who provides a cure for our illness; and as a result of being healed, we are able to change our patterns of living and lifestyles, gradually breaking free from the hold of sin.

One more point needs to be made. For every Christian concept of salvation, there is a corresponding concept of sin. We have already seen how sin can be understood as *illness*, and salvation as *healing*. Others could be noted, and used apologetically. Salvation is about *reconciliation* to God, just as sin is about *alienation* from God. Salvation is about being *redeemed* from captivity or bondage, just as sin is about being *trapped* in captivity or bondage. The apologist has access to a rich range of images in exploring both the Christian understanding of the human predicament, and the transformative effect of the gospel.

Apologetic Aspects of the Incarnation

Thus far, we have considered how the Christian understanding of salvation has significant apologetic implications, offering important points of contact and connection with the human situation, and the notion of sin. But what of the doctrine of the incarnation? At the heart of the New Testament is the belief that something *new* and life changing has happened in Jesus Christ. The opening of the first letter of John captures this sense of astonishment at the new world opened up by the life, death, and resurrection of Christ:

> We declare to you what was from the beginning, what we have heard, what we have seen with our eyes, what we have looked at and touched with our hands, concerning the word of life – this life was revealed, and we have seen it and testify to it, and declare to you the eternal life that was with the Father and was revealed to us (1 John 1:1–2).

The doctrine of the incarnation speaks of a direct transformative personal encounter between God and humanity that is made possible by the Son of God coming amongst us as one of us in a visible and tangible manner. Yet while the incarnation has long been recognized as a central focus of the Christian faith, its apologetic aspects have often been neglected. So what use it is *apologetically?* In what follows, I shall tease out some aspects of the Christian understanding of the incarnation, and note their apologetic application.

Rethinking the Nature of God

The French philosopher Blaise Pascal (Figure 4.3) drew a sharp distinction between the "God of Abraham, God of Isaac, God of Jacob" on the one hand, and the "God of the philosophers" on the other. We need to remember that the term "God" is open to multiple interpretations. Indeed, a central theme of Christian theology is the clarification of what God lies at the heart of faith. The doctrine of the incarnation plays an important role in this process. As rethinking the nature of God was an important part of my own transition from atheism to Christianity, I shall tell my own story at this point, to clarify the apologetic significance of this issue.

I was an atheist as a teenager, partly because I believed that science and religion were at war with each other, and partly because God seemed to be a total irrelevance. God was in heaven (wherever that was), and I was on earth. It seemed to me that God was a distant reality standing behind or outside history, detached from human existential concerns and shielded from the traumas of history. I could see no intellectual or existential case for believing in a God like that. I left atheism behind me shortly after arriving at Oxford University to study the natural sciences, partly because of my growing realization of the intellectual over-ambition of the

Figure 4.3   The philosopher and mathematician Blaise Pascal (1623–1662), one of the most significant apologists of the seventeenth century. Adobe Stock Image 32208863.

forms of atheism I had earlier embraced, but also as I came to realize that Christianity offered a way of making sense of the world I observed around me and experienced within me.

Christianity offered me a rationally plausible and imaginatively compelling "big picture" of reality that brought my worlds and concerns into focus. It is not so much a collection of isolated individual beliefs, but a web of interconnected beliefs, which gains its strength and appeal partly because of its comprehensiveness, and partly because of its intellectual and imaginative resilience. Christian theology weaves together the threads of biblical truth to disclose a pattern of meaning – like a tapestry, which brings many individual threads together, thus allowing their deeper significance and interconnections to be appreciated.

A central theme of this "big picture" is the incarnation. While the doctrine of the incarnation helps us grasp the significance of Jesus Christ for humanity, it also tells us something about the kind of God that Christians love and worship. The biblical affirmation that the "word became flesh and lived among us" (John 1:14) offers a radically different concept of God – not the abstract and remote "God of the Philosophers," but a God who cares for us, not as a passive distant observer, but as an active fellow traveler and constant companion within the historical process. God is someone we can know and address in worship and prayer.

One of my objections to Christian belief as a teenager had been my feeling that God was existentially irrelevant. I conceived this nonexistent God as a distant figure, without any involvement in the world. God was in heaven – wherever that was. And I was located in the flow of space and time that we call human history. Since God was absent from the flow of history, God seemed to me to be an irrelevance.

My teenage atheism was partly a result of my rationalist understanding of God as a static, impersonal, and indifferent being, who stood over and above human history. The philosopher Roger Scruton perceptively summarized this way of thinking about God and its consequences: "The God of the philosophers disappeared behind the world, because he was described in the third person, and not addressed in the second." As I reflected on the doctrine of the incarnation, I could see that this idea was a game changer. If this doctrine was right, the Christian experience of God was very different from my dull rationalist preconceptions of what God ought to be like.

The incarnation thus gives us both a new way of *thinking* about God, and a new way of *visualizing* God. God is like Christ, who is the "image of the invisible God" (Col 1:15). God is with us in history – not merely in the sense of being on our side, but also in the sense of standing alongside us, sharing our story, and journeying with us. God was not a distant and disinterested autocrat, who watched the sufferings of the world indifferently from a safe distance. *This* God chose to enter into our world, to share its pain and sorrow, to enter human history in human form, with all the risks this involved. Why? Because we matter to God, and that is what God is like.

Seeing the Face of God

Christians hold that they can see the face, not merely know the character, of God. Albert Einstein, however, famously considered God to be an impersonal and disembodied "mind" that lies behind the observed universe. Einstein repeatedly refers to an "intelligence," "mind," or "force," which lies behind or beyond the universe, and identifies this with God. "This firm belief in a superior mind that reveals itself in the world of experience, represents my conception of God." For Einstein, God is faceless, a mysterious impersonal presence within the universe that is shrouded in mystery and cannot be known or visualized, familiar to readers of C. S. Lewis's late novel *Till we Have Faces*. This inscrutable God, indifferent to the fate of humanity, cannot be observed or known.

The idea of knowing God "face to face," however, is of major importance to both Christian theology and spirituality. This rich analogy, with its deep imaginative and relational emphases, points to the serious theological deficits of notions of a "faceless" God. The philosopher Roger Scruton recently highlighted the importance of this point, noting that human identity is linked with the capacity to form meaningful relationships with persons – with those who have *faces*, which in some way disclose who they are. For Scruton, God is the *logos* "which relates object to subject as a smile relates you to me."

Scruton's views find their echo in the writings of the US philosopher Paul Elmer More (1864–1937). As a young man, More was fascinated and initially deeply satisfied by the ideal world of beautiful Platonic forms, the silent, majestic yet totally impersonal world of the purely ideal. Yet More began to experience a sense of unutterable bleakness and loneliness in this still, silent realm. "The thought of a naked soul journeying forever on and on through inanimate idea, with no personal guide or consoler … send a shudder and a chill through me." He longed for those impersonal forms to become personal, to disclose a face. For More, the world of Platonic forms was alienating, in that it seemed impersonal and faceless. "My longing for some audible voice out of the infinite silence rose to a pitch of torture. To be satisfied I must see face to face, I must, as it were, handle and feel."

More's longing to find a personal reality at the heart of reality was finally met through grasping the significance of the Christian doctrine of the incarnation. Here, More declared, God was disclosed in personal form; here is God with a face; here is a God who can be seen, known, touched, and named. The theological, spiritual, and artistic importance of this point was brought out clearly by the Scottish art historian Neil MacGregor: "Unlike Muslims and Jews, Christians (or at least the early Christians) have *seen* their God; for Christianity is the religion of the Word made flesh, and, largely as a consequence, it is also a religion of the image."

This desire to see the face of God – and a corresponding fear that God's face might be hidden or inaccessible – is deeply embedded in the faith of ancient Israel and in the New Testament. The Psalmist longed to see God – to behold the face of God in the land of the living. "I thirst for God, the living God; when shall I go to see the face of God?" (Psalm 42:2). The medieval writer Nicholas of Cusa summed up the importance of seeing God *and being seen by God* in a neat maxim: "I am because you look upon me" (Latin: "Ego sum quia tu me respicies.") Yet how can God be seen? In particular, how could the beauty of God be represented in ancient Israel's theological culture marked by an explicit rejection of the construction or use of images of the divine in any form of personal or corporate worship?

In the light of these concerns, we can understand why the incarnation is a game changer in this matter. The doctrine of the incarnation affirmed that God, who cannot be seen or touched, chose to enter into the world in a *visible and tangible form*. This electrifying declaration is central to the New Testament's witness to the significance of Christ. Christ enables believers to see God face to face, knowing God not as an object, but as a person. In Christ, God is embodied – made tangible, visible, and audible, and thus made accessible to humanity.

The New Testament's insistence that Christ is the "image of the invisible God" (Colossians 1:15) speaks of God choosing to self-disclose in Christ. This striking and theologically profound way of speaking, when taken together with the assertion that all things "hold together" in Christ (Colossians 1:17), offers a Christological framework both for visualizing the divine and affirming the intrinsic coherence of the created order. As the US theologian Katherine Sonderegger notes, the New Testament clearly indicates that Christ "is the grounding Logic of the whole creation."

The apologetic implications of the incarnation, when this is seen as disclosing the face of a God who wants to be *known*, rather than merely *known about*, will be clear. More's feeling of alienation and detachment from a faceless world of Platonic forms – especially his deep longing to "see face to face," to "handle and feel" the transcendent – is an important starting point for a wider discussion of the Christian understanding of the incarnation.

Christianity and the Human Quest for Meaning

The British novelist Jeanette Winterson is one of many writers to highlight the significance of finding meaning in life for human beings. This, she argues, sets us apart from animals, and defines what really matters in life.

> A meaningless life for a human being has none of the dignity of animal unselfconsciousness; we cannot simply eat, sleep, hunt and reproduce – we are meaning seeking creatures. The Western world has done away with religion but not with our religious impulses; we seem to need some higher purpose, some point to our lives – money and leisure, social progress, are just not enough.

Modern psychology suggests that there seems to be a global human sense of a need for meaning. Most human beings want to understand what they experience and to feel that their lives have significance and purpose. And while empirical psychology is not able to determine the meaning of life, it has clearly established how important the notion of "meaning" is for human beings, and the difference that it makes to human flourishing and wellbeing. The psychologist Michael F. Steger, Director of the Center for Meaning and Purpose, and Professor of Psychology at Colorado State University, suggests that we can thinking of "meaning in life" as "the extent to which people comprehend, make sense of, or see significance in their lives, accompanied by the degree to which they perceive themselves to have a purpose, mission, or overarching aim in life." Meaning is about the way in which people make sense of the world, see significance in their lives, and locate themselves within a greater scheme of things.

While many families of philosophical traditions deriving from Aristotelianism and Stoicism have much to say about the nature of meaning in life, it is widely recognized that religion in general, and Christianity in particular, has a distinctive capacity to provide people with a comprehensive and integrated framework of meaning, which both helps to make sense of their observations and experiences, while at the same time providing a way of helping them to transcend their own limited experience and situation, and connect up with something greater.

In a perceptive lecture delivered at Cambridge University in 1990, the novelist Salman Rushdie argues that religion has met three types of needs that have failed to be satisfied by secular, rationalist materialism. First, it enables us to articulate our sense of awe and wonder, partly by helping us grasp the immensity of life, and partly by affirming that we are special. Second, it provides "answers to the unanswerable," engaging the deep questions that so often trouble and perplex us. And finally, it offers us a moral framework, within which we can live out the good life. For Rushdie, the "idea of God" provides us with a "repository of our awestruck wonderment at life, and an answer to the great questions of existence." Any attempt to describe or define human beings "in terms that exclude their spiritual needs" will only end in failure.

So what sort of "meaning" are we talking about? In what follows, we shall consider a number of issues of apologetic importance, and explore how these are connected with core themes of the Christian faith.

Finding a Secure Base in Life

A central theme of classical Christian thinking about the nature of the life of faith is the importance of "taking hold of Christ (*apprehendere Christum*)" or "being united with Christ (*unio cum Christo*)." For writers such as John Calvin and Martin Luther, faith involves the believer becoming attached to Christ, or united with Christ, thus initiating a process of transformation and renewal. Many spiritual writers of the Middle Ages recognized the importance of the theme of "attachment to Christ." In the late twentieth century, however, this has come to be expressed particularly in terms of "attachment theory," which points to the importance of a "secure base" for a young child resulting from parental attachment. This arose from the work of the social psychologist John Bowlby, particularly his 1988 work *A Secure Base*, which highlighted the importance of parental attachment to positive personal development, and the negative impact of separation. The potential of such a model for illuminating the affective aspects of the notion of the parental care of God, embodied in Christ, will be clear. God is the one who accompanies us through life, and is the "secure base" that enables us to cope with life's ambiguities and complexities.

Finding Fulfilment

Many people regard the search for personal and communal authenticity and fulfilment as being of central and critical importance. The idea that Christianity both articulates and enables such fulfilment seems to have been present from its beginning. Christianity did not present itself as an enemy of Judaism (within which it initially emerged), but rather as representing its climax and fulfilment. "Do not think that I have come to abolish the Law or the Prophets; I have not come to abolish them but to fulfil them" (Matthew 5:17). Yet as Christianity established itself in Roman and Greek culture in the late first century, early Christian writers pointed out how Christianity was the fulfilment of the classic human quest for wisdom, and highlighted the way in which Christianity resonated with themes in the writings of philosophers such as Plato and Plotinus.

Other early Christian writers located the significance of Christianity at a more existential level. For Augustine of Hippo, Christianity offered a vision of a God who was able to fulfil the deepest longings of the human heart. This is expressed in his famous prayer: "You have made us for yourself, and our heart is restless until it finds its rest in you." Augustine held that human beings have some inbuilt longing to relate to God (which he linked with bearing the "image of God"), so that finding and embracing God is thus about becoming what we are meant to be, and finding joy and peace in doing so. In this sense, it is perfectly reasonable to speak of a "Christian humanism" – as opposed to, for example, a secular humanism, which argues that religion is an improper and dysfunctional imposition upon humanity.

Inhabiting a Coherent World

The philosopher Iris Murdoch is one of many writers to bring out the importance of appreciating the "calming" and "healing" effect of ways of looking at the world that make it seem rational and meaningful. One of the benefits of thinking of Christianity as a "big picture" – rather than as an assembly of individual doctrinal components – is that this makes it clear that Christianity is a coherent way of thinking. Christian theologians have, since the earliest times, argued that such seeming irrationalities as the presence of suffering in the world do not constitute a challenge to the notions of meaning and purpose that are embedded within the Christian faith. Augustine of Hippo, for example, set out an approach to the presence of evil within the world, which affirmed the original integrity, goodness, and rationality of the world. Evil and suffering arose from a misuse of freedom, the effects of which are being remedied and transformed through redemption. Augustine argues that the believer is enabled to make sense of the enigmas of suffering and evil in the world by recalling its original goodness, and looking forward to its final renewal and restoration in heaven.

Yet many in contemporary western culture echo the view of the physicist Steven Weinberg that the natural sciences disclose a meaningless universe. "The more the universe seems comprehensible, the more it seems pointless." Yet this is simply a belief, a perception rather than an objective fact or justified conclusion. The New Testament takes a different perspective, speaking of all things "holding together" or being "knit together" in Christ (Colossians 1:17), thus suggesting that a hidden coherence lies beneath the external semblances of our world. Christianity provides a framework which allows an affirmation of the *coherence of reality*. However fragmented our world of experience may appear, there is a half-glimpsed "bigger picture" that holds things together, its threads connecting together in a web of meaning that might otherwise seem incoherent and pointless.

This is a major theme in one of the finest Christian literary classics – Dante's *Divine Comedy*. As this great Renaissance poem draws to its close, Dante catches a glimpse of the unity of the cosmos, in which its aspects and levels are seen to converge into a single whole. This insight, of course, is tantalizingly denied to him from his perspective on earth; yet once grasped, this perspective enables him to see his life in a new way. Dante's insight is this: there is a hidden web of meaning and connectedness behind the ephemeral and seemingly incoherent world that we experience.

A Sense of Self-worth

Being loved and valued is of critical importance to many people. The poet Raymond Carver illustrates this well, speaking of his longing "to know myself beloved, to feel myself beloved on the earth." This helps us appreciate why so many people regard personal relationships as being of such significance, and find their sense of self-worth affirmed and validated through them. Yet this thought is constantly subverted by reflecting on the apparent insignificance of humanity, when seen in its broader cosmic context. Sigmund Freud famously argued that scientific advance has led to a radical reevaluation of the place and significance of humanity in the universe, deflating human pretensions to grandeur and uniqueness. As our knowledge of our universe expands, we realize how many galaxies lie beyond our own. The human lifespan is insignificant in comparison with the immense age of the universe. We can easily be overwhelmed by a sense of our own insignificance, when we see ourselves against this vast cosmic backdrop.

So what answers might be given to this sense of despair and pointlessness? Is our self-worth undermined, if not destroyed, by these reflections? Some would argue that we need to face up to our situation, whether in a bold act of intellectual defiance, or a gracious resignation to a bleak emptiness as we contemplate our limited role in the greater scheme of things. Christian writers regularly engage these questions, often speaking of the transvaluation of human life through being "touched" by God – a theme that is found, for example, throughout the poetic writings of George Herbert. Herbert likens the graceful "touch" of God to the fabled "philosopher's stone" of medieval alchemy, which transmutes base metal into gold (a theme to which we shall return later, pp. 173–75). Through inhabiting the Christian narrative, we come to see ourselves, as the medieval writer Julian of Norwich famously put it, as being enfolded in the love of Christ, which brings us a new security, identity, and value. Our self-worth is grounded in being loved by God.

Earlier, I noted the importance of personal relationships in affirming a human sense of self-worth. Perhaps this helps us understand why the Christian idea of a personal God who loves individual human beings, and demonstrates that love through the acts of incarnation and atonement, is seen as so important by many spiritual writers. God is one who relates to us, and thence transforms our sense of value and significance precisely through this privilege of relationship. We matter to God.

This point is brought out by Marilynne Robinson (Figure 4.4), in an apologetically insightful essay entitled "Psalm Eight." Robinson here engages the deep human feeling of insignificance in the face of the temporal and spatial vastness of the universe by drawing on some of the opening verses of this Psalm:

> When I look at your heavens, the work of your fingers,
> the moon and the stars that you have established;
> what are human beings that you are mindful of them,
> mortals that you care for them? (Psalm 8:3–4).

Figure 4.4   The novelist Marilyn Robinson pictured with President Obama in the White House at the 2012 National Humanities awards in 2013. Alamy Image 2DYRJ8G.

Robinson suggests that the fact that we are created by God reassures us that we are, at least in some sense, *special*.

> The strategy of the Psalmist is to close the infinite distance between God and human-kind by confounding all notions of scale. If the great heavens are the work of God's fingers, what is small and mortal man? The poem answers its own question this way: Man is crowned with honor and glory. He is in a singular sense what God has made him, because of the dignity God has conferred upon him, splendor of a higher order, like that of angels.

Yet Robinson then supplements this with a second insight – that this "infinite distance between God and humankind" is intentionally and graciously bridged by God. Robinson's point is that, in the act of incarnation, God "visits" humanity, deeming us worthy of such a divine act of humility and compassion. Both God's works of creation and redemption affirm that human beings matter to God. *They* are special; *we* are special.

In this chapter, we have considered some important themes relating to the way in which Christianity connects with and engages some fundamental concerns. In the next chapter, we shall take this exploration further, and consider the idea of "points of contact" and their apologetic significance.

Study Questions

1. Is it irrational to appeal to human longing in apologetics?
2. Set out, in your own words, the apologetic potential of these aspects of the Christian understanding of salvation: redemption; healing; adoption.
3. Set out, in your own words, how you might develop the apologetic potential of the incarnation.
4. In what ways does the incarnation affirm that humanity really matters to God?

For Further Reading

Aitken, James K., Hector M. Patmore, and Ishay Rosen-Zvi, eds. *The Evil Inclination in Early Judaism and Christianity.* Cambridge: Cambridge University Press, 2021.

Clifford, Richard J., and Khaled Anatolios. "Christian Salvation: Biblical and Theological Perspectives." *Theological Studies* 66, no. 4 (2005): 739–69.

Colijn, Brenda B. *Images of Salvation in the New Testament.* Downers Grove, IL: IVP Academic, 2010.

Davidson, Ivor J., and Murray Rae. *God of Salvation: Soteriology in Theological Perspective.* Farnham: Ashgate, 2011.

Dunn, James D. G. *The Theology of Paul the Apostle.* Grand Rapids, MI: Eerdmans, 1998.

Eberhart, Christian A. *The Sacrifice of Jesus: Understanding Atonement Biblically.* 2nd ed. Eugene, OR: Wipf & Stock, 2018.

Filtvedt, Ole Jakob. "The Transcendence and Visibility of the Father in the Gospel of John." *Zeitschrift für die Neutestamentliche Wissenschaft* 108, no. 1 (2017): 90–118.

Green, Joel B. *Practicing Theological Interpretation: Engaging Biblical Texts for Faith and Formation.* Grand Rapids, MI: Baker Academic, 2011.

Greggs, Tom. *The Breadth of Salvation: Rediscovering the Fullness of God's Saving Work*. Grand Rapids, MI: Baker Academic, 2020.

Heim, Erin M. *Adoption in Galatians and Romans: Contemporary Metaphor Theories and the Pauline Huiothesia Metaphors*. Leiden: Brill, 2017.

Holcomb, Justin S. *Christian Theologies of Salvation: A Comparative Introduction*. New York, NY: New York University Press, 2017.

Hollander, Harm W. "Seeing God 'in a Riddle' or 'Face to Face': An Analysis of 1 Corinthians 13.12." *Journal for the Study of the New Testament* 32, no. 4 (2010): 395–403.

Jongeneel, Jan A. B. "Hendrik Kraemer's *Christian Message in a Non-Christian World*: A Magnum Opus after Seventy-five Years." *International Bulletin of Mission Research* 37, no. 4 (2013): 203–6.

Lewis, Robert Brian. *Paul's "Spirit of Adoption" in Its Roman Imperial Context*. London: Bloomsbury T&T Clark, 2018.

MacKenzie, Michael J., and Roy F. Baumeister. "Meaning in Life: Nature, Needs, and Myth." In *Meaning in Positive and Existential Psychology*, edited by Alexander Batthyany and Pninit Russo-Netze, 25–38. New York, NY: Springer, 2014.

Marion, Jean-Luc. "Seeing, or Seeing Oneself Seen: Nicholas of Cusa's Contribution in *De Visione Dei*." *Journal of Religion* 96, no. 3 (2016): 305–31.

Martin, Thomas F. "Paul the Patient: *Christus Medicus* and the 'Stimulus Carnis' (2 Cor. 12:7): A Consideration of Augustine's Medicinal Christology." *Augustinian Studies* 32, no. 2 (2001): 219–56.

McGrath, Alister E. "The Owl of Minerva: Reflections on the Theological Significance of Mary Midgley." *Heythrop Journal* 61, no. 5 (2020): 852–64.

McGrath, Alister E. "Place, History, and Incarnation: On the Subjective Aspects of Christology." *Scottish Journal of Theology* 75, no. 2 (2022): 137–47

McTavish, James. "Jesus the Divine Physician." *Linacre Quarterly* 85, no. 1 (2018): 18–23.

Moberly, R. W. L. "Salvation in the Old Testament." *Journal of Theological Interpretation* 15, no. 2 (2021): 189–202.

Montgomery, James Warwick. *History and Christianity*. Minneapolis: Bethany House, 1964.

Montgomery, James Warwick. *Defending the Gospel in Legal Style: Essays on Legal Apologetics and the Justification of Classical Christian Faith*. Bonn, Germany: Culture and Science, 2017.

Nunziato, Joshua S. *Augustine and the Economy of Sacrifice: Ancient and Modern Perspectives*. Cambridge: Cambridge University Press, 2019.

Ryan, Robin. *Jesus and Salvation: Soundings in the Christian Tradition and Contemporary Theology*. Collegeville, MN: Liturgical Press, 2015.

Steger, Michael F. "Meaning in Life." In *Oxford Handbook of Positive Psychology*, edited by Shane J. Lopez, 679–87. Oxford: Oxford University Press, 2009.

Swain, Scott R. *Trinity, Revelation, and Reading: A Theological Introduction to the Bible and Its Interpretation*. London: T & T Clark International, 2011.

Toit, David du, Christine Gerber, and Christiane Zimmermann, eds. *Sōtēria: Salvation in Early Christianity and Antiquity*. Leiden: Brill, 2019.

van der Watt, J. G., ed. *Salvation in the New Testament: Perspectives on Soteriology*. Leiden: Brill, 2005.

5

Exploring Points of Contact for the Christian Faith

Sociologists and theologians have long spoken of "signals of transcendence" (Peter Berger) or "deep symbols" (Edward Farley) – human experiences or intuitions that seem to point beyond themselves to a greater vision of reality. For Berger, these "signals of transcendence" are elements of everyday life that seem to exhibit a connection to the transcendent, human experiences or intuitions that are marks or indications of a truly "other" of some sort. Modern secular culture has not "lost a propensity for awe, for the uncanny, for all those possibilities that are legislated against by the canons of secularized rationality." Yet when seen within a Christian interpretative framework, these cease to be seen as human projections or constructions, and are instead seen as divinely implanted intuitions, grounded in the theological insight that human beings bear the "image of God."

Christian apologetics aims to identify possible points of contact for the gospel that are already embedded in human culture and experience, and use these to open up the transformative capacity of the Christian faith. Christian theology provides an organizing framework for apologetics that enables us to notice, highlight, and interpret certain aspects of common human experience, and develop an intellectual bridge from the ordinary to the transcendent realms.

Having highlighted the cultural significance of "signals of transcendence," Berger suggests that theologians and apologists ought to give more thought to how these might be explored and used. Berger's description of such "signals" merits close study, and underlies the approach to apologetics explored in this chapter. For Berger, apologists ought to

seek out what might be called signals of transcendence within the empirically given human situation. And I would further suggest that there are prototypical human gestures that may constitute such signals. By signals of transcendence, I mean phenomena that are to be found within the domain of our "natural" reality but that appear to point beyond that reality.

Christian Apologetics: An Introduction, First Edition. Alister E. McGrath.
© 2024 John Wiley & Sons Ltd. Published 2024 by John Wiley & Sons Ltd.

In the previous chapter, we considered the apologetic importance of exploring how Christianity is able to make significant and meaningful connections with human experience and existence. In this chapter, I shall use the term "points of contact" to describe these kinds of human instincts, intuitions, and interests that can be repurposed or redirected so that they serve as pathways to transcendence – to something that is *beyond* our world of experience and observation.

The Concept of a "Point of Contact"

Sometimes the apologist has to do some creative thinking in working out how to help audiences see how the Christian faith connects up with their lives and situations. One of the hallmarks of a good preacher is the ability to invent, borrow, or repurpose powerful narratives or illustrations that help make connections between the Christian faith and the audience for the sermon. Yet sometimes those points of contact are already there, built into the fabric of the natural world or the deep structure of the human soul – yet pointing beyond them, reflecting their ultimate origins in God. The Christian doctrine of creation, for example, has a rich intrinsic apologetic potential, which is too easily overlooked.

Christians hold that human beings are created in the "image of God" (Genesis 1:17). This rich idea has many aspects, which have been widely explored by Christian theologians. For example, the "image of God" can be seen as a reminder of the authority of God over humanity. In the ancient near East, monarchs would often display images of themselves as an assertion of their power in a region (see, for example, the golden statue of Nebuchadnezzar, described in Daniel 3:1–7). Two influential ways of understanding the "image of God" have particularly significant apologetic implications.

First, humanity bearing the "image of God" means that there is some kind of correspondence between human reason and the rationality of God as creator. For John Calvin, this correspondence may be damaged or obscured by sin, but it remains part of the human condition. On this understanding of things, there is an intrinsic resonance between the structures of the world and human reasoning. This approach is set out with particular clarity in Augustine of Hippo's major theological writing *On the Trinity*:

> The image of the creator is to be found in the rational or intellectual soul of humanity ....
> [The human soul] has been created according to the image of God in order that it may use reason and intellect in order to apprehend and behold God.

For Augustine, we have been created with the intellectual resources that can set us on the way to finding God by reflecting on the creation. It is relatively easy for the apologist to build bridges from *God's creation* to *God*; from *God's work* to *God's person*. Theoretically, this move is grounded in the Christian doctrine of creation; practically, it means that we are invited to discern rather than invent ways of making connections between the created world around us and the Christian faith.

And second, the "image of God" refers to a *created capacity to relate to God*. The human longing for God is not a human invention, but is grounded in God's work of creation. We are *made* and *meant* to think in this way. God has created humanity with a specific goal – namely, to relate to God. To be created in the "image of God" is to possess the potential to enter into a relationship with God. This theme has played a major role in Christian spirituality and apologetics. Why? Because it establishes a secure theological link between God and the human experience of longing. We have been created in order to relate to God. Augustine expressed this idea in a famous prayer to God, which has found its way into countless Christian liturgies and devotional works:

> To praise you is the desire of humanity, a small piece of your creation. You stir humanity to take pleasure in praising you, because you have made us for yourself, and our hearts are restless until they find their rest in you.

For Augustine and many other Christian writers, this deep human sense of longing has its origins in God, and can only find its fulfilment in God. To come home to God is to find the peace and fulfilment that nothing in this world can offer. God is the one we have been looking for all our lives, without knowing it. Although Anselm of Canterbury is best known for his "ontological argument" for the existence of God (pp. 44–6), he understood the rationality of faith to be demonstrated not simply in human reasoning processes, but in the deep structures of human longing and desire.

All of this can be seen as an elaboration of the basic New Testament insight that God is not without a witness in history, culture, or human experience (Acts 14:17). The apologetic task is to try to identify that inbuilt and indirect witness and use it as a point of contact for the proclamation of the Christian gospel. A good example of the apologetic use of such a "point of contact" is found in the Paul's Areopagus address, recorded in the Acts of the Apostles (Acts 17:16–34). Paul here makes an appeal to his Athenian audience through a "sense of divinity" present in each individual as a point of contact for the Christian faith. By doing this, Paul connects with existing Greek theistic assumptions, while at the same time demonstrating how the Christian gospel goes beyond these, making good their deficiencies. What the Greeks held to be unknown (and possibly unknowable), Paul proclaims to have been made known through the resurrection of Christ. Paul is able to connect up with the experiential and cognitive world of his audience, using intellectual bridges that are part of the Christian "big picture."

This idea of an inbuilt "sense of divinity" has been adapted and developed by many Christian writers down the centuries. John Calvin is an excellent example of a theologian who makes use of this notion to highlight that religious belief is natural.

> There is within the human mind, and indeed by natural instinct, a sense of divinity (*divinitatis sensus*). This we take beyond controversy. To prevent anyone from taking refuge in the pretense of ignorance, God himself has implanted in everyone a certain understanding of his divine majesty. … a sense of divinity is by nature engraved on human hearts.

For Calvin, human beings have a natural awareness of God, built into the structure of the human mind through creation, which needs to be directed towards its proper fulfilment in Christianity. This important theological observation plays a significant role in the "Reformed epistemology" of Alvin Plantinga (born 1932; Figure 5.1), which has become increasingly significant in the early twenty-first century.

Figure 5.1   The US philosopher Alvin Plantinga speaking at Notre Dame University in 2005. Alamy Image 2MW0R00.

Six "Points of Contact": Reflection and Application

So what "points of contact" might be important for apologetics? In this chapter, we shall consider six of these, exploring their distinct identities and how they might be used practically. How can we present these as what C. S. Lewis famously termed "clues to the meaning of the universe"? In each case, we shall explore two core questions. What is the experience being addressed? And what is its apologetic interpretation and application? We begin with one "point of contact" that has already been touched on in this volume – a sense of longing for something of supreme importance. As this is the first such "point of contact" to be considered, the interpretative questions noted earlier will be considered in greater detail than in subsequent sections.

A Sense of Longing

One of the more important of Augustine's theological insights is that God alone is the heart's true desire, the origin and goal of human longings. This theme has been developed by may Christian spiritual writers and apologists – such as Pascal, Jonathan Edwards, and C. S. Lewis. To begin with, we shall try to clarify what kind of experience is under consideration here.

Many people have a deep sense of yearning for something that seems to be really important, but which eludes us. The German term *Sehnsucht* is often used to describe this general sense of longing for something that presents itself as both undefinable and unattainable. The English poet Matthew Arnold described this as a "wistful, soft, tearful longing." It is important to appreciate that this poignant desire for something agonizingly elusive is a common human experience, and is not limited to individuals who are "religious" or "spiritual." The atheist philosopher Bertrand Russell, for example, describes this kind of experience well.

> The centre of me is always and eternally a terrible pain … a searching for something beyond what the world contains, something transfigured and infinite – the beatific vision, God – I do not find it, I do not think it is to be found – but the love of it is my life … it is the actual spring of life within me.

This experience "searching for something beyond what the world contains" is clearly a significant point of contact. So how is it to be accounted for? And, perhaps more importantly, what does it mean? Where does it take us? How can the apologist use this in building bridges for faith?

Precisely because this is a widely encountered human experience, Christian theologians have written extensively about how it can be accommodated and interpreted within a Christian framework, both in terms of its *origin* and its *goal*. The medieval spiritual writer Julian of Norwich represents this tradition of interpretation well, depicting God as both the origin and ultimate goal of desire. "I am who makes you to love, I am who makes you to long, I it am, the endless fulfilling of all true desires." Julian's medieval English may seem a little awkward to modern readers; the spiritual and apologetic point that she is making is, however, both clear and important.

So how is this experience to be used apologetically? The important point is that this experience needs to be named – and one of the best ways of doing this is to *describe* it, even though it is difficult to reduce it to words. Russell's sketchy account of something that is "beyond what the world contains" is a useful starting point. So is C. S. Lewis's account in his autobiography *Surprised by Joy* of his childhood experiences of intense longing for something unknown and elusive, which seemed to point to something of ultimate importance that lay beyond his horizons of knowledge. Lewis, in describing this early experience of longing, makes it clear that he was unable to make sense of it at the time. It was only later, looking back at this experience from the perspective of his Christian faith, that he was able to understand what had really happened, and grasp its full significance.

> It is difficult to find words strong enough for the sensation which came over me. … It was a sensation, of course, of desire; but desire for what? And before I knew what I desired, the desire itself was gone, the whole glimpse withdrawn, the world turned commonplace again, or only stirred by a longing for the longing that he just ceased.

There is an interesting parallel here with the Old Testament narrative of the calling of Samuel. The central core of this narrative (1 Samuel 3:4–20) is that a natural event or experience is able to point beyond itself, to its true origins and goal. Samuel hears his name being spoken four times during the night. On the first three occasions, he believes that Eli is calling him, and runs to find him. Eli suggests he ought to interpret this natural phenomenon as originating from God. On the fourth occasion, Samuel responds appropriately. Most scholarly accounts of this passage fail to see that the central issue is *discernment*. An event within nature is interpreted in a new manner, and seen to possess a new significance as a result of this interpretation.

The Old Testament scholar Walter Moberly rightly identifies this central concern, and summarizes its significance as follows: "God then speaks to Samuel. But His speaking instantly poses the central issue of the story, that is discernment. For when God speaks, Samuel does not recognize the voice as God's voice." Moberly notes that there is nothing intrinsic to the experience that identifies it as supernatural or specifically divine. The call of God may not be initially recognizable as such, in that it is mediated in and through the natural realm.

The point of contact is thus something that is experience or observed, described, and above all *appropriately interpreted* – in other words, it is seen as a signpost to a goal, rather than being a goal in itself. Instead of becoming fixated on the experience itself, we need to ask what it *means*. What does it point towards? By interpreting this experience as a *signpost*, the experience is located within a framework of meaning that both gives significance to this sense of longing, and at the same time acts as a gateway to something of existential significance. What we really desire is what this experience of longing points to. Lewis's "argument from desire" is based on the insight that nature cannot, and is not meant to, satisfy our deepest desires. Natural experiences are a sign of something beyond themselves to "that indescribable something of which they become for a moment the messengers."

As with all points of contact, the essential apologetic task is thus the interpretation of an experience or observation that is already present in the individual or community's consciousness, so that it becomes not a self-referential object of interest in its own right, but a pointer to something else – the reality of the Christian faith on the one hand, and its capacity to connect up with the existential realities of human existence on the other. The theologian Josef Pieper is one of many writers who notes how our natural hopes and longings were grounded in something that lies beyond us, yet that is not alien to us. "All our natural hopes tend towards fulfilments that are like vague mirrorings and foreshadowings of, like unconscious preparations for, eternal life."

So what is the status of this, or any other point of contact? Does it prove anything? No. It is one of a number of possible explanations of what we observe or experience – yet which, if true, changes everything. It is suggestive, a clue that is meant to "arouse our suspicions" (as Lewis put it), encouraging audiences to wonder whether there is something that they have suppressed, overlooked, or ignored. It is a clue, which takes its place among other such clues, pointing to a coherent way of understanding the world and our place within it. As the Cambridge physicist Alexander Wood perceptively observed, "our first demand of religion" is that it should "illumine life and make it a whole."

This needs to be connected with our earlier reflections on "inference to the best explanation" (pp. 51–4), a philosophical approach to the interpretation of evidence that explicitly acknowledges that such experiences can be interpreted in several ways. The question is which such interpretation is the most elegant, simple, and comprehensive – capable not only of making sense of a single experience, but of as many as possible elements of the broad range of "points of contact" that we shall consider in this chapter.

The Beauty of the World

Beauty has been a neglected theme in modern Christian apologetics, partly because of the rationalizing tendencies of the "Age of Reason." Many thinkers of this period valued "objective" rational arguments, and believed that discussion of the significance of beauty was hopelessly subjective, and hence lacked any rational or evidential value. What one person might find attractive may seem to be dull and uninteresting to someone else. Beauty, as we are often reminded, resides in the "eye of the beholder."

Yet beauty was an important element of early and medieval Christian apologetics. Throughout the early Christian era and the Middle Ages, beauty was generally considered to be a "transcendental quality of being," along with truth and goodness. The beauty of nature was, it was argued, derived from the greater beauty of God its creator. Natural beauty was thus a pointer towards the beauty of God, and an invitation to discover and experience this. The medieval theologian Bonaventura of Bagnoregio made this point particularly clearly.

> All creatures in this visible world lead the spirit of the contemplative and wise person into the eternal God. For creatures are shadows, echoes, and pictures of that first, most powerful, most wise, and most perfect Principle, of that eternal Source, Light, Fullness, of that efficient, exemplary and ordering Art.

The apologetic power of natural beauty is an important theme in the preaching of Jonathan Edwards, the leading American theologian who played a major role in the "Great Awakening" of the eighteenth century. For Edwards, the Christian faith allows the human experience of delight at the beauty of the natural world to be channeled towards Christ. This is particularly evident in one of Edwards's most lyrical descriptions of nature:

> When we are delighted with flowery meadows and gentle breezes of wind, we may consider that we only see the emanations of the sweet benevolence of Jesus Christ; when we behold the fragrant rose and lily, we see his love and purity. So the green trees and fields, and singing of birds, are emanations of his infinite joy and benignity; the easiness and naturalness of trees and vines [are] shadows of his infinite beauty and loveliness; the crystal rivers and murmuring streams have the footsteps of his sweet grace and bounty.

The Christian vision of reality, according to Edwards, allows us to see nature in such a way that its beauty can be recognized as "emanations, or shadows, of the excellencies of the Son of God." Beauty thus becomes an intellectual or imaginative channel, a bridge connecting the human experience of beauty with its ultimate source in Christ, as God's agent of creation. The noted British philosopher of religion F. R. Tennant was also aware of the apologetic importance of the beauty of nature. For Tennant, the universe possesses a natural beauty that exceeds anything that is necessary for human survival, and thus cannot be accounted for by a Darwinian account of the development of the living world.

The apologetic power of beauty is particularly evident in one of the gospel "Parables of the Kingdom," usually known as the "Parable of the Pearl of Great Price" (Matthew 13:45–46). "The kingdom of heaven is like a merchant in search of fine pearls; on finding one pearl of great value, he went and sold all that he had and bought it." While this parable has multiple layers of meaning, one of these is the power of beauty to elicit desire. A retelling of the parable may help make this point clearer.

The parable tells us of merchant who notices a pearl and decides to sell everything in order to possess it. Why? Because he has found something that is supremely worth possessing. In its light, everything he already possesses has created and then intensified an appetite for beauty that they have proved incapable of satisfying. The merchant believes those possessions were the goal of his quest; in fact, they were merely a stage in his search for something of transcendent and permanent value. The good simply makes the merchant yearn for the best – something that he knows he has not yet found. Until, of course, he saw that special pearl. Experiencing its beauty opened up some deep questions. What was he really looking for? And what really possesses the power to satisfy our deepest longings?

Many early Christian writers recognized the capacity of beauty to attract people. We might have to argue the truth of a philosophical idea; yet beauty is self-evidencing, its probative force sufficient to fascinate us, and draw us towards it. Many, for example, have found themselves captivated by the sense of beauty and transcendence that is so often evoked by J. R. R. Tolkien's *The Lord of the Rings*, sensing that this is something *real* that points beyond the everyday world, and somehow draws us towards it. It is this capacity of beauty to attract us that underlies its apologetic importance.

Tolkien's Oxford colleague C. S. Lewis argued that human beings possess an instinct of transcendence, which is stimulated by memory, beauty, and longing. For Lewis, beauty evokes an ideal that is more real than anything we encounter in this transitory world, evoking a sense of longing for a half-remembered realm from which we are presently exiled. This homing instinct is a desire "for something that has never actually appeared in our experience," yet which is constantly suggested and intimated by the beauty of what we do experience.

Lewis thus argues that the perennial human "quest for beauty" is actually a quest for the *source* of that beauty, which is only mediated through the things of this world. Lewis's point is that "objects of beauty," which are actually vehicles for conveying beauty, too easily become the objects of our devotion and attention. "The books or the music in which we thought the beauty was located will betray us if we trust to them: it was not *in* them, it only came *through* them." Yet more importantly, Lewis saw that beauty invites *participation*, rather than *understanding*.

> We do not want merely to see beauty, though, God knows even that is bounty enough. We want something else which can hardly be put into words – to be united with the beauty we see, to pass into it, to receive it into ourselves, to bathe in it, to become part of it.

For Lewis, to discover beauty is to be pointed towards its ultimate source and goal – God.

Yet the natural world offers at least two other apologetic "points of contact," the first drawing on the ordering and complexity of the natural world, and the second on the sense of wonder that many experience at the vastness of the natural world. We shall consider both of these in this chapter.

The Ordering of Nature

Human beings have always been impressed by the order of the world. In the ancient world, Babylonian astronomers worked out the regular movements of the planets against the background of fixed stars, and used these to structure time and develop calendars. The world seemed to have a deep structure. But why? And what did this point to? For many writers, discovering the ordering of the universe was a step on the road to wisdom, a clue to the deeper meaning of life. And for Christian apologetics, it offers a "point of contact" with a wider audience to affirm the rationality of faith, and its capacity to illuminate our world.

It is important to appreciate that the success of the natural sciences depends on both an ordered cosmos on the one hand, and a human mind which is capable of grasping and representing this ordering on the other. The British theoretical physicist and theologian John Polkinghorne (1930–2021; Figure 5.2) rightly notes that, from a Christian perspective, our ability to make sense of our universe, according to the Christian "big picture," is not a piece of good luck, but the consequence of God's act of creation. Human beings bear the "image of God," which means that there is some kind of resonance between the human mind and the structure of the universe. Polkinghorne's point is that the Christian faith offers a map of reality, a "big picture" that allows us to make sense of these observations. Both the rationality of the human mind within us and the rational transparency of the universe beyond us have their common origin in a deeper rationality, the "mind of God."

Figure 5.2   The British theoretical physicist and theologian John Polkinghorne speaking at the Hay Festival in Wales in 2011. Alamy Image C44FEW.

Apologetics is about showing how the Christian "big picture" makes sense of our ordered world – including helping us to understand the *successes* of the natural sciences on the one hand, and their *limits* on the other. Christianity holds that God has created an ordered world. So why can human beings discern this ordering? Why are they able to represent it so elegantly using mathematical equations? The natural sciences regularly raise important questions that transcend the capacity of the scientific method to answer them. If these questions are to be answered, we have to go beyond the scope of the sciences. And that's why it is important to emphasize that the Christian faith offers a "map of meaning," which makes this profoundly comprehensible.

Why is this "point of contact" helpful apologetically? There are a number of ways in which this can inform apologetic conversations. First, it emphasizes the capacity of the Christian faith to make sense of things – to "chime in" with what is observed within the world, and the deeper picture of reality that emerges from the natural sciences. Second, it offers an important point of contact with the natural sciences. Although science and faith are sometimes presented as being in conflict, it is better to think of faith offering a deeper context to the scientific method. It offers an explanation of why science works in the first place, rather than asking us to accept this as a happy accident or miracle.

Second, it provides a viable alternative to what is sometimes called the "God of the gaps" approach to apologetics, which argues that God can be invoked to fill gaps in scientific explanation or understanding. Rather than appealing to gaps in scientific explanation, it is much more help to ask why scientific explanation is possible in the first place. Albert Einstein recognized the importance of this point, arguing that the greatest mystery about the universe was the fact that we can make so much sense of it. The Christian "big picture" offers an explanation of both the explanatory success of the natural sciences, grounding this in the doctrine of creation. As the theologian Thomas F. Torrance points out, this order is *contingent*, not *necessary*. "The whole universe of created being was thought of as given an authentic reality and integrity of its own, and as endowed by God with a creaturely rational order grounded beyond itself in his own transcendent reality." The cosmos reflects the divine structuring of God's act of creation, which enables our universe to disclose something of the divine rationality.

> [The notion of contingent order] is the direct product of the Christian understanding of the constitutive relation between God and the universe, which he freely created out of nothing, yet not without reason, conferring upon what he has made and continues to sustain a created rationality of its own dependent on his uncreated transcendent reality.

The apologist can thus explore how the many aspects of the universe – such as its beauty and ordering – disclose the beauty and rationality of God. The order that is discerned within the world – and, indeed, upon which so much scientific reasoning is dependent – is thus to be understood as a consequence of the creative action of God.

Discussions about the apologetic importance of the ordering of creation have been given added impetus through the growing appreciation of the phenomenon of "fine-tuning" in nature. Put simply, this is the observation that small changes in the fundamental constants of nature would have led to the emergence of a universe in which life was not possible. Yet this observation is open to several interpretations. A theist could argue that the observation of the "fine-tuning" of the universe is consistent with belief in God; an atheist would suggest this is simply a matter of good luck. While this does not amount to a *proof* of the existence of God, it certainly adds to a cumulative series of considerations that points to a creator God. As Richard Swinburne and others have noted, the plausibility of belief in God rests on a series of considerations – not a single observation, piece of evidence, or argument.

A Sense of Wonder: The Night Sky

In his important study of a lingering human intuition of transcendence in a secular culture, Peter Berger emphasized the importance of "signals of transcendence," pointing to a richer vision of life than those offered by naturalism and materialism. A sense of wonder at the cold brilliance of the night sky is perhaps the most familiar of these. Most people find themselves overwhelmed with a sense of awe or amazement when confronted with the beauty or majesty of nature, which seems for a moment to intimate a grander vision of reality, perhaps lying beyond the horizons of our experience. It is as if, for only a moment, a veil is removed and we catch a half-glimpsed sight of a promised land, waiting to be mapped and explored.

This experience of wonder seems to be acknowledged and channeled towards God in a familiar passage from one of the Psalms: "The heavens declare the glory of God" (Psalm 19:1). The word "glory" here conveys the sense of being imaginatively overwhelmed by the vastness of God, as seen in the brilliance of the night sky. Yet this Psalm does not suggest that we can *prove* God's existence by looking at the heavens. After all, Israel already knew about the existence of its God. The recognition that God's creation declares God's glory is not presented in this psalm as a mandate for deducing the existence and character of God by looking at the heavens. Rather, the text affirms that the God who was already well known to Israel might be known in an aesthetically richer or imaginatively extended way by reflection on what God has created – such as the night sky.

So how might this sense of wonder in the presence of the vastness of the natural order be explored apologetically? Let me offer a personal reflection here. I remember well a journey I made across Iran when I was a research student in the late 1970s. I was travelling on a night bus through the vast empty desert between the cities of Shiraz and Kermān. The bus broke down. We all left the coach while its driver tried to fix it. As I wandered through the ruins of an abandoned caravanserai that night, I saw the stars that night as I had never seen them before – brilliant, solemn, and still, in the midst of a dark and silent land. I experienced an overwhelming feeling of awe at the brilliant spectacle above me. Although I had been a Christian for several years at that time, and was reasonably well settled in my faith, I still registered a strong feeling of the beyondness of things – a sense that I was standing on the borderlands of a strange and wonderful world, which I had yet to enter fully.

This feeling leads many to search for an expansion of their vision of reality. Perhaps this idea is most familiar from some words of the great natural philosopher Isaac Newton, written towards the end of his life. Newton here recognizes the existence of a greater horizon, hinted at by what we see, yet too easily overlooked. The discovery that we stand on the shore of an "ocean of truth" allows us to see things – and ourselves – in a new way.

> I seem to have been only like a small boy playing on the sea-shore, diverting myself in now and then finding a smoother pebble or a prettier shell than the ordinary, whilst the great ocean of truth lay all undiscovered before me.

Newton's image suggests that the apologist's role is to help people see beyond the pebbles and shells on the shoreline of our world, and seek for the greater reality that lies beyond them.

A Sense of Moral Obligation

The philosopher Immanuel Kant (Figure 5.3) singled out two aspects of the natural world that seemed to him to be particularly significant. "Two things fill the mind with ever new and increasing admiration and awe, the more often and steadily we reflect upon them: the starry heavens above me and the moral law within me." Many share Kant's sense that human moral intuitions can serve as "points of contact," allowing helpful and productive conversations about the importance and the ultimate grounding of ethics.

As we noted earlier (pp. 8–11), C. S. Lewis presents Christianity as a "big picture" that is able to frame our observations of the external world and our internal experiences. This can be clearly seen from his famous popular statement of the "argument from morality" in the opening pages of *Mere Christianity*. This offers us a helpful way

Figure 5.3   Monument to the philosopher Immanuel Kant (1724–1804) in his home town of Kaliningrad. Adobe Stock Image 209280059.

of exploring another point of contact – the moral sense that so many people experience within them. Lewis here invites us to reflect on two people having an argument. Any attempt to determine who is right and who is wrong depends on recognition of some norm or standard that stands over and above both of them, and which both implicitly recognize as binding and authoritative. Lewis suggests that everyone has some sense of there being something "higher" than us – an objective norm to which we appeal, and which we expect others to observe; a "real law which we did not invent, and which we know we ought to obey."

Yet although everyone knows about this law, Lewis suggests that they fail to live up to it. "The foundation of all clear thinking about ourselves and the universe we live in" consists in our knowledge of a moral law, and an awareness of our failure to observe it. This awareness ought to "arouse our suspicions" that there "is Something which is directing the universe, and which appears in me as a law urging me to do right and making me feel responsible and uncomfortable when I do wrong." Lewis suggests that these moral intuitions – or, to use Kant's phrase, this "moral law within us" – point to an ordering mind governing the universe.

Lewis is clearly not arguing that our moral intuitions *prove* that there is a God. His point is more subtle: Christianity is able to accommodate these intuitions in an intel-lectually satisfying way. Right and wrong can be understood within a Christian frame-work as "clues to the meaning of the universe." Clues, taken by themselves, prove nothing; their importance lies rather in their cumulative and contextual force. For Lewis, the best explanation of our deep intuition of the existence of objective moral truths is that the knowledge of right and wrong within us is grounded in an intelligence behind or beyond nature that acts as the foundation for the objectivity of our moral judgments.

Lewis suggests that, if there is a God, this provides both and explanation of, and a firmer foundation for, the deep human instinct and intuition that objective moral val-ues exist, and a defense of morality against more irresponsible statements of ethical relativism. God, for Lewis, is made known through our deep moral and aesthetic intui-tions. For Christians, God offers an objective foundation for moral values, which is not subject to the whims of powerful elites or the changing moods of public opinion. The philosopher Iris Murdoch made the important moral point that a transcendent notion of goodness is essential if defensible human notions of "right" and "justice" are to be maintained. Otherwise, we just end up rooting morality in populist politics, local situ-ations, or cultural trends, so that social acceptance becomes the foundation of moral thinking. The atheist philosopher Paul Kurtz noted this problem of with particular clarity: "The central question about moral and ethical principles concerns this onto-logical foundation. If they are neither derived from God nor anchored in some trans-cendent ground, are they purely ephemeral?"

A historical example will help to make the moral force of this point clearer. In 1933, the Nazis seized power in Germany, and promptly set about using the law to impose totalitarian rule. New laws were brought in, enforcing a Nazi ideology. The only way of challenging the Nazi approach was to argue that there existed a higher moral author-ity than the German state, to which its laws were ultimately accountable. A new interest thus emerged in the notion of "natural law" – namely, a higher form of justice that cannot be manipulated by states for their own ends, and that mandates the correction of oppressive human laws.

The disturbing questions raised by the rise of the Third Reich and its aftermath have not gone away. Indeed, they have been raised again by a "pragmatic" approach to morality, such as that associated with the influential philosopher Richard Rorty. For Rorty, humanity creates its own values and ideas, and is not accountable to any external objectivity (natural law) or internal subjectivity (conscience) for the outcome of this creative process. The truth of moral values depends simply upon their existence and acceptance within society. This view has been severely criticized as adopting an uncritical approach concerning prevailing social conventions. "We figure out what practices to adopt first, and then expect our philosophers to adjust the definition of 'human' or 'rational' to suit." Rorty argues that a consequence of this communitarian or pragmatic approach to truth must be the recognition that "there is nothing deep down inside us except what we have put there ourselves, no criterion that we have not created in the course of creating a practice, no standard of rationality that is not an appeal to such a criterion, no rigorous argumentation that is not obedience to our own conventions."

Truth and morality are thus grounded in transitory social conventions, which are created – not *discerned* – by human communities. As Richard Bernstein and others have argued, Rorty simply reifies social practices, and treats these as being synonymous with "truth," "goodness," or "justice." Yet if Rorty is right, what ultimate justification could be given for opposing Nazism? Law is simply a reification of social practice. This being the case, Rorty admits, then he has to acknowledge that:

> When the secret police come, when the torturers violate the innocent, there is nothing to be said to them of the form "There is something within you which you are betraying. Though you embody the practices of a totalitarian society, which will endure forever, there is something beyond those practices which condemns you."

All these concerns point to the need for a transcendent ground of morality. Otherwise, we are trapped in the shifting sands of influential power groups, with morality being redefined to suit the needs of those with influence. Apologetic arguments that appeal to morality tend to fall into two slightly different groups: those which appeal to the intellectual advantage of belief in God as a foundation for moral values, and those which appeal to the practical value of belief in God in securing the stability of moral values. A Christian "big picture" gives us a toolkit for engaging questions of morality, and providing a basis for right living in changing and uncertain times.

Existential Anxiety and Alienation

Many people experience a sense of bewilderment at being placed within this universe, feeling that this is not where they are meant to be. They feel that they are lost in a strange world in which they do not really belong. Pascal offers one of the best descriptions of this sense of unease and confusion, mingled with a deep sense of existential anxiety:

> When I consider the short duration of my life, swallowed up in the eternity before and after, the little space which I fill, and even can see, engulfed in the infinite immensity of spaces of which I am ignorant, and which know me not, I am frightened, and am

astonished at being here rather than there; for there is no reason why here rather than there, why now rather than then. Who has put me here? By whose order and direction have this place and time been allotted to me?

Later in this work, we shall consider the Canadian philosopher Charles Taylor's influential account of the emergence of an "immanent frame" (pp. 187–89). This involves a move away from a cosmos that has a transcendent basis, and is charged with meaning towards a "closed universe," constructed by the human mind, which is haunted by the sense of loss of meaning and transcendent. Taylor regards this sense of loss as apologetically significant, pointing towards the existential inadequacy of this "immanent frame." The loss of a transcendent basis to life means that we feel rootless, unanchored in something stable and significant. The existentialist philosopher Martin Heidegger used the German term *Geworfenheit* ("being thrown") to describe this feeling of existential unease. We had no say in entering thus strange and pointless world; we have been "thrown" into it, and have no way of getting out of it or finding our way to where we really belong.

The Old Testament scholar Walter Brueggeman argues that we now live in a "rootless" world, and need to ground ourselves in our histories if we are to discover who we are and where we belong. Peter Berger takes this further, speaking of the crisis of meaning that results from "finding oneself stranded, alone, in a remote corner of the universe bereft of human meaning." We feel we don't really belong here, and that our true destiny lies somewhere else. But *where*?

Many Christian apologists have noted the growth of this sense of historical and cultural dislocation and reflected on how this might act as a "point of contact" with the Christian ideas of worldly existence as an "exile" from our true homeland (pp. 116–17). G. K. Chesterton is one of many apologists to point to the importance of this intuition that we don't really belong here. "We have come to the wrong star ... That is what makes life at once so splendid and so strange. The true happiness is that we *don't* fit. We come from somewhere else. We have lost our way."

So where do we really belong? Where is our real homeland? Alex Haley's 1976 novel *Roots: The Saga of an American Family* is a good illustration of this longing for roots. *Roots* became a publishing sensation, topping the *New York Times* best seller list. As a Black American, Haley wanted to know where he really belonged. He traced his origins back to Kunta Kinte, a young man who was taken from the Gambia in west Africa when he was seventeen and sold as a slave in Maryland. Although the factual reliability of Haley's narrative is now known to be questionable, *Roots* highlighted the cultural importance of feeling that we are rooted in history. The fragmentation of older cultural certainties can create a sense of rootlessness and restlessness, where many people feel that they are wandering pointlessly through a strange landscape, with no goal and no purpose. There is no "home" for them to find.

Christianity affirms that believers belong here *for the time being*. They are "strangers and sojourners" (Leviticus 25:23), people who pass through this world but do not belong there. Yet though presently located in this history and this place, Christians nevertheless possess the status of being "citizens of heaven" (Philippians 3:20). For this reason, they really belong in heaven, where they have the right both to *enter* and *inhabit* this special place. They belong there; it is their homeland.

The Christian faith offers multiple perspectives on our situation. It allows us to realize that we are in exile on earth, while we anticipate our return to heaven. It helps us realize that we are in captivity in Egypt, awaiting our entry into the Promised Land. Though physically located in one place, we mentally inhabit another, where we believe that we truly belong. Though we live here on earth, this world is not our true homeland but rather a place into which we have been "thrown." Our quest is to find our way back to where we are *meant* to be. This sense of existential unease or dislocation helps us realize that this world is not our true homeland; we really belong in heaven (Philippians 3:20–1). This, of course, is a leading theme in the sermons and homilies of many early Christian writers – for example, Cyprian of Carthage's famous declaration that "paradise is our homeland (*patria*)."

Thus far in this chapter, we have sketched six "signals of transcendence," and outlined how these "points of contact" might be used apologetically. Many more could be added. Yet there is one further step that needs to be taken – developing a context within which these can be presented and explored. As I have emphasized throughout this book, the Christian faith itself provides a "big picture" of reality, an interpretive framework that allows such "signals of transcendence" to be seen as pointing towards core gospel themes. Some apologists, however, prefer to use an intermediary "neutral" framework to begin to explore the significance of these "signals of transcendence." The most interesting of these is the image of a dark underground cave, set out by the classic Greek philosopher Plato in his dialogue *The Republic*, written some 375 years before the birth of Christ. In what follows, we shall examine this image, and see how it can help to frame apologetic discussions which make use of these "points of contact."

Plato's Cave: A Neutral Framework for Framing "Points of Contact"

The image of Plato's cave has been hugely influential in philosophy, theology, and popular culture (Figure 5.4). Its themes are prominent in movies such as the film *The Matrix* (1999), and frequently find their way into C. S. Lewis's fictional works, particularly his *Chronicles of Narnia*. To appreciate and work with this image, set out in Plato's famous dialogue *The Republic*, we have to set aside our preconceptions, and enter into its imaginative world. At points, we may feel that the image is somewhat improbable; yet we need to allow the analogy to establish its own framework of discussion, and see where it takes us.

To begin with, we need to set the scene for Plato's reflections on the limits on human knowledge. Socrates invites his disciple Glaucon to imagine a group of prisoners who are chained facing the back wall of a great underground cave. They have been there all their lives, and they are unaware of the existence of any world other than the cave. Behind them, a fire is burning, providing both heat and light within the cave. People are moving about the smoky cavern, talking to each other and holding up shapes of people and animals so that they cast shadows on the cave wall. The prisoners can hear echoes of the conversations of others within the cave, but cannot understand them, as the sounds are reflected and distorted by the cave's walls. They believe that these echoes and shadows constitute and determine reality, being unaware of the existence of a very different world beyond the cave.

Figure 5.4   Statue of the philosopher Plato by the Italian sculptor Piccarelli in front of the National Academy building, Athens. Adobe Stock Image 115496308.

Plato's image raises two really interesting philosophical and theological questions. Do we know only a world of darkness and flickering shadows, believing that this is all that there is to reality? And if so, how might we find our way to a better world that lies beyond the cave? You might like to pause your reading at this point, and try the following mental experiment. *Think* yourself into the scenario of Plato's cave. Try to imagine the dark, smoky cave, and the flickering shadows on its walls. Now *locate* yourself within the analogy: you are one of the chained prisoners. How might you discover that there is a world beyond the cave? What strategies might you come up with?

There are two obvious possibilities. One is that the structure of the cave may include features that suggest there is a world beyond its walls – for example, you might notice strange objects that don't seem to belong in the cave, and might therefore come from a world beyond the cave. The second is that you might experience some deep intuition that this is not your true home, and come to believe that they belonged somewhere else. What if this world is only a shadowland? You might, for example, experience a sense of longing for something that nothing within the cave is able to satisfy, or sense that there has to be more than this severely limited world.

Those are the kind of "points of contact" that we have been exploring in this chapter and elsewhere in this book. C. S. Lewis's "argument from desire" focusses on the human sense of longing for something that is satisfying, stable, and secure, and the apparent inability of our present world to provide this. Lewis's argument (see pp. 49–51) is that this intuition is a *clue* (not a *proof*) to the existence of a grander vision of reality, within which we have a place. There are three points that need to be appreciated here, in developing this line of reflection and exploration with your audience. First, these are only clues. Yet, as C. S. Lewis points out, these clues plant seeds in our mind, opening us up to wider and deeper visions of reality than we find in a secular mindset. Second, while an individual clue may not carry great evidential weight, a *series of clues* is highly suggestive. And third (and perhaps most important), the Christian "big picture" can accommodate these clues, just as successful scientific theory is able to accommodate multiple observations.

Yet there is another question that can be helpfully explored using the framework of Plato's cave. What if someone from a world beyond this cave were to enter into its shadowy world, telling its occupants of this strange and wonderful world beyond its walls, and offering to lead those trapped in the cave into its bright sunlit realm? This involves, to use the language of Christian theology, both *revelation* and *salvation*. It is about informing or persuading people that there is a world beyond the cave, and removing obstacles and barriers to *discerning* and *entering* that new world.

Many early Christian writers were familiar with the various forms of Platonism that were popular in late classical antiquity, and could see how to use a Platonic framework to help explain certain central Christian affirmations about the significance of Christ. Their strategy was to use a neutral interpretative framework, familiar to their audiences, as an intermediary step in commending Christianity itself. The apologist can present this as a mental experiment, inviting audiences to enter into this story of the prisoners in the cave, and reflect on whether they too are imprisoned within a limiting worldview.

In the next chapter, we shall turn to consider the growing interest in the apologetic importance of stories, evident in the rise of "narrative apologetics."

Study Questions

1. Set out, in your own words, the nature and value of "points of contact." How are they helpful? Do you think they have a downside?
2. Imagine that you are writing an apologetic talk. How might you appeal to a sense of longing in writing such a talk? What points would you make? What questions could you open up?
3. Which of these six points of contact did you find particularly interesting? Why?
4. What are the advantages of using Plato's image of the cave as an intermediary in exploring some themes of the Christian faith?

For Further Reading

Adams, Edward. "Calvin's View of Natural Knowledge of God." *International Journal of Systematic Theology* 3, no. 3 (2001): 280–92.

Bailey, Justin Ariel. *Reimagining Apologetics: The Beauty of Faith in a Secular Age.* Downers Grove, IL: InterVarsity, 2020.

Berger, Peter L. *A Rumor of Angels: Modern Society and the Rediscovery of the Supernatural.* New York, NY: Doubleday, 1969.

Berger, Peter L. *The Many Altars of Modernity: Toward a Paradigm for Religion in a Pluralist Age.* Berlin: de Gruyter, 2014.

Blowers, Paul M. "Beauty, Tragedy and New Creation: Theology and Contemplation in Cappadocian Cosmology." *International Journal of Systematic Theology* 18, no. 1 (2016): 7–29.

Collins, Robin. "The Teleological Argument: An Exploration of the Fine-tuning of the Cosmos." In *Blackwell Companion to Natural Theology*, edited by William Lane Craig and J. P. Moreland, 202–81. Oxford: Blackwell, 2009.

Conzelman, Hans. "The Address of Paul on the Areopagus." In *Studies in Luke-Acts: Essays Presented in Honor of Paul Schubert*, edited by Leander E. Keck and J. Louis Martin, 217–32. Nashville, TN: Abingdon Press, 1966.

Cootsona, Gregory S. "How Nature and Beauty can Bring Scientists and Theologians Together." *Theology and Science* 9, no. 4 (2011): 379–93.

Coutras, Lisa. *Tolkien's Theology of Beauty: Majesty, Splendor, and Transcendence in Middle-Earth*. New York, NY: Palgrave Macmillan, 2016.

Dubay, Thomas. *The Evidential Power of Beauty: Science and Theology Meet*. San Francisco: Ignatius Press, 1999.

Edwards, L. Clifton. *Creation's Beauty as Revelation: Toward a Creational Theology of Natural Beauty*. Eugene, OR: Pickwick Publications, 2014.

Evans, C. Stephen. *Natural Signs and Knowledge of God: A New Look at Theistic Arguments*. Oxford: Oxford University Press, 2010.

Farley, Edward. *Deep Symbols: Their Postmodern Effacement and Reclamation*. Valley Forge, PA: Trinity Press International, 1996.

Fuller, Robert C. *Wonder: From Emotion to Spirituality*. Chapel Hill, NC: University of North Carolina Press, 2006.

Gibson, Michael D. "The Beauty of the Redemption of the World: The Theological Aesthetics of Maximus the Confessor and Jonathan Edwards." *Harvard Theological Review* 101 (2008): 45–76.

Hall, Dale. "Interpreting Plato's Cave as an Allegory of the Human Condition." *Apeiron: A Journal for Ancient Philosophy and Science* 14, no. 2 (1980): 74–86.

Lightman, Alan P. *Searching for Stars on an Island in Maine*. New York, NY: Pantheon Books, 2018.

McGrath, Alister E. *A Fine-tuned Universe: The Quest for God in Science and Theology*. Louisville, KY: Westminster John Knox Press, 2009.

McGrath, Alister E. "Place, History, and Incarnation: On the Subjective Aspects of Christology." *Scottish Journal of Theology* 75, no. 2 (2022): 137–47.

McLaughlin, Sara Park. "Beauty without End: C. S. Lewis and Theological Aesthetics." *The Lamp-Post of the Southern California C. S. Lewis Society* 25, no. 3 (2001): 9–12.

Ordway, Holly. *Apologetics and the Christian Imagination: An Integrated Approach to Defending the Faith*. Steubenville, OH: Emmaus Road Publishing, 2017.

Rochberg, Francesca. "Reasoning, Representing, and Modeling in Babylonian Astronomy." *Journal of Ancient Near Eastern History* 5, no. 1 (2018): 131–47.

Siniscalchi, Glenn. "Fine-tuning, Atheist Criticism, and the Fifth Way." *Theology and Science* 12, no. 1 (2014): 64–77.

Sommer, Benjamin D. "Nature, Revelation, and Grace in Psalm 19: Towards a Theological Reading of Scripture." *Harvard Theological Review* 108, no. 3 (2015): 376–401.

Sommers, Claire. "School of Shadows: The Return to Plato's Cave." *Arion: A Journal of Humanities and the Classics* 25, no. 3 (2018): 131–46.

Stump, Eleonore. "Faith, Wisdom, and the Transmission of Knowledge through Testimony." In *Religious Faith and Intellectual Virtue*, edited by Timothy O'Connor and Laura Frances Callahan, 204–30. Oxford: Oxford University Press, 2014.

Testoni, Ines, Emilio Paolo Visintin, Dora Capozza, Maria Concetta Carlucci, and Malihe Shams. "The Implicit Image of God: God as Reality and Psychological Well-being." *Journal for the Scientific Study of Religion* 55, no. 1 (2016): 174–84.

Stump, Eleonore. "Beauty as a Road to God." *Sacred Music* 134, no. 4 (2007): 13–26.

Walker, Andrew. "Scripture, Revelation and Platonism in C. S. Lewis." *Scottish Journal of Theology* 55, no. 1 (2002): 19–35.

6

Narrative Apologetics

Why Telling Stories Matters

Every preacher know that stories give imaginative accessibility and depth to what otherwise might be rather dense and dull sermons. It will come as no surprise that using stories in apologetic sermons, lectures, or writings makes them much more interesting! Yet narrative apologetics involves much more than the pragmatic recognition of the usefulness of stories in sustaining the attention of a sometimes restless audience. It rests on a deep appreciation that the Christian Bible makes widespread use of stories to explain who we are, what is wrong with us, and what can be done about this. Yet for reasons that we will consider in the opening section of this chapter, this aspect of the Bible tended to be overlooked or marginalized during the "Age of Reason."

In this chapter, we shall consider the new interest in narrative apologetics in recent decades, focusing on two of the most significant Christian writers to make use of this approach – J. R. R. Tolkien and C. S. Lewis. We will consider both the rich theological foundation on which narrative apologetics rests, and the practical question of how best it may be developed and applied.

The Rediscovery of Narrative Apologetics

Apologetics is a rich and multifaceted discipline, which has taken various forms throughout Christian history, often in response to certain specific cultural concerns or pressures. During the Middle Ages, works of Christian apologetics – such as Thomas Aquinas's *Summa contra Gentiles* – aimed to bring out the intrinsic reasonableness of faith, in effect showing how the Christian faith was consistent with human rationality. The rise of the "Age of Reason" in western Europe, however, led to a narrowing of apologetic focus. As we noted earlier (pp. 24–6; 33–5), the early modern period saw an

Christian Apologetics: An Introduction, First Edition. Alister E. McGrath.
© 2024 John Wiley & Sons Ltd. Published 2024 by John Wiley & Sons Ltd.

increased focus on rationality, with a diminishing concern for aesthetic, emotional, and relational considerations. One of the most striking aspects of the forms of Christian theology and apologetics that emerged during the "Age of Reason" was their tendency to downplay and marginalize the fact that the Bible tells stories – stories that communicate the character and purposes of God. Enlightenment writers saw the Bible as teaching certain theological or philosophical truths, and occasionally using narratives to make these more interesting or memorable. Only what Enlightenment writers referred to as "pre-critical" theologians took these stories seriously; enlightened theologians realized that the stories were secondary and ultimately unnecessary ways of communicating rational truths. They were simply means of access to rational truth, which could be discarded once that truth had been attained.

H. Richard Niebuhr's work *The Meaning of Revelation* (1941) played an important role in the theological and apologetic retrieval of narratives. This work included a chapter entitled "The Story of our Lives," focusing on the narrative that lay at the heart of Christianity. For Niebuhr, the preaching of the early church did not take the form of arguments for the existence of God, but was essentially a recital of the basic elements of the story of the historical appearance of Jesus Christ and how the community of disciples understood this and responded to it. The Christian narrative centers on Jesus Christ, which it presents as an "intelligible event which makes all other events intelligible."

One of the most important developments in recent decades has been a growing appreciation of the critical role that narrative – the telling of stories – plays in human culture in general, and the religious life in particular. We "understand what reality is, who we are, and how we ought to live by locating ourselves within the larger narratives and metanarratives that we hear and tell, and that constitute what is for us real and significant." We are not simply "animals who make stories" but also "animals who are *made by* our stories." We both tell stories, and dwell within stories.

This trend towards the recovery of narrative as a means of transmitting history and perceptions of historical significance was given a new impetus by Hans Frei's landmark study *The Eclipse of Biblical Narrative* (1974). Frei pointed out the theological impoverishment resulting from the neglect of biblical narratives, and is widely seen as clearing the way for the recovery of taking narrative seriously as an authentically biblical and theological category. A narrative need no longer be seen as some kind of literary embellishment of the basic ideas of Christian theology; rather, it can be considered as a primary form of disclosure of God's identity and character, which emphasized its rooting in the actualities of history. Frei's work is part of a wider cultural retrieval of the importance of stories in human culture.

The US Catholic theologian Edward Oakes helpfully identifies four factors that help us understand why "narrative theology" has gained such influence in recent years, as well as laying the foundations for developing a "narrative apologetics."

1. Narrative can be seen as the "ideal genre for theology to establish contact with literary and humanistic studies in general, helping to pull it out of its academic ghetto." This clearly has implications (and applications) for apologetics, in that it highlights how the use of narratives could enable connection between the Christian faith and a wide range of cultural discourses.

2. Narrative enables an "easy transition to each believer's autobiography," which allows a storied approach to theology to relate more directly to human pastoral needs more effectively than traditional academic theology. The critical apologetic consequence of this is that narrative apologetics can relate the Christian story to each individual's personal story, enabling a form of connection that is otherwise much more problematic if the Christian faith is seen in cerebral or purely conceptual forms.
3. Narrative "highlights aspects of the Bible that are much more central to its identity than traditional theology made room for." Oakes here encourages apologetics to make use of a wide range of biblical genres.
4. "When revelation is interpreted as a form of narrative, it is then more easily seen as simply a more intense and clarifying narrative, one that structures and gives meaning to all the other narrative lines that make up a human life." This is Oakes's most important point, highlighting how narrative apologetics is able to establish connections with the other "narrative lines" that make up an individual human existence, and in doing so, is able to redirect and transform these.

So how does this renewed theological interest in narratives work out in the field of apologetics? In a thoughtful reflection on the nature of apologetics, John Milbank suggests that apologetics inevitably – and rightly – entails *narration*. Christian apologetics is a form of argumentation or reasoning that tells stories.

> *Apologein* in Greek means "to tell fully" and therefore simply to narrate, with a fullness that is acquired from a slightly detached perspective, as indicated by the prefix "apo" meaning "away from", "off", or "standing apart". Therefore the very word would suggest that an *apologia* is the primary narrative testament of faith … If an *apologia* is indeed an argument, then it is also a narrative.

Milbank's vision of apologetics weaves together narrative, argument, confession and imaginative witness. It distinguishes the plotline of a narrative and the sequential unfolding of a logical case, while presenting both as integral elements of a vision of reality that was historically actualized in the incarnation. For this reason, Milbank concludes, apologetics must "always remain Christological."

Paul Fiddes makes the point that narratives have a particularly important capacity to show that faith is a *living historical reality*, rather than as an abstract system of thought. Christianity is about living a real life, not simply thinking certain thoughts. Stories embody a concept of truth that demands *manifestation* rather than logical verification, offering its hearers an invitation to "participate in the story of the triune God." This shifts the apologetic focus in two ways. First, it emphasizes the importance of *witness*, rather than *argumentation*. An individual can narrate the difference that faith makes to their lives, rather than become trapped in ponderous argumentative detail. Christians can testify to the vitality of their faith and its impact on their lives. And second, building on this point, the Christian faith is not presented as a set of beliefs to be affirmed but as a "promise of participation in a new kind of existence."

Fiddes's analysis merits close attention, as it emphasizes the ability of the Christian gospel to transform lives, not simply change the way we think. Where older apologists often limited themselves to presenting intellectual arguments for the truth of Christianity, there is increasing interest in focusing on the capacity of the Christian faith to transform lives – a transformation that can best be described through the telling of a life-story. Our personal stories are redirected and reorientated by the Christian narrative. Narrating personal transformation or the discovery of meaning is a significant component of Christian apologetics, which highlights the critical role of personal testimony in bearing witness to the ability of Christianity to change and redirect someone's life so that they may have "life in all its fulness" (John 10:10). This point is particularly well conveyed in the gospel accounts of Christ's encounter with individuals, which often lead to their personal transformation – as in the narrative of Zacchaeus (Luke 19:1–10).

Christianity as a Grand Narrative?

Christianity tells a story that has the potential to interpret, illuminate, and transform individual narratives across history. This story that makes sense of all other stories – a "Grand Narrative" or "metanarrative" – shows how individuals encounter, embrace, and are transformed by the Christian faith. Yet the suggestion that Christianity offers some form of metanarrative raises the concern, found particularly in the writings of the French philosopher and literary theorist Jean-François Lyotard, that metanarratives are relics of an oppressive past. Lyotard rightly points out that many political ideologies – such as Nazism and Stalinism – impose their own version of "truth" on others. But things are not as simple as Lyotard suggests.

Postmodernism is right to reject the forceful or authoritarian *imposition* of a master narrative on the complexities of experience, which is then used to control and limit our understandings of the world. But it is difficult to see any legitimate objection to the *discernment* of a specific metanarrative as a means of coordinating multiple stories into a coherent whole. In any case, many now argue that postmodernity itself represents a metanarrative, seeks to impose a *suppression* or *marginalization* of other metanarratives, irrespective of their evidential foundations. The sociologist Christian Smith makes this point in his careful analysis of the role of narratives in contemporary culture. "Postmodernism itself is a narrative, hardly providing an escape from story-based knowledge and meaning." Lyotard's suspicion of metanarratives actually subverts his own position.

There are two issues here, one pragmatic, the other theoretical. Pragmatically, human beings find stories useful, engaging, and satisfying; theoretically, there is a growing body of evidence that human beings seem to be hardwired to use, develop, and transmit narratives. So how might stories be used *apologetically*? Perhaps the most helpful point at which to begin is to consider the influential narrative approaches to apologetics developed by Lewis and Tolkien in more detail, before exploring some case studies that will help clarify how narratives can be used practically in apologetics.

Narratives and Apologetics: C. S. Lewis and J. R. R. Tolkien

J. R. R. Tolkien (Figure 6.1) argued that God has hardwired humanity to *tell* stories and to *respond* to stories that had the capacity to capture the imagination. Since humanity bears the "image of God," we have a created natural capacity to tell stories that

Figure 6.1   J. R. R. Tolkien (1892–1973), author of *The Hobbit* and *The Lord of the Rings*, photographed in 1967. Alamy Image F5PET8.

point to their true origin in the mind of God. "Fantasy remains a human right: we make in our measure and in our derivative mode, because we are made: and not only made, but made in the image and likeness of a Maker." Tolkien thus seems to conceive the "image of God" as a kind of narrative template, implanted by God within humanity so that we have a natural inclination to use stories for a range of purposes. Tolkien's approach helped C. S. Lewis grasp how thinking of the Christian faith as a story could serve as the basis of his own apologetics.

In September 1931, Lewis hosted Tolkien and their mutual friend Hugo Dyson at a dinner at Magdalen College, Oxford. Afterwards, they walked around the college grounds discussing the place of stories in the Christian faith – more precisely, the nature and importance of the category of "myth." Tolkien used the term "myth" to refer to a specific form of narrative that conveys "fundamental things," rather than (as in the popular sense of the term) a fabricated untruth, a story that was devoid of historical basis.

Yet this was not a dry and disinterested academic conversation, but an exploration of an existential theme that had been troubling Lewis after his conversion in 1929. While Lewis now believed in God, he could not see how to integrate Christ into his new way of thinking. He was, he recalled, unable to understand or explain "how the life and death of Someone Else (whoever he was) 2000 years ago could help us here and now."

What had been holding me back [from embracing Christianity] has not been so much a difficulty in believing as a difficulty in knowing what the doctrine *meant*: you can't believe a thing while you are ignorant *what* the thing is. My puzzle was the whole doctrine of Redemption: in what sense has the life and death of Christ "saved" or "opened salvation to" the world.

Tolkien helped Lewis solve this problem by reframing Christian faith primarily as a *narrative*, rather than a set of abstract ideas or doctrines. Tolkien had a particularly high regard for Nordic pagan myths, which he held to offer "a far-off gleam or echo of *evangelium* in the real world." Tolkien helped Lewis to see that Christianity was not *primarily* a set of doctrines or moral principles, but a controlling grand narrative – a myth, in the true sense of the term – which generated and sustained doctrines and moral principles. The story of Christ was thus a "true myth" – that is to say, a myth that functions in the same manner as other myths, yet which *really happened*. Lewis realized that Christianity possesses the literary form of a myth, but with the critical difference that it was *true*. This true story generated doctrinal statements, which Lewis came to see as "translations into our *concepts* and *ideas* of that which God has already expressed in a language more adequate, namely the actual incarnation, crucifixion, and resurrection." Christianity, rather than being one myth alongside many others, is thus to be seen as representing the fulfilment of all myths – the "true myth" towards which all other myths merely point.

In his 1944 essay "Myth Became Fact," Lewis argued that God *authorizes* the use of myth as a means of captivating the human imagination and engaging the human reason (Figure 6.2). Since "God chooses to be mythopoeic," Lewis suggests, then we in our turn should be "mythopathic" – that is to say, receptive to God's myth, recognizing and acknowledging its "mythical radiance," and offering it an "imaginative welcome." And, since God uses myths (again, understood in the proper sense of the term) as a means of communicating both truth and meaning, why should not Christian apologists do the same? If God has created us in such a way that we are receptive to stories, why not use such stories to explain and commend the Christian faith?

In a perceptive account of Lewis's use of stories, the Lutheran theologian Gilbert Meilaender highlights what he believes to be Lewis's most important achievement – telling "stories which expand the imagination" and allow us to appreciate "the quality, the feel, of living in the world narrated by the biblical story." Lewis had realized that Christianity told a story that made sense of things, without being restricted to what could be understood or grasped by human reason. The Christian story allows us to see ourselves and our world in a new way, as if a sun had dawned on an otherwise shadowy and misty landscape.

Lewis saw such imaginative approaches based on narratives as *supplementing* their rational counterparts, operating at different levels, and potentially appealing to different audiences. For Lewis, the human imagination was the gateway to the soul, enabling the apologist to evade the "watchful dragons" of rationalism. *The Chronicles of Narnia* represent Lewis's mature and most successful work of literary apologetics. Though cast in the form of children's stories, these seven works aim to capture their readers' imaginations, and generate a new receptivity towards core themes of the Christian story.

Figure 6.2 The Oxford literary scholar and apologist C. S. Lewis in 1919, the year in which he began his undergraduate studies at University College, Oxford University, after having served in the British Army during the First World War. Alamy Image RDNXJN.

Yet many feel that it is Tolkien who offers a deeper and more satisfying account of why narratives are both appropriate and effective in Christian apologetics. For Tolkien, the human instinct to tell stories of meaning is grounded in the Christian doctrine of creation, in that humanity has been endowed with both a capacity and propensity to tell stories, which tacitly echo God's story of creation and redemption. Both the human love of narration and our capacity to create stories such as the great fantasy epic of the *Lord of the Rings* result from being created in the "image of God." For Tolkien and Lewis, Christianity tells a better, more illuminating and more persuasive story about humanity and the cosmos than its rivals. We shall explore this point further in the next section, focusing on Lewis's 1941 sermon "The Weight of Glory."

Apologetics as Telling a Better Story

As we have seen, Christian apologetics aims to show the deeper appeal and capaciousness of the Christianity, which tells a better story than its secular rivals. Earlier in this work, we looked at how the philosopher Richard Swinburne developed an apologetic approach based on the scientific idea of "inference to the best explanation" (see pp. 51–4). This approach evaluates rival scientific theories by exploring how well they accommodate the observational evidence, using criteria such as simplicity, elegance, and comprehensiveness. The important point that this is a relative judgement. Explanations are being compared with each other to determine which is the "best," rather than proved to be true. So might a similar approach can be used for evaluating the capacity of a *metanarrative* for accommodating the complexity of the world and human experience? Which is the *best* story?

So how do we decide which story is to be preferred? The sociologist Christian Smith points out that "it is difficult rationally to adjudicate between divergent stories. How do you tell which one is more deserving of assent and commitment than others?" The process of comparing narratives involves asking which appears to provide the best account of what we observe and experience. This does not amount to a proof that Christianity is true, but rather a demonstration that the Christian story offers a more satisfactory framework for making sense of things than – for example – its materialist counterpart. Lewis argues that a materialist account of human rationality is both circular and self-defeating. It contradicts itself. A similar point is made by the philosopher Alvin Plantinga in several of his works, including *Where the Conflict Really Lies: Science, Religion, and Naturalism* (2011).

Someone who embraces naturalism thus has to deal with a potentially fatal flaw in their own narrative, in that naturalism calls into question the reliability of human rational processes. The importance of this point can be seen from a comment by J. B. S. Haldane, a materialist scientist who was well aware of the internal inconsistency of this position:

> If my mental processes are determined wholly by the motions of atoms in my brain I have no reason to suppose that my beliefs are true. They may be sound chemically, but that does not make them sound logically. And hence I have no reason for supposing my brain to be composed of atoms. In order to escape from this necessity of sawing away the branch on which I am sitting, so to speak, I am compelled to believe that mind is not wholly conditioned by matter.

So how can the cultural dominance of a materialist metanarrative be broken? In his classic 1941 sermon "The Weight of Glory," Lewis suggested that this metanarrative has cast a spell over western culture, normalizing the idea that there is no transcendent dimension to life. So how can its spell be broken? Lewis's answer is significant apologetically: *to break a spell, you have to weave a better spell.* "Spells are used for breaking enchantments as well as for inducing them. And you and I have need of the strongest spell that can be found to wake us from the evil enchantment of worldliness that has been laid upon us for nearly a hundred years." To break the spell of one story, you need to tell a better story, capable of capturing the imagination and opening the mind to alternative possibilities.

While he was an atheist during the 1920s, Lewis found himself reflecting on the varying capacities of various metanarratives to do justice to the complexity of reality. Despite sharing their atheism, he considered modernist writers such as George Bernard Shaw (1856–1950) and H. G. Wells (1866–1946) to be "a little thin." Lewis considered that their cultural metanarratives possessed "no depth," and seemed incapable of adequately representing the "roughness and density of life." Yet Lewis found the

Christian poet George Herbert (1593–1633) remarkably successful in "conveying the very quality of life as we actually live it," apparently on account of "mediating" reality through what Lewis then termed "the Christian mythology." Perhaps, Lewis mused, this metanarrative was to be preferred to those of Shaw and Wells, on account of its capacity to enfold the complexity and granularity of human experience. For Lewis, a story needs to "chime in" with the human experience of reality if it is to carry weight, and open up new possibilities.

The philosopher Alasdair MacIntyre offers an analysis that helps to clarify Lewis's point. MacIntyre considered classical Thomism to offer the most satisfactory account of human moral reflection. But why? For MacIntyre, the answer was clear: "that narrative prevails over its rivals which is able to include its rivals within it, not only to retell their stories as episodes within its story, but to tell the story of the telling of their stories as such episodes." If you can fit someone else's story inside your story, this shows the greater explanatory capaciousness of your narrative, and hence the authority of your narrative over the other. Lewis, like MacIntyre before him, realized that the Christian narrative could fit in other accounts of the world. The Christian apologist is thus called to out-narrate the dominant stories that shape our culture, by exposing their weaknesses or showing how they are enfolded or eclipsed by the more luminous and compelling story offered by Christianity.

So what is this Christian "story"? There are a number of ways of telling this story, all of which build upon the rich biblical witness to the presence and activity of God in the world, and how this is focused on the life and ministry of Christ. Each of them offers an answer to some of the most pressing questions of humanity, including who we really are; where we are; what has gone wrong; and what can be done to put things right. To explore how the Christian story might be used apologetically, we shall consider how the New Testament scholar N. T. (Tom) Wright sets it out:

> The story is about a creator and his creation, about humans made in this creator's image and given tasks to perform, about the rebellion of humans and the dissonance of creation at every level, and particularly about the creator's acting, through Israel and climactically through Jesus, to rescue his creation from its ensuing plight. The story continues with the creator acting by his own spirit within the world to bring it towards the restoration which is his intended goal for it.

So how would Wright answer the four questions noted above? Perhaps the best way of exploring this issue is simply to set out Wright's own answers.

1. *Who are we?* "We are humans, made in the image of the creator. We have responsibilities that come with this status."
2. *Where are we?* "We are in a good and beautiful, though transient, world, the creation of the god in whose image we are made."
3. *What is wrong?* "Humanity has rebelled against the creator. This rebellion reflects a cosmic dislocation between the creator and the creation, and the world is consequently out of tune with its created intention."
4. *What is the solution?* "The creator has acted, is acting, and will act within his creation to deal with the weight of evil set up by human rebellion, and to bring his

world to the end for which it was made, namely that it should resonate fully with his own presence and glory. This action, of course, is focused upon Jesus and the spirit of the creator."

Yet Wright makes a further point, paralleling the approach of Christopher Morse, a professor of theology at Union Theological Seminary in New York City. In his work *Not Every Spirit: A Dogmatics of Christian Disbelief* (2009), Morse makes the point that a set of beliefs or an informing metanarrative is not simply about what we are obliged to *affirm*; it also concerns what these beliefs or this metanarrative commit us to *denying*. The question here is not primarily what is *affirmed*, but what is *excluded*. Wright points out that each of the four affirmations arising from the Christian story has a parallel denial. For example, in responding to the second of his questions, Wright sets out beliefs that the Christian is right to reject, on the basis of this informing narrative: "We are not in an alien world, as the Gnostic imagines; nor in a cosmos to which we owe allegiance as to a god, as the pantheist would suggest." Wright helpfully shows the apologist that the Christian story can be used both to make sense of the world and to identify false or inadequate accounts of life.

The Apologetic Application of Biblical Narratives

The Bible is rich in narratives, each of which can be thought of as a thread that can be woven into a grander biblical metanarrative – a story about creation, fall, the calling of Israel, and the death and resurrection of Jesus Christ. Many apologists focus on this overall "grand narrative," which gives individual human stories meaning and value by locating them within this greater story. Yet it is important to realize that many of the stories that are brought together in this single narrative web have an important apologetic role to play in their own right. Each narrative thread needs to be respected and appreciated for what it is, and not merely for being part of a greater whole.

One important apologetic point is that biblical narratives provide a much more engaging account of faith than arguments, making it easier for people to make connections with their own individual stories than might be possible if relying on more abstract theological ideas. To appreciate this point, let us consider how we might try to communicate the love of God to a secular audience. Theologians will rightly want to point out that God's love is so vast that human language is simply not capable of expressing it. This may be true, but it is not particularly helpful apologetically. It creates the impression that we are incapable of talking about, let alone commending, the love of God. Instead, we can draw on the imaginative power of an incarnational narration of the life of Christ, drawing on a significant statement in the New Testament:

> God is love (*agapē*). God's love was revealed among us in this way: God sent his only Son into the world so that we might live through him. In this is love, not that we loved God but that he loved us and sent his Son to be the atoning sacrifice for our sins (1 John 4:8–10).

This familiar passage makes two distinct types of statement about the love of God. The first is framed almost as a timeless ahistorical truth: "God is love." It is an important theological insight, which is woven into the fabric of Christian theology. Think, for example, of the Christian interpretation of the cross of Christ, traditionally explored using "theories of the Atonement." The well-known popular Christian writer John Stott ably identifies the central role of the love of God in such theories: "It cannot be emphasized too strongly that God's love is the source, not the consequence, of the atonement. ... God does not love us because Christ died for us; Christ died for us because God loved us."

Yet there is an apologetic issue here, which concerns the manner of *presentation* of this theme, not its truthfulness. The love of God is here presented and explored in a theoretical and abstract manner, which appeals primarily to the mind, while failing to engage the imagination or emotions. We are assured that "God is love," but are left unsure what this word "love" means, and how it is shown. The affirmation of a timeless theological principle will doubtless help some to think about divine love; others, however, will simply not get what it is all about.

So we turn to the second of those theological statements: "God sent his only Son into the world so that we might live through him." It is impossible to miss the dramatic change in imagery and genre that takes place here. Metaphysics is replaced by a *narrative*. We are reminded of what God *did* to demonstrate both the nature and constancy of the divine love. This terse statement calls to mind the gospel accounts of the passion of Christ, which invites us to turn over in our minds and savor elements of that narrative, seeing in our mind's eye the deeply moving scene of Christ's crucifixion, and helping us appreciate what was done to transform our situation.

An incarnational narration of our faith tells us that the "love of God" can be compared to someone laying down their lives so that those who they love might live (cf. John 15:13). The apologist thus does not appeal primarily to God's love in the form of an abstract timeless propositional statement, but rather retells the imaginatively compelling story of the passion of Christ, inviting the audience to enter into that narrative, and to try to understand both what is going on, and how it relates to them. The passion narrative has its own distinct integrity and given added depth by using artistic images of the crucifixion, which help us focus on the event of Christ's death, and its significance.

So what other narratives could be used? In what follows, we shall explore several representative possibilities.

The Apologetic Application of Narratives: Some Examples

Up to this point, we have considered mainly the theoretical justification of narrative apologetics. So how do we move from the science to the art of narrative apologetics? In what follows, I shall explore three broad narratives to open up the possibilities that this approach opens up. We begin by considering a familiar biblical narrative, and consider its apologetic implications.

A Biblical Narrative: The Babylonian Exile

One of the most significant events in the history of Israel is generally known as the "Babylonian Deportation" or "Babylonian Exile" of the sixth century BCE. Following a failed rebellion by the kingdom of Judah against the Babylonian empire, Nebuchadnezzar besieged the city of Jerusalem, and deported most of its inhabitants over the period 597–581 to Babylon. They would remain in exile until the fall of Babylon to the Persian king Cyrus the Great in 539 BCE. Although some Jews remained in Babylon following the collapse of the Babylonian empire, most appear to have made their way back to Jerusalem, taking advantage of Cyrus's decree that all those who had been deported were now free to return to their native cities. Most of the people of Jerusalem returned to rebuild the fallen city walls and its Temple. This event was a landmark in Israel's history.

While there are several ways in which the narrative of Exile can be developed apologetically, perhaps the most winsome and engaging of these is to correlate it with the deep sense that we don't really belong here. (We considered this "point of contact" in the previous chapter: pp. 100–2). Our true identity lies somewhere else, and we will not be satisfied until we find and enter our true homeland. So if you were giving an apologetic talk, you might invite your audience to imagine that they are inhabitants of Jerusalem who have been deported to Babylon. Can you feel the sense of longing to go home where you really belong? To sign the songs of Zion at home in Jerusalem, rather than in exile in Babylon?

This line of imaginative and empathetic exploration will help you explore the idea of being trapped in a place where you do not belong; the need for someone to set you free; and the hope of entering into the place where you really belong, your liberator having gone ahead before you to prepare the way. The French theologian and philosopher Simone Weil saw the notion of being "rooted" as a core "need of the soul." Yet to be "rooted" does not mean belonging *here*; rather, it is about belonging *somewhere*, which makes existing *here* bearable.

You can develop all of these points in your own way as your expression of the art of apologetics. The important point to appreciate is that a story creates a framework that allows you to explore some central themes of the Christian faith in an intellectually hospitable manner – not imposing them upon people, but inviting them to step inside this way of thinking about and imagining the human situation, and appreciating its appeal and significance. This approach affirms that we really belong elsewhere. This world is our place of transit, in which we begin to realize that something lies beyond it. Like the prisoners in Plato's dark underground cave (pp. 102–4), we sense there must be more to reality than this world of shadows, and become aware of "signals of transcendence" pointing to a world beyond the darkness of the cave.

A Cultural Narrative: The Relation of Science and Faith

Science and faith are important elements of modern western culture, and it is perhaps not surprising that they regularly find themselves in competition for intellectual authority and cultural influence. The movement known as the "New Atheism," which emerged in 2006, can be seen as asserting the sole authority of the natural sciences in cultural matters, including religion (pp. 159–61). So are science and faith really inconsistent with each other, so that their relationship can only be framed in terms of conflict or warfare? Or can they be seen as important, yet different, aspects of human knowledge, capable of enriching each other when properly understood and correlated?

In a later chapter, we shall consider the intellectual aspects of this matter, considering three representative ways of understanding their relationship (pp. 161–4). Yet there is another way of exploring this relationship, which many consider to be more effective and engaging – namely, telling the stories of prominent individuals who hold science and faith together. In a recent study, sociologists Christopher Scheitle and Elaine Howard Ecklund assessed the influence of "Science Popularizers" on the public's view of religion and science. One particular aspect of their analysis stands out: the role of cultural exemplars who model a positive relationship between science and faith. Their study focused on the impact of Francis C. Collins (born 1950; Figure 6.3) on the public perception of the relation of science and faith.

Collins is a US biologist who was Director of the Human Genome Project, before being nominated by President Obama to be Director of the National Institutes of Health in 2009, a position he continued to hold under two subsequent presidents. Collins had earlier (2006) authored a personal memoir of his own religious journey from atheism to Christian faith, entitled *The Language of God: A Scientist Presents Evidence for Belief*. Scheitle and Ecklund found that Collins's personal story was influential in shifting people away from the popular stereotype of the "warfare" of science and religion "toward a collaboration view of religion and science." The apologetic importance of this observation is clear: the personal story of a significant public figure who has found a way of holding science and faith together is significant in encouraging others to think along the same lines.

Figure 6.3 Francis C. Collins, Director of the National Institutes of Health from 2009–2021, and author of *The Language of God* (2006). Alamy Image T7KGNM.

Now let's be clear: the example of Collins does not resolve the intellectual issue of whether science and faith are compatible, or can exist in positive relationship. Rather, Collins's own story demonstrates that someone with significant credentials in this field had found his way to what he considers to be a workable solution – and thus encourages others to follow through on his approach, to see if they can make it work for themselves. In doing so, they are likely to explore and engage the kinds of arguments that we will consider later in this volume (pp. 159–69). Other examples could be given, most notably the physicist John Polkinghorne and the astronomer Jennifer Wiseman.

Literary Analogies: Making Theology Real

As we have already noted, the apologist has a wide range of literary analogies to draw on in exploring apologetic questions. Both J. R. R. Tolkien and C. S. Lewis knew the importance of narratives for engaging life's deepest questions, and it is no accident that *The Lord of the Rings* and *The Chronicles of Narnia* are rich in stories that can be put to apologetic use. One example will help illustrate the potential of narrative approaches to apologetics: the need to find a way of visualizing sin, and the way in which human beings can be entrapped within situations from which they cannot extricate themselves, classically described in Paul's letter to the Romans: "I can will what is right, but I cannot do it. For I do not do the good I want, but the evil I do not want is what I do" (Romans 7:18–19). But how can this be *imagined*? Sin is too easily perceived as an abstract idea, rather than as an entrapping force.

Lewis's answer is to make us imaginatively receptive to the idea of sin by telling a story that illustrates how our own desires can master and overwhelm us. In the *Voyage of the Dawn Treader*, Lewis tells of how Eustace Scrubb longs to be rich, only to find that this desire spirals out of control, eventually enslaving him. Drawing on an old Nordic tradition, which saw dragons as symbols of greed, Lewis depicts Scrubb turning into a dragon, ensnared within his own imagined and self-serving story of success and wealth. Yet as disillusionment sets in, Scrubb realizes that he cannot break free from his identity as a dragon. Scrubb becoming trapped in the body of a dragon is a powerful visual narrative representation of the power of sin to entrap, captivate, and imprison. There seems to be no hope of salvation.

Yet Aslan now appears, tears away at Scrubb's dragon flesh with his claws, and finally plunges the wounded bleeding boy into a well from which he emerges purified and renewed, with his humanity restored. Lewis's narrative enables his readers to visual sin as an enslaving force that cannot be overcome by human agency. We are held captive by our own desires. Only Christ as savior and liberator can break sin's power, and restore us to full humanity. Lewis's story provides a framework for "seeing" or "imagining" sin, understanding both its capacity to enslave, and how it may be overcome. Other ways of depicting sin using stories are, of course, available – but Lewis's narrative is an excellent starting point.

In the next chapter, we shall turn our attention to the importance of our audiences in developing apologetic approaches. It's an important theme, too easily overlooked. How does the history and identity of the people we are speaking to shape the approaches we adopt, the analogies that we use to explain Christian ideas, and the questions that we might find ourselves being asked about?

Study Questions

1. Using your own words, explain why the importance of stories was downplayed during the "Age of Reason."
2. Why is it important for apologists to show that Christianity has a "better story" to tell than secularism? What criteria might you use to decide which is the "better" story?
3. How might you use the story of the Exodus apologetically?
4. Choose three "parables of the Kingdom," and consider what apologetic points you might make using these.

For Further Reading

Baynes, Kenneth. "Self, Narrative, and Self-Constitution: Revisiting Taylor's 'Self-Interpreting Animals.'" *Philosophical Forum* 41, no. 4 (2010): 441–57.

Burley, Mikel. "Narrative Philosophy of Religion: Apologetic and Pluralistic Orientations." *International Journal for Philosophy of Religion* 88 (2020): 5–21.

Chatraw, Josh. *Telling a Better Story: How to Talk about God in a Skeptical Age*. Grand Rapids, MI: Zondervan, 2020.

Coutras, Lisa. *Tolkien's Theology of Beauty: Majesty, Splendor, and Transcendence in Middle-Earth*. New York, NY: Palgrave Macmillan, 2016.

Fewell, Danna Nolan, ed. *The Oxford Handbook of Biblical Narrative*. Oxford: Oxford University Press, 2016.

Flieger, Verlyn. *Splintered Light: Logos and Language in Tolkien's World*. 2nd ed. Kent, OH: Kent State University Press, 2002.

Frei, Hans. *The Eclipse of Biblical Narrative: A Study in Eighteenth and Nineteenth Century Biblical Hermeneutics*. New Haven, CT: Yale University Press, 1974.

Gottschall, Jonathan. *The Storytelling Animal: How Stories Make Us Human*. Boston: Houghton Mifflin Harcourt, 2012.

Halík, Tomáš. *Patience with God: The Story of Zacchaeus Continuing in Us*. New York, NY: Doubleday, 2009.

Hogenson, George B. "The Controversy around the Concept of Archetypes." *Journal of Analytical Psychology* 64, no. 5 (2019): 682–700.

Hultgren, Stephen. "Narrative Christology in the Gospels: Reflections on Some Recent Developments and Their Significance for Theology and Preaching." *Lutheran Theological Journal* 47, no. 1 (2013): 10–21.

Jacobs, Alan. *Original Sin: A Cultural History*. New York, NY: HarperOne, 2008.

Malbon, Elizabeth Struthers. *Mark's Jesus: Characterization as Narrative Christology*. Waco, TX: Baylor University Press, 2009.

Markos, Louis. *Apologetics for the Twenty-First Century*. Wheaton, IL: Crossway, 2010.

McGrath, Alister E. "A Gleam of Divine Truth: The Concept of Myth in Lewis's Thought." In *The Intellectual World of C. S. Lewis*, 55–82. Oxford: Wiley-Blackwell, 2013.

McGrath, Alister E. *Narrative Apologetics: Sharing the Relevance, Joy, and Wonder of the Christian Faith*. Grand Rapids, MI: Baker Books, 2019.

Morse, Christopher. *Not Every Spirit: A Dogmatics of Christian Disbelief*. 2nd ed. New York, NY: Continuum, 2009.

Niebuhr, H. Richard. "The Story of Our Lives." In *The Meaning of Revelation*. New York, NY: Macmillan, 1960, 43–90.

Oakes, Edward T. "Apologetics and the Pathos of Narrative Theology." *Journal of Religion* 72, no. 1 (1992): 37–58.

Ochs, Elinor, and Capps, Lisa. *Living Narrative: Creating Lives in Everyday Storytelling*. Cambridge, MA: Harvard University Press, 2001.

Ordway, Holly. *Tales of Faith: A Guide to Sharing the Gospel through Literature*. Park Ridge, IL: Word on Fire Institute, 2022.

Padley, Jonathan, and Kenneth Padley. "'From Mirrored Truth the Likeness of the True': J. R. R. Tolkien and Reflections of Jesus Christ in Middle-Earth." *English* 59, no. 224 (2010): 70–92.

Plantinga, Alvin. *Where the Conflict Really Lies: Science, Religion, and Naturalism*. New York, NY: Oxford University Press, 2011.

Scheil, Andrew P. *Babylon under Western Eyes: A Study of Allusion and Myth*. Toronto: University of Toronto Press, 2016.

Scheitle, Christopher P., and Elaine Howard Ecklund. "The Influence of Science Popularizers on the Public's View of Religion and Science: An Experimental Assessment." *Public Understanding of Science* 26, no. 1 (2017): 25–39.

Seiple, David. "Faith for Faithful Disbelievers: Christopher Morse as Systematic Theologian." *Union Seminary Quarterly Review* 65 (2014): 156–70.

Shuster, Marguerite. *The Fall and Sin: What We Have Become as Sinners*. Grand Rapids, MI: Eerdmans, 2004.

Smith, Christian. *Moral, Believing Animals: Human Personhood and Culture*. Oxford: Oxford University Press, 2009.

Sommer, Kristin L., Roy F. Baumeister, and Tyler F. Stillman. "The Construction of Meaning from Life Events: Empirical Studies of Personal Narratives." In *The Human Quest for Meaning: Theories, Research, and Applications*, edited by Paul T. P. Wong. New York, NY: Routledge, 2012, 297–314.

Stökl, Jonathan, and Caroline Waerzeggers, eds. *Exile and Return: The Babylonian Context*. Berlin: De Gruyter, 2015.

Stump, Eleonore. *Wandering in Darkness: Narrative and the Problem of Suffering*. Oxford: Clarendon Press, 2010.

Ward, Michael. "The Good Serves the Better and Both the Best: C. S. Lewis on Imagination and Reason in Apologetics." In *Imaginative Apologetics: Theology, Philosophy, and the Catholic Tradition*, edited by Andrew Davison, 59–78. London: SCM Press, 2011.

7

The Importance of the Audience

Who is the audience for apologetics? What kind of people do apologists think they are speaking to? And what difference does an understanding of the aspirations, concerns, and anxieties of the audience make to the approach that the apologist develops? In his reflections on evangelism and apologetics, the leading British evangelical writer and preacher John Stott (Figure 7.1) insisted that while there was "only one basic apostolic tradition of the gospel," it was important to appreciate that "the apostolic approach was 'situational'" – in other words, that New Testament writers realized that "different situations called forth different treatments." The same gospel might thus be proclaimed in one manner to one specific audience, and in another to a different audience.

Stott illustrates this point by inviting his readers to compare the very different approaches adopted by Paul in his sermon in the synagogue in Antioch (Acts 13) and his address to the Areopagus in Athens (Acts 17). The same gospel was being presented in different audience-specific ways. Stott's strategy of "double listening" was designed to enable a universal gospel to be particularized to a specific audience. We shall develop this point further later in this chapter by comparing the approaches adopted by Peter in his Pentecost address (Acts 2) and Paul's Areopagus address (Acts 17).

Some older apologists argued that the identity of the audience was not of any importance; it was simply necessary to proclaim the Christian faith, which was universally relevant, and hence could be proclaimed in exactly the same way in every cultural context. Yet their own favored ways of proclaiming or defending the gospel usually turned out to be rooted in their own cultural context, so that their preaching often amounted to an implicit demand to adopt their cultural norms as much as an explicit invitation to adopt the Christian faith. Happily, the situation has changed, and there is now a much greater awareness of the need for cultural empathy and patience as a prerequisite for effective apologetics. There is a widespread recognition that apologetics needs

Christian Apologetics: An Introduction, First Edition. Alister E. McGrath.
© 2024 John Wiley & Sons Ltd. Published 2024 by John Wiley & Sons Ltd.

Figure 7.1   The noted preacher and writer John R. W. Stott (1921–2011), Rector of All Soul's Langham Place, London. Alamy Image E12XN8.

to recognize and respond to the different starting points, plausibility structures, and questions of different audiences. Francis Spufford's *Unapologetic*, for example, is clearly written for an audience that finds Christianity weird, outdated, or culturally unintelligible. This audience sees Christianity both as embodying yesterday's values and causing today's problems. Spufford's apologetic approach reflects both the starting points of his thoroughly post-Christian readers, and the lines of argument and reflection that might carry weight with them – but which would not work well with other audiences.

In this chapter, we shall reflect on the importance of the audience for apologetics, whether this is a specific individual, or a wider group of people. How do we take into account the specific nature of our audience in preparing apologetic talks? I have some colleagues who argue that you can use the same address over and over again, no matter who you are speaking to. If it worked for one audience, it will work just as well for others. In this chapter, we shall consider the reasons for being critical of this viewpoint. The art of apologetics involves crafting approaches that are attuned to the questions asked by specific groups of people, which need to be answered in terms they can understand. The audience needs to feel you are speaking to *them*, and not to *someone else*.

Let's use Paul's metaphor of salvation as adoption as an example of this point. The image of "adoption" is clearly helpful in opening up some aspects of the Christian faith (see pp. 73–4). Paul uses this image in some of his letters in the expectation that his readers would be familiar with it and be able to see how it illuminates the way in which the Christian gospel changes the human situation. But the practice of adoption was culturally specific in the New Testament world. While it was a legal category familiar throughout the Greco-Roman world at this time, it was largely unknown in the Jewish world. This helps us understand why Paul uses this image in letters written to churches in Rome and other regions in the Greco-Roman world – such as the city of Ephesus and the region of Galatia (Romans 8:15, 23; 9:4; Galatians 4:5; Ephesians 1:5). Yet no New Testament writer uses this image when writing to a *Jewish* readership. Why not? Because it would probably have been unintelligible to such an audience, except for those with a good knowledge of Roman culture.

Apologetics is thus an art, not simply a science. It requires a good knowledge of the Christian faith on the one hand and of the audience you are speaking to (or writing for) on the other, along with a generous amount of wisdom and cultural empathy to be able to connect up the two. It is pointless to adopt an apologetic approach that is culturally unintelligible to its audience. In what follows, we will explore this point further, beginning with a reflection on how the New Testament witnesses to the importance of the audience in apologetics.

Greeks and Jews: The New Testament and the Importance of the Audience

The two main people groups that are envisaged and engaged by the writers of the New Testament are Greeks and Jews. In Paul's first letter to the Corinthians, for example, "Greeks" are set alongside "Jews" as a defining group of considerable apologetic importance (1 Corinthians 1:22). Yet these are two very different groups of people, with different histories, mindsets, and expectations. So how did early Christian apologists engage these two quite different audiences?

The Acts of the Apostles is one of the most important New Testament works for the apologist, as it offers us as offers us not only insights about how the early church developed, but accounts of some early Christian sermons that clearly have an apologetic focus. In this section, I shall consider Peter's Pentecost sermon to a Jewish audience (Acts 2) and Paul's address on the Areopagus at Athens (Acts 17), and ask what we might learn from them about how a universal faith can be particularized to connect up with a specific audience.

The audience for Peter's Pentecost sermon was "devout Jews from every nation under heaven living in Jerusalem" (Acts 2:5). The core theme of this sermon is that the coming of Christ fulfils the prophecies of the Old Testament. Peter's apologetic address is framed in terms of themes that were both important to a Jewish audience, and could be easily understood by them. Peter demonstrates that Christ meets the specific expectations and hopes of Israel, appealing to specific authorities (here, prophetic passages in the Old Testament), which would have carried weight with his audience to argue that Christ fulfils Old Testament prophecy. Peter uses language that would readily have been accepted and understood by his audience – such as his specific reference to Jesus of Nazareth as "Lord and Christ." No explanation of these two technical terms "Lord" and "Christ" was needed, as these ideas were familiar (and significant) to his Jewish audience.

To appreciate the importance of these points, we need to contrast Peter's approach with that of Paul in his speech on the Areopagus (or "Mars Hill") in Athens (Acts

Figure 7.2   The Areopagus, one of the most important buildings in ancient Athens, which was the site of the apostle Paul's apologetic address recorded in the Acts of the Apostles. Adobe Stock Image 59170115/.

17:16–34) (Figure 7.2). Although Athens had been a major political and cultural center in the classical period, it was little more than a provincial city within the Roman Empire by the time of Paul's visit. Yet Athens still possessed an iconic significance as the heart of Greek thought and culture. So how could Paul connect up Christianity with this audience, which knew nothing of the Old Testament, and would in any case not have considered it to have any significance for them? Whereas Peter's Pentecost sermon was addressed to a Jewish audience, deeply steeped in a knowledge of the Old Testament, Paul's sermon at Athens engaged people from a very different cultural context. Although Paul's letters are full of appreciative references to the Hebrew Bible (later designated the "Old Testament" by Christian writers), his Athenian audience would simply not have been familiar with this text, nor would they have seen it as significant. Paul rightly discerned that in order to connect up with this specific audience, he would have to develop a different approach that was specific to *this* audience, speaking to *their* situation.

Paul thus found himself in a situation in which he had to proclaim the gospel without being able to contextualize this within the history and hopes of Israel. Where Peter appealed to the "book of Scripture," Paul turned instead to the "book of nature." It is an idea whose roots are deeply embedded in the Old Testament: "The heavens are telling the glory of God; and the firmament proclaims his handiwork" (Psalm 19:1). Paul believed passionately in the theological truth and apologetic importance of this insight (see especially Romans 1–2). An appeal to God as creator thus becomes a way of channeling the theme of redemption in Christ.

Paul is clearly aware of the distinct identity and characteristics of his audience, and uses local beliefs and landmarks as anchors for his apologetic presentation. Since his audience did not know anything about the Hebrew Bible, Paul draws upon literary authorities with which they were familiar – in this case, the Athenian poet Aratus, widely regarded as one of the great cultural icons of his day. (Aratus dates from the late fourth and early third centuries before Christ, and it is thought that he was born in Paul's own province of Cilicia, a region in southern Anatolia in modern-day Turkey.)

Paul's citation from Aratus is intended both to connect up with this specific audience, and to highlight the importance of the theme of the proximity of God: "[God] is not far from each one of us. For 'In him we live and move and have our being'; as even some of your own poets have said, 'For we too are his offspring'" (Acts 17:27–8). Paul here quotes a half-line from Aratus to reinforce – not to establish – his own point about God being close to hand. He cites a local author, partly to show respect for his audience, but also to use Aratus as a gateway for the ideas that he wants to present. Without using these specific terms, Paul's address to the Athenians appeals to a "sense of divinity" present in each individual as a "point of contact" for the Christian faith. What the Greeks held to be unknown (and possibly unknowable), Paul proclaims to have been made known through Christ.

Paul also references a local Athenian landmark – the inscription "to an unknown god" on an altar (Acts 17:23). Diogenes Laertius and other contemporary writers refer to "anonymous altars" of this kind around this time. Paul here argues that a god of whom the Greeks had some implicit or intuitive awareness is now being made known to them by name and in full in the Christian gospel. The god who is known indirectly through the created order can be known fully through the resurrection of Jesus Christ. Paul here picks up on the apologetic potential of a local landmark, which again became a gateway to his proclamation of the gospel.

Paul's apologetic address at Athens offers important insights about how to adapt the proclamation of the gospel to a local audience. Peter's approach to a Jewish audience in Jerusalem would not have connected with Paul's audience in Athens, any more than Paul's approach in Athens would have resonated well with Peter's audience in Jerusalem. Paul adapts his rhetoric to the local situation, citing a local authority (the poet Aratus), exploiting the apologetic potential of a local landmark (an "anonymous altar"), and developing a line of thought that chimed in with some Athenian ideas about the presence of the divine in the natural order. This approach can easily be adopted and adapted today.

The theme of fulfilment is important in both these addresses, but is interpreted in different ways. Peter's Pentecost sermon in Jerusalem is about the fulfilment of the hopes of Israel and God's promises of the gift of the Holy Spirit in Christ. Paul's sermon in Athens was about the fulfilment of the classical longing for wisdom. For others, such as C. S. Lewis, Christianity is about the fulfilment of the heart's desire.

The two examples from the Acts of the Apostles considered earlier in this chapter point to the importance of audience-specific approaches in explaining and proclaiming a universal Christian faith. The critical point to appreciate is that, though universal in its scope and reach, Christianity is capable of connecting in different ways with specific audiences. This does not mean that there are multiple *Christianities*; it rather means that there are multiple *possible points of entry or access* to Christianity. Apologetics focusses on identifying those points of entry and helping people to find them; preachers and catechists then focus on helping them grow and flourish in the new world of faith.

Peter and Paul may have focused on two quite distinct (and important!) people groups (Jews and Greeks) in the two addresses we have considered. Yet they were clear that, through faith, they had become part of a single new "people group" – the Christian community or church – within which both were welcome, yet which was not defined by their ethnic pasts. Christians gradually positioned themselves as members of an *ethnos* or *genos* distinct not merely from Judaism, but also from Roman and Greek historical and ethnic norms.

Apologetics as an Art: The Balcony and the Road

The best apologetics is based upon a knowledge both of the Christian faith and the audience that is being engaged. This requires an immersion in the rich tradition of Christian reflection on the Bible, and reading widely to get a sense of how the Christian faith can be articulated faithfully and sensitively in different historical and cultural contexts. Apologetics is thus a *science*, demanding a familiarity with the Christian faith, as this has been developed over the ages in response to the many challenges that have arisen.

Yet apologetics is also an *art*. It demands an understanding of the audience, both as individuals and groups, and a willingness to learn their languages, step into their situations, and identify the aspects of the Christian faith that might connect up with them. It means listening to their concerns, bewilderment, and difficulties, in order to be able to navigate a way of addressing these compassionately, carefully, and convincingly. It is about taking trouble to understand their concerns, and being sensitive to what are often misunderstandings about the nature of faith in general, and certain Christian beliefs in particular. To take these concerns seriously is not to agree with them; it is to recognize them as shaping your audience's assumptions, and helping you identify helpful starting points and approaches.

Apologetics thus works at two quite different levels. On the one hand, we have to contend with genuine intellectual difficulties. Here, the issue is *intelligibility*. How can Christianity make sense of the world? How can the world make sense of Christianity? Here, the great classical tradition of Christian apologetics has much to offer. On the other hand, we have the questions and problems that arise directly from experience of life – its traumas, its anxieties, and its hopes. The questions here focus on *relevance* and an ability to correlate the Christian faith with the needs and situations of individuals and people groups. Apologetics now becomes an art, a craft – a skill, soundly based upon a science, yet attentive to the diversity and specificity of its audiences, requiring the apologist to be able to make connections between the Christian faith and their audiences.

There is an obvious parallel here with the practice of medicine. This rests on a deep knowledge of how the human body works, how various drugs function, and how to diagnose what is wrong with someone. But this is only part of the problem. Physicians have to learn the art of relating to people as individual human beings, winning their confidence as they try to work out what is wrong with them, and being able to explain both the problem and its cure in everyday language, rather than the more precise and technical language of medical journals. It is about journeying with them during the therapeutic process, encouraging them and supporting them. Medicine is thus a *relational*, not simply a *professional*, matter. The art of medicine is acquired over time, through experience.

A framework that is helpful in exploring the different levels at which apologetics functions was developed by John A. Mackay, a former President of Princeton Theological Seminary. This framework draws a distinction between two different perspectives on life, which Mackay terms "The Balcony" and "The Road." The imagery is drawn from early twentieth century urban life in Spain, where Mackey spent a significant period of his life studying the Spanish language. Here is how he describes these two very different perspectives.

> By the Balcony ... I mean that little platform in wood or stone that protrudes from the upper window of a Spanish home. There the family may gather of an evening to gaze spectator-wise upon the street beneath, or at the sunset of the stars beyond . . . By the Road, I mean the place where life is tensely lived, where thought has its birth in conflict and concern, where choices are made and decisions are carried out. It is the place of action, of pilgrimage, of crusade, where concern is never absent from a wayfarer's heart. On the Road a goal is sought, dangers are faced, life is poured out.

The two different perspectives proposed by Mackay are those of a detached inquisitive spectator on the balcony, and of the active engaged participant below on the road. Those sitting comfortably on the Balcony can watch those below them with a detached disinterest as they struggle in their journey, unaffected by their concerns. Those on the Road, however, are facing real issues, and have to make real decisions that will affect their future and their welfare as they struggle to cope with their journey and reach its goal. But those above them on the Balcony merely observe their problems. They are not affected, except in a vaguely theoretical way, by the outcome of what is going on below them.

Recent apologetics tends to be dominated by "Balcony" perspectives – a belief that human beings are able to offer a rational criticism of God's nature and purposes on the basis of our capacity to make complete sense of our world. (As we noted earlier, James K. A. Smith terms this outlook "epistemic Pelagianism:" p. 54.) Inevitably, this means that apologists, in trying to respond to such charges of irrationality, often find that they have to operate within this framework, and thus come to normalize its core assumptions within the community of faith. In his magisterial account of the rise of a secular culture, Charles Taylor points out how this analysis helps us understand – and perhaps counter – the "increased preoccupation with theodicy," which seems to be a feature of our age.

> This is, of course, the classic stand of disengagement, laying out the universe as a tableau, from which the thinker is disintricated.... How does this effect the religion and apologetics of this time? Well, perhaps the confident way in which God's purposes are being read off the Universe, and his good intentions demonstrated, reflects precisely this stance of the World-picture, the disengaged grasp of the whole, which has put behind it the sense that the higher levels may not be fully scrutable.

For Taylor, this cultural development has led to the emergence of a rationalist apologetics, better at defending Deism than Christianity, which seems to lose sight of many distinctively Christian insights that are essential to coping with suffering (such as the person of Jesus Christ). It is helpful to consider the quite distinct approaches to the problem of suffering associated with the Balcony and the Road. The Balcony approach offers academic responses to what is perceived primarily as a rational problem, assessing various ways (often involving obscure technical distinctions) in which suffering can be seen as consistent with the intentions of an almighty and loving God. Now this needs to be done, if Christianity is to remain a credible option in our culture. But there is clearly a danger here – namely, that this does not connect up with the concerns of those on the Road.

For the problem, seen from the Road, is rather different. Those on the Road are suffering, and are wondering how on earth they may cope with it, master it, and persevere in the life of faith. They are participating in suffering, not observing it at a critical and safe distance. They are looking for practical wisdom, not an abstract theoretical analysis. And somehow, the apologist has to develop the art of speaking wisely to those on the Road, while being rooted in the rich wisdom of the Christian faith and the experience of applying this to the Christian life. The apologetic importance of Mackay's distinction is brought out clearly by C. S. Lewis, as we shall see in the next section.

Understanding the Audience: Thoughts from C. S. Lewis

C. S. Lewis, widely regarded as one of the most effective and winsome recent Christian apologists, wrote two books that engage the issue of suffering: *The Problem of Pain* (1940), and *A Grief Observed* (1960). While their intellectual arguments are actually quite similar, their tone and voice are very different. To use the framework developed by John Mackay, set out in the previous section of this chapter, *The Problem of Pain* offers a view of suffering seen from the Balcony; *A Grief Observed* offers an account seen from the Road.

The core theme of *The Problem of Pain* is often summarized in a single citation: "God whispers to us in our pleasures, speaks in our conscience, but shouts in our pains: it is his megaphone to rouse a deaf world." Lewis was quite clear why he wrote *The Problem of Pain*: he wanted to "solve the intellectual problem" that is raised by suffering. This focus leads Lewis to treat pain in an overintellectualized way, which has caused puzzlement to some of his readers. Surely Lewis knew that suffering was more than some kind of intellectual crossword puzzle?

A Grief Observed is totally different in its tone and approach. On Monday 23 April 1956, Lewis married Joy Davidman in a civil ceremony at Oxford's Register Office; on 13 July 1960, Davidman died of cancer with Lewis by her bedside at the Radcliffe Infirmary, Oxford. Lewis was devastated, and penned a passionate, searing, and emotionally intense account of his feelings. It remains one of the finest explorations of the process of grieving. *A Grief Observed* rejects many of the ideas Lewis developed in *The Problem of Pain* as inadequate and unsatisfactory. Someone experiencing the trauma of suffering and bereavement would find them useless.

Yet although these two works "feel" very different, they reach more or less the same intellectual conclusion. Suffering does not call into question the "big picture" of the Christian faith. It reminds us that we do not see the whole picture, and are thus unable to fit all of its pieces neatly into place. In 1940, Lewis focused on the intellectual discomfort this caused Christians in general; in 1961, he refocused on the emotional distress it caused him in particular. This distinction is of major importance in relation to developing the *art* of apologetics. Some audiences are looking for a detached and disinterested Christian reflection on the place of suffering in life – in other words, a view from the Balcony; others are in spiritual anguish, and want someone who knows their feelings to help them cope with their situation, and find meaning in their despair. They want someone who is on the Road with them, and can speak to them as a fellow traveler and fellow sufferer. Part of the art of apologetics is understanding these two perspectives, and being able to engage questions from each of them.

So what insights does Lewis offer us on engaging specific audiences? By the late 1930s, Lewis had gained a reputation as one of Oxford University's finest lecturers, packing huge audiences into lecture rooms as he spoke about Renaissance English literature to undergraduates. Yet when the Second World War broke out, Lewis found himself with an additional speaking responsibility – speaking to Royal Air Force ground crews about Christianity. Lewis initially found it difficult speak to audiences of young men who had left school at sixteen. However, he persevered, and learned to connect with them on their own levels. Lewis reflected on what he learned through this process in a 1945 lecture on Christian apologetics.

> We must learn the language of our audience. And let me say at the outset that it is no use laying down a priori what the "plain man" does or does not understand. You have to find out by experience … You must translate every bit of your theology into the vernacular. This is very troublesome … but it is essential. It is also of the greatest service to your own thought. I have come to the conclusion that if you cannot translate your own thoughts into uneducated language, then your thoughts are confused. Power to translate is the test of having really understood your own meaning.

This short passage is packed full of wisdom. Three points stand out.

First, Lewis insists that we must "learn the language of our audience." And we have to do this by getting to know them and listening to them. Instead of assuming we know how unfamiliar audiences speak and think, we need to listen to them. We need to learn the words they use, and note the words that they do *not* use. It's important that we do not present Christianity in a way that unintentionally makes them feel excluded. Good apologists learn to listen before they speak.

Second, Lewis suggests that "you must translate every bit of your theology into the vernacular." For Lewis, apologetics presents "that which is timeless (the same, yesterday, today, and tomorrow – Hebrews 8:8) in the particular language of our own age." This theological translation is time consuming and troublesome. But it makes a difference, as Lewis himself discovered.

And finally, Lewis remarks that "Power to translate is the test of having really understood your own meaning." It's a fair point. If you struggle to explain an idea in plain language, it might be that you have some more thinking and learning to do. Trying to explain a Christian theme in a new way, or at a different level, is a significant stimulus to understanding it more deeply yourself.

Lewis went on to develop three quite different apologetic strategies in his writings, each of which seems to focus on a distinct audience. In *Mere Christianity* (1952) and *Miracles* (1947), we find Lewis developing the case for the Christian faith based on an appeal to reason. But the dominant apologetic theme in *Surprised by Joy* (1955) is that the Christian faith is the fulfilment of human longing. And, of course, in the celebrated *Narnia* novels (1950–1956), Lewis appeals to stories and to the imagination as the gateway to the human soul. Lewis clearly learned how important individual audiences were, and gave much thought to how best to engage them.

Seekers and Dwellers: A New Context for Apologetics

In an important study of shifts in US religious culture, US sociologist Robert Wuthnow drew a distinction between two quite different self-understandings that he observed, which he categorized in terms of a "seekers versus dwellers" paradigm (see p. 133). At the beginning of the twentieth century, he suggested, virtually all US citizens practiced their faith within a settled Christian or Jewish framework. At the end of that century, a major shift can be seen. Many continue to see themselves as "dwelling" – that is, settled inhabitants of a Christian institution and conceptual space. Yet there is a growing trend towards "seeking" – an often private and personal quest to find significance and meaning, which involves exploration. Wuthnow set out this distinction as follows:

> A spirituality of dwelling emphasizes habitation: God occupies a definite place in the universe and creates a sacred space in which humans too can dwell; to inhabit sacred space is to know its territory and to feel secure. A spirituality of seeking emphasizes negotiation: individuals search for sacred moments that reinforce their conviction that the divine exists, but these moments are fleeting; rather than knowing the territory, people explore new spiritual vistas, and they may have to negotiate among complex and confusing meanings of spirituality.

Interestingly, Wuthnow makes the important point that older approaches to spirituality (such as the monasticism of Benedict of Nursia) are often able to hold these two aspects together, recognizing that "dwelling and seeking are both part of what it means to be human." It was possible to be seeker within a settled community.

So what is the apologetic significance of this distinction? In my view, it offers a very helpful framework for exploring some strategic questions about engaging multiple audiences. In what follows, I shall reflect on some of these issues and note their potential apologetic application.

1. Although Wuthnow tends to depict "dwellers" as characterized by the security of their beliefs, Taylor's analysis of our "secular age" (see pp. 185–88) – and personal experience – suggests that many "dwellers" will now experience the "fragilization" of belief, as they discover that they are seen as "contestable." This leads to an important conclusion, which is perhaps not given enough attention: apologetics is

part of the ministry of a church *to its own members*, who will need both reassurance that their core beliefs are defensible, and to be equipped to answer the critical questions of their friends beyond the community of the church concerning matters of belief. This might take place through sermons, teaching days, or study groups.

2. Church communities have a particular role in offering intellectual hospitality to "seekers," who often attach themselves to such communities as a means of exploring their questions. The British sociologist Grace Davie is one of many to note the emergence of this pattern of "belonging without believing," which is now clearly evident in many western nations. Part of the hospitality offered by church communities can take the form of sharing its beliefs, and explaining the difference that this makes to "sojourners" or "seekers" who have chosen to join them. We will consider a particular example of how a church might adapt to this ministry in the next section of this chapter, when we consider the recent ministry of Tomáš Halík in the "Academic Parish of Prague" (pp. 136–38). Halík developed a regular ministry to seekers, which respected their distinct identity and engaged their specific questions. Other models exist, including the idea of a "guest service" (for example, in the form of "safe place" for outsiders introduced by John Stott at All Souls, Langham Place, London in the 1960s).

3. Since apologetics is mainly conducted by "dwellers," and is mainly directed towards "seekers," it is clearly important for apologists to step into the mindset of a "seeker" and understand their aspirations and longings on the one hand, and their potential difficulties relating to Christianity. The importance of personal friendship with "seekers" is likely to be an important part of this process of familiarization and understanding.

Apologetics and Audiences: Three Case Studies

Thus far, we have considered some ways in which apologetics can engage different audiences, using some important historical reference points. We now need to explore this important point in more detail, to help readers gain a good understanding of the issues involved, and how to develop their own personal style in engaging contemporary audiences. So how can we incorporate these ideas into our apologetic conversations, addresses, and writings? How can we understand their worldviews, anxieties, and aspirations? It is at this point that the importance of apologetics as an *art* becomes obvious. The wise application of these principles demands imagination and flair, as much as a good understanding of the situation. We shall consider three different audiences in the twenty-first century, and reflect on how the specifics of these shape and inform the apologetic approaches that were developed and adopted to engage them.

Apologetics in Secular Manhattan: Tim Keller

We begin by focusing on Tim Keller, who developed a highly effective and influential apologetic ministry while he was pastor of Redeemer Presbyterian Church in Manhattan in downtown New York. Keller was born and raised in Pennsylvania, where he was educated at Bucknell University, before studying for the pastorate at Gordon-Conwell

Theological Seminary. He served as pastor of West Hopewell Presbyterian Church in Virginia, before joining the faculty of Westminster Theological Seminary in Philadelphia. Up to this point, Keller had done little in the way of apologetics. That changed radically as a result of his accepting a call to be the founding pastor of Redeemer Presbyterian Church in New York in 1989. Keller's ministry straddled the complex and unsettling transition from the twentieth to the twenty-first century.

While there were many factors that may have contributed to the success of Keller's apologetic outreach, the most important is his intimate knowledge of this specific audience – their aspirations, fears, and misgivings about faith. As Redeemer Presbyterian Church grew steadily over the years, Keller realized that his congregations included many curious skeptics, whose questions and concerns he began to address in his sermons. This allowed him to craft an approach to apologetics that connected directly with the diverse congregations at Redeemer, meeting them on their own terms. Keller quickly realized that there were many within these congregations that were "seekers" rather than "dwellers" (to draw on Robert Wuthnow's distinction, noted earlier in this chapter). He also came to see that there were various types of "seekers," with different concerns and aspirations. He had to find ways of connecting up with these.

As an admirer of both Francis Schaeffer and C. S. Lewis, Keller could see how he could use their approaches to connect up with these secular seekers. Yet those approaches needed to be adapted to his context at Redeemer. Keller felt that their arguments were too extended and complex for the audiences he knew and engaged, who needed shorter, simpler, and more accessible approaches. Although Keller was appreciative of earlier works of apologetics, he realized that things had changed. Back in the 1950s (when Lewis's classic *Mere Christianity* was published), people might be expected to follow an extended point-by-point argument. But not anymore. Keller's experience of his Manhattan audiences convinced him that they were not able to – or willing to – cope with more extended and discursive approaches. Keller considered himself to be a *preacher*, where Lewis was clearly a *writer*. And preachers knew that you had to hold people's attention and get to the point quickly.

> When Lewis was writing, people were able to follow sustained arguments that had a number of points that built on one another. I guess I should say we actually have a kind of rationality-attention-deficit disorder now. You can make a reasonable argument, you can use logic, but it really has to be relatively transparent. You have to get to your point pretty quickly.

The point to appreciate is that although Keller appreciated the approaches of Schaeffer and Lewis, he realized that they both needed to be modified to work effectively for his own audience.

Yet though he gained acclaim as a preacher, Keller's fame as an apologist arose primarily through his books, which allowed him to reach a new audience, drawing his readers into an imaginative world and allowing them to explore and taste the new world being described to them. Keller came across this idea in an article suggesting that a book is a "textually created world. … When you give yourself to a book, you essentially let the author take you into a world for a while. Even if it's a non-fiction book, the author is basically saying, 'This is how I see what's going on in the world.'" Writing books would allow Keller to reach far beyond his own church congregation, engaging the imaginations of a wider audience.

By the late 1990s, Keller's experience of his audiences led him to conclude that they were not interested in a "long chain of syllogistic reasoning"; what they really wanted was "something of a mixture of logic and personal appeal." Lewis may have inspired Keller's apologetic approach; yet Keller adapted this to the very different apologetic context in which he found himself. As Keller himself put it, *The Reason for God* "is *Mere Christianity* for Dummies."

Keller's book *The Reason for God: Belief in an Age of Skepticism* (2008) drew on his experience of engaging these audiences. Rather than use a leading religious publisher, Keller chose to publish with Dutton, which describes itself as a "boutique imprint within the largest English-language publisher in the world." To understand Keller's subsequent success as an apologetic *writer*, we need to appreciate that his books built on his apologetic *style* that he developed as a *preacher*. Their approach is emotionally intelligent and verbally economical, showing a remarkable capacity to connect with the experience and concerns of his audience. Like G. K. Chesterton before him, Keller did not set out to "prove" Christianity in the strong sense of the term. Keller rather argued that Christianity should be compared to rival worldviews to see which of them offered the best account for what we see and experience in the world. This was a comparative, not an absolute judgement, paralleling the search for the "best explanation" in the natural sciences (see pp. 51–4).

Reading Keller's writings dating from the 2010s, such as *Making Sense of God*, makes it clear that he has read, digested, understood, and applied much of Charles Taylor's analysis of secularism in *A Secular Age*, and Alasdair MacIntyre's account of tradition-mediated rationality, particularly in relation to questions of adjudication between rival traditions. Yet while Keller's writing is *informed* by these discussions, it is not *weighed down* by them. Having grasped their apologetic significance, Keller has internalized this wisdom, and allowed it to shape his approach without losing his own distinctive voice, and capacity to reach and engage his intended audience. In many ways, Keller models an apologetic approach that is both wise and accessible – steeped in experience and reading contemporary scholarship, yet still retaining a clear and focused argument without the verbal density and conceptual opaqueness that can so easily arise from engaging academic writers. We shall return to this point in Chapter 9, as we explore Francis Schaeffer's apologetic approach, and note how Keller was able to reappropriate and repurpose this for a Manhattan audience in the early 2000s.

Connecting with Black America: Urban Apologetics

In recent years, apologists have become increasingly aware of the distinct identities of ethnic groups in the western world, particularly in the cities of the United States, and the need to develop apologetic and pastoral strategies that are adapted to their histories and situations. One question has emerged with particular force: how can Christianity engage the needs and situations of Black American communities, especially in US inner cities? The rise of "Urban Apologetics," pioneered by Eric Mason and others, deals with the specific and important question of how Christianity meets the unique *needs* and answers the specific *questions* of Black people. This means reading the New Testament through a Black urban lens, and formulating apologetic approaches with this specific community in mind.

The distinct approach of this movement can be seen in *Urban Apologetics: Restoring Black Dignity with the Gospel* (2021), a collection of essays edited by Mason, addressed specifically to Black America. The background to this collection is the long history of segregation, slavery, and racism experienced by Black people, which is often articulated in the belief that Christianity is a "white man's religion," which is nonindigenous to people of color, failing to address the needs and interests of Black people.

Mason, the founding and lead pastor of Epiphany Fellowship in Philadelphia, argues that "urban apologetics" focuses on the unique experiences and reality of African Americans and other minorities, particularly in the inner cities. All too often, traditional apologetics has defended and proclaimed a "white Jesus" and a "whitewashed" Christianity, which many Black American Christians find alienating. Addressing these difficulties, Mason argues, not only reconnects the Black community with the Christian faith; it enables white people to grasp a gospel that has been seen through a specific racial and cultural lens, and thus become impoverished and distorted.

In an earlier work, Mason raised some important questions about a "colorblind church." His point is that churches which claim to be "colorblind" tend to overlook the specificity of the ethnic groups within their congregations, and thus fail to engage the needs, concerns, and aspirations of Black people.

> Catholicity means precisely the opposite of colorblindness – celebrating the inclusion of all ethnicities in Christ. … Colorblind theology undermines unity in the church by refusing to acknowledge significant ethnic differences or address significant problems.

Some questions might be raised about this way of thinking. For example, the Black pastor Voddie T. Baucham Jr. offers a rather different way of viewing ethnicity and Christian identity that acknowledges a diversity of "Black perspectives." Yet this debate highlights the importance of understanding the many audiences for apologetics, rather than simply reducing them to familiar cultural stereotypes.

Once more, the importance of apologetics as an art can be seen: you need to discover your audience, rather than accept someone else's categorization of that audience. And one of the best ways of doing this is being part of that audience. Apologetics needs to engage the specific needs of individual ethnic groups in congregations and society at large, rather than homogenize them into some allegedly universalized community that can be engaged by an allegedly universal apologetics. Recognition of the specificity of ethnic groups within US culture is essential if Christian apologetics is to connect with the real issues faced by the Black community, particularly in the light of religious challenges from groups such as the "Nation of Islam," "Hebrew Israelites," "Kemeticism," and "Black Atheism."

Urban apologetics, though focusing on the needs of Black Americans, highlights the importance of speaking to individual communities, knowing their histories and aspirations, and using language and imagery that have not been developed with other audiences in mind. While indigeneity is not a reliable marker of apologetic effectiveness, it is important to realize that members of a specific ethnic community or people group are likely to be the most effective apologists to this community, in that they are more likely to be accepted by that community on the one hand, and speak its language and know its questions on the other.

Post-Christian Apologetics in Prague: Tomáš Halík

Finally, we turn to consider an approach to apologetics in a post-Christian context that emerged from within European Catholicism. The Czech public intellectual and Catholic priest Tomáš Halík (born 1948; Figure 7.3) has established himself as one of the most thoughtful advocates of public apologetics in a time of change and uncertainty in central Europe. Although Halík is not well known outside Europe, his ideas and the strategies that he developed to implement them are of wider theoretical and practical importance, especially to churches in the west wanting to develop forms of ministry adapted to their changing situation. His writings from 2000 onwards specifically engage the question of how individual Christians and churches can engage an audience that is losing contact with its Christian heritage. So how can Christianity reconnect with a post-Christian audience?

Halík's distinct approach reflects both his own personal history, and his knowledge of the specific audience he hopes to engage. As professor of philosophy at Charles University (founded in Prague in 1348), Halík knew a specific audience well – a group of spiritually curious individuals who were intellectually intrigued by Christianity yet who were alienated from its institutions and practices. To make this situation more complex, this audience was deeply suspicious of false certainties, such as the Marxist

Figure 7.3   The Czech academic and churchman Tomáš Halík (born 1948) at a news conference in London in 2014, following his award of the Templeton Prize. Alamy Image 2D0B2Y4.

ideology that was aggressively promoted during the period of Soviet hegemony in eastern Europe.

So how could Halík engage this audience apologetically? Halík developed a strategy which involved recognizing his audience's anxieties and concerns, particularly their spiritual restlessness, their suspicion of institutions, and their disillusionment with simplistic answers that did not adequately meet their deep questions. First, Halík created a "zone of questions and doubts," a safe space in which seekers could explore their questions at a distance from the institution of the church. Halík suggests that the gospel narrative of the encounter between Zacchaeus and Christ (Luke 19:1–10) opens up a way of envisaging the tasks and strategies of a church in this age of uncertainty.

For Halík, Zacchaeus is a classic example of a "curious seeker" who dwells on the fringes of belief, watching from a distance and maintaining that distance. Like many seekers of today, Zacchaeus was neither "indifferent nor hostile" to faith. Though clearly drawn to Christ, Zacchaeus chose to stand at a safe distance from him as he reflected on what to make of him. Many of those on the margins of the church are seekers who have *chosen* to remain within their own safe places. These seekers

are still on the journey, dusty and far from the goal. They are not yet 'ready' to display themselves to others in the full light of day, maybe because they find themselves in a blind alley on their life's journey. ... And yet they sense the urgent moment when something of importance passes by them. It has a force of attraction, as it had for Zacchaeus, who longed to set eyes on Jesus.

This leads Halík to emphasize the importance of the "fringe" – the liminal zone at the interface between the church and the world. This "fringe" is a "zone of questions and doubts" through which a "seeking church" can encounter and engage seekers who are both curious and hesitant, preferring to remain on the margins of the institution of the church, which many of them distrust. The maintenance of this fringe is thus essential to the continuing ministry of the church, not least in providing a space within which those whose original faith has been shaken or has faded can arrive at a deeper faith that is able to cope with uncertainty. For Halík, the gospel story of Zacchaeus helped him to frame his own particular mission and vocation – not as a missionary seeking to convert people, but as an understanding neighbor who could show and explain what faith was all about.

Halík put his own approach into practice in his own "Academic Parish of Prague," based at the church of St Salvador in the center of the Czech capital city. With the permission of his local Catholic bishop, Halík was able to create a community of exploration, which both respected and engaged the doubts and questions of a distinct audience of urban and educated people. By engaging an audience that he knew, and whose concerns he understood, Halík ensured that a large constituency sharing those concerns would be drawn to hear him. Halík's homilies – which were typically 15 minutes long – were supplemented by a more detailed "Basics of Faith Course." The sociological specificity of the audience for Halík's homilies thus became a strength, rather than a weakness. Halík knew this audience and their concerns, and his academic position at Charles University gave him the academic standing he needed to speak to these professional audiences as their equal.

Yet while the institutional context is an important part of Halík's public apologetic ministry, it is also important to note the distinctive voice of Halík himself as a "personal convinced doubter," who presented himself as someone who was more concerned to explore questions than to offer "concrete and restrictive answers." Halík's essay "Befriending the Nonbeliever Within" sets out the apologetic strategy that lies behind this approach, helping us understand how Halík aims to step into the *persona* of an atheist or doubter, and explore those concerns sympathetically as one who understands, and at times perhaps even shares, such concerns and difficulties – yet was able to resolve and transcend these.

Halík's specific apologetic approach was crafted to engage the situation in the Czech Republic in the opening decade of the twenty-first century, ensuing that the needs of an important group of seekers could be engaged effectively and sensitively. Yet many aspects of his approach are culturally transferable, being capable of transplanted, with appropriate adjustments, in other contexts.

Theological Translation: Explaining Christianity to Secular Audiences

At the beginning of this work, we looked at the importance of "theological translation" – the task of explaining or expressing Christian ideas using a "cultural vernacular," a vocabulary that connects up with a wider culture. Christianity uses a rich range of terms that are often confusing or impenetrable to secular audiences. The apologist has to master the task of unpacking and exploring these ideas in terms that will be understood by those beyond the church.

We have already noted the London preacher John Stott, who was highly regarded for his ability to explain the Christian faith. Stott himself clearly grasped the importance of translating theology into the cultural vernacular. One of his best attempts to do this is found in his 1982 book *Between Two Worlds*, in which he explores the role of the preacher as the one who bridges the gap between the Bible and the contemporary world, allowing some core themes of Christianity to be grasped and appreciated by a modern audience. It is an outstanding work of its kind, showing how the significance of Jesus Christ can be "translated" into the idioms of the culture of the 1980s. A short extract will help illustrate this point.

> To encounter Christ is to touch reality and experience transcendence. He gives us a sense of self-worth or personal significance, because He assures us of God's love for us. He sets us free from guilt because He died for us and from paralyzing fear because He reigns.

All of these statements are thoroughly grounded in the New Testament. Yet Stott, using his framework of "double listening" has succeeded in "translating" them, not simply in the sense of making them *intelligible*, but in the deeper sense of enabling the gospel to *connect* with the cultural concerns, moods, and anxieties of the 1980s. Stott does not use technical theological terms, but words that would make sense within the culture of his day, particularly in relation to perceptions of self-worth. So how might we do this more extensively? How might we unpack some core Christian terms, so that a wider audience might be able to grasp something of their meaning? And, given that Stott's reflections relate to London in the 1980s, how might his approach be updated to take account of cultural shifts since then, and be applicable to a wider cultural context?

In what follows, I shall offer simple and short cultural translations of three core Christian ideas – not to shut down discussion of how these might be explained, but to help my readers do two things: first, explain and express these ideas in ways that they are completely comfortable with, rather than use mine uncritically; and second, to have in mind a specific audience, and allow this to shape the form and terms of your "translation." I have chosen three familiar Christian terms; after reading my translation, think about how you could explain them to the audience you will be engaging. Try to limit yourself to a few minutes, and pack as much useful information as you can into that short explanation, laying the groundwork for a longer conversation. Each of my short explanations takes no more than two minutes to set out, well within the attention span of most people. Remember, my explanations are simply intended to stimulate you to develop your own approach! They are not "model" explanations, but simply examples to stimulate your own thinking. You will notice how they incorporate some themes and approaches that we have already considered in this volume.

Faith

For a lot of people, faith means running away from evidence, burying your head in the sand, and refusing to think. That's not the way Christians understand the word. For Christians, faith is about discovering a way of thinking and living that makes sense. It's not just about believing that God exists, but discovering that this God is wise, loving, and good – and choosing to embrace this God as our travelling companion. Faith is about *trust* in someone, not just a belief that they exist. It's about loving God in our hearts, not just knowing God is there in our minds. Faith is not merely *cognitive* ("I believe that this is true"), but is also *relational* and *existential* ("I trust this *person*"). And this faith is not irrational. Faith is not a blind leap into the dark, but a joyful discovery of a bigger picture of things, of which we are part. For C. S. Lewis, faith in God is the lens that brings reality into sharp focus, the sun that lights up the world so that it may be seen more fully and clearly. Belief in God makes sense in itself, and it makes sense of everything else. It helps us live meaningfully and authentically in this complicated and strange world.

Salvation

This term is used frequently in the New Testament (see Acts 13:26; Ephesians 1:13; Hebrews 1:14). The basic meaning of the word includes deliverance, healing, preservation, or rescue from a dangerous situation. To be "saved" is about being rescued or delivered from a dangerous situation, just as the Israelites were delivered from their captivity in Egypt at the time of the Exodus. In much the same way, Christ is understood to deliver humanity from the fear of death and the penalty and power of sin. The biblical understanding of "salvation" is enormously rich, and includes the ideas of "wholeness" or "health." There is a very close relation between the ideas of salvation and wholeness. In many languages, the words for "health" and "salvation" are one and the same. Thus it is sometimes difficult to know whether a passage should be translated in terms of salvation or wholeness. An example of this can be seen at Mark 5:34. Should the words of Jesus in this passage be translated as "Your faith has made you whole" or "Your faith has saved you"? The Greek word used here can bear both these meanings. So the Christian gospel is about healing, about making us *whole*. In many respects the gospel is like a medicine – something that heals and restores us.

Adoption

Paul uses this word to help explain the benefits that he believes result from Christ's death (Romans 8:15; 8:23; 9:4; Galatians 4:5; Ephesians 1:5). Paul uses the term 'adoption' to indicate that faith brings about a change in our status before God. We are adopted into the family of God, with all the benefits that this brings. What benefits? For a start, if we are adopted as children of God, we share what Christ inherited from God. Just as Christ suffered and was glorified, so shall we. Suffering is real – but it leads to glory. And second, adoption into the family of God brings a new sense of belonging. Everyone needs to feel that they belong somewhere. Social psychologists have shown the need for a "secure base," a community or group that gives people a sense of purpose and an awareness of being valued and loved by others. In human terms, this need is usually met by the family unit. For Christians, this real psychological need is met through being adopted into the family of God. Believers can rest assured that they are valued within this family, and are thus given a sense of self-confidence, which enables them to work in and witness to the world.

You might like to try two further exercises in constructing your own approach to apologetics. First, you might like to extend this process beyond these specific examples, and develop the art of translating other significant Christian terms into everyday language. Here are some possibilities for you to develop: incarnation, atonement, sin, and revelation. And second, you might like to identify two very different audiences, and produce short descriptions of any of these terms with the needs of these audiences in mind.

In the next chapter, we shall move on to consider some of the major apologetic questions that often arise in conversation or debate. While it is impossible to deal with all such questions, it is hoped that the representative questions that will be discussed will be helpful in helping you to develop your own apologetic style and approach.

Study Questions

1. Explain, in your own words, the problems in using the same apologetic talk for a variety of different audiences.
2. Contrast the approaches used by Peter in his Pentecost sermon in Jerusalem, and Paul in his address at Athens.
3. What did you find interesting about the way in which Tim Keller developed his own distinct apologetic approach? What might be learned from this?
4. How does "Urban Apologetics" deal with the question of its specific Black audience? And how might these ideas find wider application?

For Further Reading

Alexander, Loveday. "The Acts of the Apostles as an Apologetic Text." In *Apologetics in the Roman Empire: Pagans, Jews, and Christians*, edited by Mark Edwards, Martin Goodman, and Simon Price, 15–44. Oxford: Oxford University Press, 1999.

Baucham, Voddie T. *Fault Lines: The Social Justice Movement and Evangelicalism's Looming Catastrophe*. Washington, DC: Salem Books, 2021.

Brooks, Christopher W. *Urban Apologetics: Why the Gospel is Good News for the City*. Grand Rapids, MI: Kregel Publications, 2014.

Chapman, Alister. "Secularisation and the Ministry of John R. W. Stott at All Souls, Langham Place, 1950–1970." *Journal of Ecclesiastical History* 56, no. 3 (2005): 496–513.

Charles, J. Daryl. "Engaging the (Neo)Pagan Mind: Paul's Encounter with Athenian Culture as a Model for Cultural Apologetics (Acts 17:16–34)." *Trinity Journal* 16, no. 1 (1995): 47–62.

Chatraw, Joshua D. "Timothy Keller: The Pastor as Apologist." In *The History of Apologetics: A Biographical and Methodological Introduction*, edited by Benjamin Forrest, Joshua D. Chatraw, and Alister E. McGrath, 800–18. Grand Rapids, MI: Zondervan, 2020.

Davie, Grace. *Religion in Britain since 1945: Believing without Belonging*. Oxford: Blackwell, 1994.

Escobar, Samuel. "The Legacy of John Alexander Mackay." *International Bulletin of Missionary Research* 16, no 3. (1992): 116–22.

Gärtner, Bertil. *The Areopagus Speech and Natural Revelation*. Uppsala: Almqvist & Wirksells, 1955.

Gray, Patrick. "Implied Audiences in the Areopagus Narrative." *Tyndale Bulletin* 55, no. 2 (2004): 205–18.

Halík, Tomáš. *Patience with God: The Story of Zacchaeus Continuing in Us*. New York, NY: Doubleday, 2009.

Hansen, Colin. *Timothy Keller: His Spiritual and Intellectual Formation*. Grand Rapids, MI: Zondervan, 2023.

Hurtado, Larry W. "Christology in Acts." In *Issues in Luke-Acts: Selected Essays*, edited by Sean A. Adams and Michael Pahl, 217–37. Piscataway, NJ: Gorgias Press, 2012, 217–37.

Jipp, Joshua W. "Paul's Areopagus Speech of Acts 17:16–34 as both Critique and Propaganda." *Journal of Biblical Literature* 131, no. 3 (2012): 567–88.

Johnson, Aaron P. *Ethnicity and Argument in Eusebius' Praeparatio Evangelica*. Oxford: Oxford University Press, 2006.

Kočí, Martin, and Pavel Roubík. "Searching the Altar of an Unknown God: Tomáš Halík on Faith in a Secular Age." In *A Czech Perspective on Faith in a Secular Age*, edited by Tomáš Halík and Pavel Hošek. Washington, DC: Council for Research in Values and Philosophy, 2015, 97–126.

Koll, Karla Ann. "The Theology of John A. Mackay as *Praeparatio Liberationis*." *Theology Today* 73, no. 2 (2016): 105–16.

Loades, Ann. "C. S. Lewis: Grief Observed, Rationality Abandoned, Faith Regained." *Literature and Theology* 3 (1989): 107–21.

Mason, Eric. *Woke Church: An Urgent Call for Christians in America to Confront Racism and Injustice*. Chicago: Moody, 2018.

Mason, Eric. *Urban Apologetics: Restoring Black Dignity with the Gospel*. Grand Rapids, MI: Zondervan, 2021.

Maxwell, Kathy Reiko. "The Role of the Audience in Ancient Narrative: Acts as a Case Study." *Restoration Quarterly* 48, no. 3 (2006): 171–80.

McGrath, Alister E. "Listening and Engaging: John Stott on the Gospel and our Culture." In *Mere Discipleship: On Growing in Wisdom and Hope*. London: SPCK, 2018, 101–11.

McGrath, Alister E. "On the Threshold of Mystery: Tomáš Halík on Cultural Witness in an Age of Uncertainty and Change." *Religions* 14 (2023): 399.

Metzger, John Mackay. *The Hand and the Road: The Life and Times of John A. Mackay.* Louisville, KY: Westminster John Knox Press, 2010.

Puosi, Eric E. "A Systematic Approach to the Christology of Peter's Address to the Crowd (Acts 2:14–36)." *New Blackfriars* 87, no. 1009 (2006): 253–67.

Rossi, Philip J. "Sojourners, Guests, and Strangers: The Church as Enactment of the Hospitality of God." *Questions Liturgiques* 90, no. 2–3 (2009): 120–30.

Schnabel, Eckhard J. "Contextualising Paul in Athens: The Proclamation of the Gospel before Pagan Audiences in the Graeco-Roman World." *Religion & Theology* 12, no. 2 (2005): 172–90.

Stackhouse, John G. "Audience-Specific Apologetics." In John G. Stackhouse, *Humble Apologetics: Defending the Faith Today.* Oxford: Oxford University Press, 2002, 145–60.

Tino, James. "Paul's Greatest Missionary Sermon: A Lesson in Contextualization from Acts 17." *Lutheran Mission Matters* 25, no. 1 (2017): 165–75.

Tromp, Paul, Anna Pless, and Dick Houtman. "'Believing Without Belonging' in Twenty European Countries (1981–2008): De-institutionalization of Christianity or Spiritualization of Religion?" *Review of Religious Research* 62 (2020): 509–31.

Witherington, Ben, and Jason A. Myers. *New Testament Rhetoric: An Introductory Guide to the Art of Persuasion in and of the New Testament.* 2nd ed. Eugene, OR: Cascade Books, 2022.

Wuthnow, Robert. *After Heaven: Spirituality in America since the 1950s.* Berkeley, CA: University of California Press, 1998.

8

Responding to Questions
Some Apologetic Debates

In the opening sections of this work (pp. 1–4), we considered the three main tasks of Christian apologetics, noting in particular the need to respond to questions and concerns relating to Christianity. Many of these critical questions are raised by people outside the Christian community; yet some are also raised by members of the community of faith, often reflecting the persistence of unresolved issues in the life of faith that need to be engaged and resolved. Every apologist needs to be able to engage such questions helpfully, in their own distinct way and using their own voice.

Dealing with questions is an art, a skill that has to be learned through experience. It is important to take these questions seriously, and not attempt to ridicule them or evade them. Each of them can be the gateway to a helpful exploration of issues. People who use evasion or ridicule in dealing with questions simply create the impression that they are incapable of answering them. In this chapter, we shall consider a set of 10 representative questions that often arise in Christian apologetics, and offer sketches of what might be said in response. These should not be treated as model or definitive responses to these questions, but rather as a brief exploration of the issues that you may find helpful as you develop your own answers. We begin by considering a classic objection to belief in God: that this is simply an invention, designed to console inadequate people.

God as Wish-fulfilment? Freud's Critique of Faith

In his influential work *The Future of an Illusion* (1927), Sigmund Freud (Figure 8.1) argued that religious beliefs are simply "illusions, fulfilments of the oldest, strongest and most urgent wishes of human beings." Although Freud popularized these ideas in the early twentieth century, their intellectual roots can be traced back to the German

Christian Apologetics: An Introduction, First Edition. Alister E. McGrath.
© 2024 John Wiley & Sons Ltd. Published 2024 by John Wiley & Sons Ltd.

Figure 8.1   Sigmund Freud (1856–1939), the Austrian neurologist and founder of psychoanalysis, photographed in London during the final year of his life. Alamy Image AY2Y4B.

philosopher Ludwig Feuerbach's *Essence of Christianity* (1841). Feuerbach argued that "God" is a subconscious creation of the human mind, a projection of human longings and ideals onto an imaginary screen, as a result of which human beings enslaved themselves to their own creations.

Feuerbach's critique is important, and achieved considerable cultural influence in western Europe, in effect offering an intellectual justification for the rejection of religious belief. Yet Feuerbach's hypothesis that "God" is simply the reification or objectification of human experience does not rest upon a rigorous empirical or rational foundation. In fact, its critics suggest that it actually rests on a simple logical fallacy. It is certainly true that things do not exist because we desire them. But it does not follow from this that, because we desire something, it does not exist, or that it cannot exist precisely because we desire it. As C. S. Lewis pointed out, natural human desires often reflect legitimate and genuine natural human *needs* – such as the need for food – which are essential to our survival.

Feuerbach's criticisms were, however, particularly effective when directed against approaches to religious belief that saw these as grounded in experience – such as that of the German theologian F. D. E. Schleiermacher, or more recent approaches within North American liberal theological traditions described by George Lindbeck as "experiential-expressivist." The theologies developed by Karl Barth or Thomas Aquinas are not vulnerable to this critique. Barth, a severe critic of Schleiermacher, held that the *reality* of God is prior to and independent of human *experience* of God. Neither Christian faith nor theology is a response solely to some subjective human experience, but rather arise from an encounter with God through Christ, mediated through Scripture.

Feuerbach's ideas were important for Freud, who saw them as confirming his ideas about the psychological origins of religious belief in the human unconscious. Freud drew a careful distinction between "errors" and "illusions"; the former were simply mistakes, but the latter were falsehoods *that arise from human wishes and desires.* "We call a belief an illusion when a wish-fulfillment is a prominent factor in its motivation." For Freud, human beings long for a God to help them cope with anxiety and insecurity. Freud thus argued that religious belief was infantile, based on human feelings of help-lessness in infancy and early childhood.

These ideas secured significant cultural traction in Europe and North America in the 1930s. Freud then came to be widely regarded as the "Darwin of the Mind," a progressive scientist who had proved that human beings invent God to meet their subconscious existential and psychological needs. In fact, however, Freud had simply proposed an unverifiable and unfalsifiable hypothesis, which chimed in with the cultural mood of his age.

Freud and Feuerbach, though in different ways, help us to understand that what we *desire* can easily morph into what we *want to be true.* Human beings are very good at constructing their own private truths, which they regard as privileged and sacrosanct. Modern scholarship on the origins of atheism in eighteenth-century Europe has high-lighted the fact that this was linked to a desire on the part of some culturally significant individuals to be liberated from any external authority.

This same basic motif is evident in recent atheist writings. The humanist philosopher Aldous Huxley, best known for his novel *Brave New World* (1932) rejected belief in God for reasons that had little to do with science or philosophy, only developing argu-ments to justify his atheism *after* he had adopted it. "I had motives for not wanting the world to have a meaning; consequently assumed that it had none, and was able without any difficulty to find satisfying reasons for this assumption." The philosopher Thomas Nagel was also explicit about the fundamental motivation for his atheism. "It isn't just that I don't believe in God, and, naturally, hope that I'm right in my belief. It's that I hope there is no God! I don't want there to be a God; I don't want the universe to be like that." Nagel's atheist philosophy seems to be a *post hoc* rationalization of his more fundamental desire for a godless universe – in other words, it is a wish-fulfilment – and hence, to use Freud's categories, an *illusion.*

Nagel's atheism amounts to a retrospective intellectual validation of a belief that had actually been determined on volitional or emotional grounds. The *wish* thus gives rise to the *belief.* This is a good example of what the psychologist Jonathan Haidt describes as the "emotional tail" wagging the "rationalist dog." People reach conclusions on intuitive or emotional grounds, and later figure out justifications for those beliefs. So yes, there is a risk that people believe in God because they want to. But there's an equal risk that people reject the idea of God because they desire total freedom and autonomy, or because they dislike the notion of ultimate accountability for their actions. They find it difficult to accept that we "are characters in a story of which we are not the author" (Gilbert Meilaender).

The Polish novelist Czesław Miłosz, who won the 1980 Nobel Prize in Literature, is one of the most perceptive and critical observers of this how this self-serving belief has become the new orthodoxy of a cultural elite: "A true opium for the people is a belief in nothingness after death – the huge solace of thinking that for our betrayals, greed, cowardice, murders we are not going to be judged." We do not like the idea of being judged for our actions; we thus invent reasons for believing that we shall *not* be judged for our actions, dismissing this as a premodern myth (or whatever other reason we come up with).

Where Freud regarded religious belief as an illusion, others – such as C. S. Lewis – have argued that Freud's atheistic materialism is self-refuting, pointing out that arguments about "projection" or "invention" cut both ways. Freud argues that God is a wish-fulfillment, in which a heavenly father takes cares of all our needs. Yet it is just as logical and evidence based to argue that Freud and other atheists deny the existence of God out of a need to escape from a father figure they don't like. After all, Freud's relationship with his own father was somewhat strained. It is not difficult to argue that his belief in the nonexistence of God springs from his deep desire that no father figure exists.

So how do these reflections help us deal with this apologetic question? Do they prove that God is not a wish-fulfilment? No – although they do call into question the too-easy secularist assumption that religion is for those who can't cope with life. The main apologetic point is that every commitment to a worldview may involve an unconscious logic of desire: this is the way people would *like* things to be, and they therefore foreground and emphasize whatever fits with this way of thinking, and downplay or ignore evidence that points in a different direction.

Is Religion the Cause of Violence?

The view that religion makes people more likely to be violent has achieved widespread circulation in recent years, especially in Christopher Hitchens's "New Atheist" manifesto *God is Not Great: How Religion Poisons Everything* (2007). This rhetorically charged message declares that the faults of the world are to be laid at the door of backward-looking superstitions, which hold the world back from its rational and scientific destiny. Eliminate religion, and the world will be a better place. Religion has led only to violence, intellectual dishonesty, oppression, and social division. Sam Harris, another influential New Atheist writer, argued that religion is generically and intrinsically evil by singling out Islam as representative of all religions, failing to take account of their very different attitudes towards violence.

Yet there are many problems with this view. For a start, "religion" is a false universal category. Individual religions exist; "religion" doesn't. The Enlightenment understandably (yet wrongly) regarded "religion" as a universal category. During the period of colonial expansion, many Europeans came across certain worldviews that differed from their own, and chose to label them as "religions." In fact, many of these are better regarded as philosophies of life, such as Confucianism; others were explicitly nontheistic, such as most forms of Buddhism. Yet the Enlightenment belief in a universal notion called "religion" led to these very different worldviews being unconvincingly forced into the same intellectual category.

In its more naïve forms, pluralism holds that all religions represent equally valid responses to the same divine reality; in its more naïve forms, the "New Atheism" holds that they all represent equally invalid and delusional responses to a fictional nonreality. In reality, the porous and imprecise concept of "religion" extends far beyond those who believe in God, embracing a wide range of beliefs and values.

It is also vitally important to make a distinction between a "religion" and a "worldview." This is a distinction that the "New Atheism" singularly fails to make or defend. Both religions (such as Christianity) and secular worldviews (such as Marxism) demand allegiance from their followers. The most successful worldviews incorporate religious elements, even if they are fundamentally secular in their outlook – as in the Soviet Union's use of quasi-religious rituals to mark essentially secular events.

The historian Martin Marty, noting the lack of any viable definition of religion, identifies five "features" that he holds to be characteristic of religion; all five, he notes, are also characteristic of political movements. It is not unreasonable to point out that, if religion is dangerous on this count, then so is politics. There can be (and are) political fanatics, just as there can be (and are) religious fanatics. The problem is fanaticism, not religion itself. The dark and aggressive tone of the "New Atheism" critique of religion suggests that fanaticism may not be limited to the ranks of those who defend religion.

The "New Atheism," of course, argues that religious worldviews offer motivations for violence that are not paralleled elsewhere – for example, the thought of entering paradise after a suicide attack. Yet this conclusion is premature, and needs very careful nuancing. For Sam Harris and Christopher Hitchens, it is obvious that religious belief leads directly to suicide bombings. Yet empirical studies of why people are driven to suicide bombings in the first place lends little support to this view. Even Richard Dawkins is cautious at this point, suggesting that religion may only be *one* of the factors involved.

Yet religion is complex, and these complexities need to be acknowledged and respected. They differ on the matter of violence. Christians, for example, hold that the face, will and character of God are fully disclosed in Jesus Christ. Christ, of course, did no violence to anyone. He was the *object*, not the *agent*, of violence. Instead of meeting violence with violence, rage with rage, Christians are asked to "turn the other cheek," and "not to let the sun go down on their anger."

The importance of the example of Christ on this matter can be seen in a tragic event in the United States in October 2006, within a week of the publication of Dawkins's *God Delusion*. A gunman broke into an Amish school in Pennsylvania, and gunned down a group of schoolgirls. Five of the young girls died. The Amish are a Protestant religious group, who repudiate any form of violence on account of their understanding of the absolute moral authority of the person and teaching of Jesus of Nazareth. When those unfortunate schoolchildren were murdered, the Amish community urged forgiveness. There would be no violence, no revenge – only the offering of forgiveness. The gunman's widow spoke, gratefully and movingly, of how this provided the "healing" that she and her three children "so desperately needed."

Yet there are other concerns about the simplistic link between religion and violence that is found in New Atheist writings. In his recent book *Seven Types of Atheism*, the atheist philosopher John Gray expresses deep unease that many atheist writers have failed to face up to the history of atheist violence against religion – for example, in the history of the Soviet Union under Lenin and Stalin. Lenin regarded the intellectual, cultural, and physical elimination of religion as central to the socialist revolution, and put in place measures designed to eradicate religious beliefs through the "protracted use of violence."

When the Bolsheviks seized power in Russia in 1917, the elimination of religious belief was a core element of their revolutionary program. This was not accidental or incidental; a "messianic atheism" was an essential aspect of the new Soviet state. Churches were closed; priests imprisoned, exiled, or executed. On the eve of the Second World War there were only 6,376 clergy remaining in the Russian Orthodox Church, compared with the prerevolutionary figure of 66,140. The most significant period of executions of priests was 1937–1938. On 17 February 1938 alone, 55 priests were executed. In 1917, there were 39,530 churches in Russia; in 1940, only 950 remained functional. The remainder had been closed, converted for secular use, or destroyed, often by dynamiting.

It is difficult to avoid the conclusion that New Atheist writers are in denial about the darker side of atheism, making them a less than credible critic of religion. Christopher Hitchens, for example, has a devout and somewhat unquestioning faith in the universal goodness of atheism, which he refuses to subject to critical examination. Yes, there is much that is wrong with contemporary religion, and much that needs to be reformed. Yet the same is also true of atheism, which still needs to subject itself to the self-searching intellectual and moral criticisms that religious systems are willing to direct against themselves. Why is it that so many atheists apply moral standards to their critique of religion that they seem reluctant to apply to atheism itself? It has often been pointed out that the "New Atheism" applies one set of evidential criteria to its own beliefs, and a more rigorous and demanding set to those of its opponents. Is the same also true of its moral critiques of religion?

Happily, there are some atheists willing to face up to this obvious evidential problem. A good example is Michael Shermer, founder of the Skeptics Society, who made the fair point that religions have been implicated in some human tragedies, such as holy wars – but then qualifies this to set this observation within a broader context.

> However, for every one of these grand tragedies there are ten thousand acts of personal kindness and social good that go unreported. ... Religion, like all social institutions of such historical depth and cultural impact, cannot be reduced to an unambiguous good or evil.

So where do these reflections take us apologetically? Perhaps one of the most important points to make is that there is a deep flaw within human beings that leads them to use violence to defend their beliefs – whether these are religious or antireligious. That is why the Christian emphasis on sin and salvation needs to be brought into this conversation. What is wrong with us? And what can be done about it?

The Problem of Suffering

Down the ages, Christian apologists and philosophers of religion have developed sophisticated accounts of how the existence of pain and suffering may be reconciled with the goodness of God. The term "theodicy" appears to have been invented by the philosopher Leibniz in 1710 to refer to an intellectual defense of the coherence and reasonableness of suffering in the world, seen from a theistic perspective. Yet there is a growing realization that the enterprise of "theodicy" is problematically linked with the rationalizing concerns of the "Age of Reason." Many earlier Christian writers – such as Irenaeus of Lyons in the second century, and Augustine of Hippo in the fifth century – offered important pastoral and spiritual reflections on the problem of suffering in the world. Modernist writers, however, have disregarded the pastoral concerns underlying these works, and forced them into the categories favored by the Enlightenment – namely, as impersonal theoretical rationalizations of the problem of evil. John Hick's work *Evil and the God of Love* (1966), for example, treats both Irenaeus and Augustine as if they were modern philosophers of religion, and fails to do justice to their clear pastoral and spiritual concerns – namely, to help people find meaning in suffering, and cope with the challenges that it raises, rather than offer highly intellectualized explanations of why suffering is present.

The philosopher Charles Taylor and others have raised questions about whether apologetics plays into, perhaps even reinforces, a secular reading of the world, in that we come to expect rational explanations of everything. Taylor's analysis of the "buffered self" suggests that we are prone to apologetic overreach. For Taylor, we too often assume that human beings have complete access to the structures of the universe and the nature of human life, and so can answer every "why" question. James K. A. Smith styles this overoptimism concerning the scope of human reason as "epistemic Pelagianism" (see p. 54) and argues that relying on such intellectual answers diminishes Christian apologetics by reducing it to a detached rationalization of the world, rather than offering hope for living meaningfully in the presence of suffering.

> This mode of "Christian" apologetics bought into the spectatorish "world picture" of the new modern order. Rather than seeing ourselves positioned within a hierarchy of forms (in which case we wouldn't be surprised if "higher levels" are mysterious and inscrutable), we now adopt a God-like, dispassionate "gaze" that deigns to survey the whole ... And it is precisely in this context, when we adopt a "disengaged stance," that the project of theodicy ramps up; thinking we're positioned to see everything, we now expect an answer to whatever puzzles us, including the problem of evil.

The difficulty that many now experience with the intellectual project of theodicy is that it seems to amount to little more than a demonstration of theism's logical consistency with evil, and fails to engage the deeper existential questions that are raised by suffering. As the philosopher Stephen Wykstra cautions, drawing on his principle of "Reasonable Epistemic Access," we need to be skeptical about any assumption that we can take a "God's eye" view of the world, being able to see everything in its totality and grasp its full significance. John Mackay's contrast between the different perspectives of the "Balcony" and the "Road" reminds us that we are not located on an elevated viewpoint, the Balcony, which gives us a total view of reality; we are on the Road, with all the limitations of vision and understanding that this entails (pp. 127–29). As William Abraham points out, the first-person experience of suffering (on the Road) cannot easily be connected with third-person intellectual abstractions (from the Balcony). "Considerations at the level of third-person perspectives fail to register; they become at best empty and hollow." Some theodicies develop well-intentioned explanations of why bad things happen to good people, but leave their readers with the impression that some people deserve suffering.

Perhaps for this reason, the US philosopher of religion Nicholas Wolterstorff found himself simply unable to read works on theodicy following the death of his son in a climbing accident in June 1983. It seemed to him that theodicy was pointless and unhelpful. "I cannot fit these pieces together. I am at a loss. I have read the theodicies produced to justify the ways of God to man. I find them unconvincing. To the most agonized question I have ever asked I do not know the answer."

It is instructive to contrast the theory-heavy theodicies of philosophers of religion with the New Testament, which recognizes the reality of living in a world shot through with suffering and evil, but declines to offer an abstract theoretical response to this. Paul does not provide a thorough or coherent theology of suffering. He rather tends to see the suffering of believers as an integral aspect of existing in the "new age" within which the "old" still remains present (Galatians 3:4; Philippians 1:28; Romans 12:9–21). Paul's intention is not to *explain* suffering by providing the core building blocks for a systematic theodicy. Nor does he follow Stoicism in conceptualizing suffering and anxiety as matters of indifference. His object is rather to offer a Christ-grounded and Christ-focused reassurance that the existence of suffering is part of a lingering old order; that to suffer does not mean that we have been abandoned or rejected by God; that Christ suffered *before* us, and *for* us; and that we may look ahead to the hope of a new order, of which we will be part. Christ enables us to discern or create some kind of meaning within apparently meaningless suffering, so that we can learn from it, live well with it, and grow as believers.

Many traditional philosophical theodicies, particularly those lacking a Christological focus, often come across as abstract, complex, and dull technocratic discussions that seem impossibly remote from the human experiences of suffering that they are meant to engage. Wolterstorff's realization that he had to learn to "live with the mystery" resonates with some of the core themes of the later section of the book of Job. In my own view, this challenging work does not offer an explanation for the existence of suffering; it rather affirms that God is present within a world that seems incoherent and unfair – in other words, that its apparent irrationality does not negate trusting God. The biblical scholar Frances Young, herself no stranger to the enigmas of a suffering world, came to a similar conclusion.

> Pondering the book of Job, that intense debate about God's goodness within the Bible, I began to discern that the answer to Job's questioning was simply the fact that he found himself in God's presence. In God's presence all the questions just fade away, as you realize the immensity of the infinite, divine reality with which you are confronted.

The book of Job offers a reflection on the problems of evil and suffering, which names the problem yet offers no easy answers. It is significant that the 2007 religious bestseller *The Shack* takes the form of a twenty-first century reimagining of the book of Job, suggesting that many today remain engaged with the issue of suffering, and are dissatisfied with the theological rationalizations that are often presented as solutions to these enigmas. What people are looking for is a meaningful engagement with suffering, enabling us to emerge from it as better people.

There will always be place in apologetics for affirming and defending the rationality of faith. Yet it is important to appreciate that such a defense can sometimes appear glib and superficial, failing to engage with the emotional and pastoral concerns of many who are troubled by suffering. The apologist needs to be sensitive to the situations that give rise to the question "how can God allow suffering?" It might be an academic question; then again, it might be a heartfelt cry of despair from someone who has just lost the love of their life. The two contexts are very different, and the apologist needs to learn how to distinguish them.

How? One way I have found helpful in responding to audience questions on the question of suffering is to affirm the importance of the question, and seek clarification on why the questioner finds it so significant. I might respond like this: "That's a good question, and I'll be glad to answer it. To help me, I wonder if you could tell me why this is an important question for you?" The questioner is usually more than happy to explain this, allowing me to work out how best to answer them – whether from the perspective of the Balcony, or the Road.

The apologist also needs to be aware of a shift in cultural mood over recent decades, which has shifted discussion of suffering away from *rationalization* towards *constructive engagement*. The question is then no longer about the abstract logic of suffering, but about how we can cope with this, and live meaningfully in a world in which suffering is an ongoing presence. In *Naming the Silences: God, Medicine and the Problem of Suffering*, Stanley Hauerwas points out that, for early Christians, suffering was not a metaphysical problem needing a philosophical solution but a practical challenge requiring a response. We need to actively engage suffering, and ask how this can transform us, making us better people. "Historically speaking, Christians have not had a 'solution' to the problem of evil. Rather, they have had a community of care that has made it possible for them to absorb the destructive terror of evil that constantly threatens to destroy all human relations."

A similar approach is taken by the Scottish pastoral theologian John Swinton, who argues that theodicy needs to be reconfigured and repurposed, shifting its emphasis away from an individual's passive acceptance of rationalizations to an active construction of meaning in life.

> Theodicy should not be understood as a series of disembodied arguments designed to defend God's love, goodness, and power. We require a different mode of understanding, a mode of theodicy that is embodied within the life and practices of the Christian community. Such a mode of theodicy does not seek primarily to explain evil and suffering, but rather presents ways in which evil and suffering can be resisted and transformed by the Christian community and in so doing, can enable Christians to live faithfully in the midst of unanswered questions as they await God's redemption of the whole of creation.

Although Swinton approaches this from the perspective of pastoral practice, the apologetic implications of his approach are significant. The question shifts from "How I can make sense of suffering?" to "How can I use the framework of the Christian faith to cope with suffering, and grow in the process?" This, it must be emphasized, is not a new approach; it represents the retrieval of early Christian thinking on this matter, dating from long before the rationalized world of the Enlightenment, which reconnects us with a rich and dynamic Christian tradition of both understanding and coping with a suffering world. The emphasis here shifts from gaining understanding to enabling personal transformation. Such an approach is found in Tim Keller's *Walking with God through Pain and Suffering* (2013), which stresses how Christianity enables us to cope with suffering, while offering some informing theological and philosophical reflections.

One final point needs to be made. At several points in this work, we have explored how aspects of the philosophy of science can be apologetically illuminating and helpful. In what follows, we shall consider an important discussion within the natural sciences that has obvious relevance to Christian reflections on suffering. Suppose than an anomaly is observed – something which does not seem to fit into a theory. Does this require us to abandon that theory as a result of the lack of empirical fit at this point?

A good example of this concerns the anomalous behavior of the planet Uranus. Within a few years of its discovery in 1781, it was noticed that Uranus's orbital motion did not correspond to what was predicted by Newtonian physics. So how might this be explained? The key question can be framed like this: was the core of Newton's theories, the idea of universal gravitation, wrong? Or was there a problem with some secondary assumption, that was not essential or central to Newton's grand theory?

In the end, it was found that the problem lay with a secondary assumption – in this case, that there was no planet beyond Uranus. It was hypothesized that a planet lay beyond Uranus, and its position was calculated on the basis of the perturbation of Uranus's orbit. In 1846, the planet Neptune was discovered. Newton's grand theory remained intact, but was modified in a minor respect.

The point is clear: an anomaly does not require a grand theory to be abandoned. Thomas Kuhn pointed out that the underdetermination of theories by evidence was such that "if any and every failure to fit were ground for theory rejection, all theories ought to be rejected at all times." Pierre Duhem suggested that a more realistic approach is to recognize that even the best explanations are attended by anomalies and difficulties. Might the puzzles and anomalies of life – such as suffering – need to be seen as *noetic* rather than *ontic*, resulting from limitations on our perception or understanding of the situation, rather than from the situation itself? Perhaps the problem partly reflects our inability to see the "big picture" with perfect clarity, so that we are instead limited to seeing things "through a glass darkly" (1 Corinthians 13:12).

Enlightenment Rationalism: Reason has Displaced God

Throughout this work, I have emphasized that Christianity is *rational*, while at the same time distinguishing this from a *rationalist* worldview, which limits human knowledge to what can be demonstrated by unaided human reason. While the "Age of Reason" (see pp. 24–6) asserted a universal human reason as the foundation of reliable knowledge, earlier writers were more cautious and critical. For example, the celebrated English poet John Donne suggested that human reason had been taken captive by sin, and was no longer a reliable guide to divine truth. Through sin, reason is unreliable and fallible.

> I, like a usurpt town, to another due,
> Labour to admit you, but, Oh, to no end,
> Reason your viceroy in me, me should defend,
> But is captiv'd, and proves weak or untrue.

Donne's point is that reason has been taken captive by sin, like a town occupied by a hostile army, and is no longer fully able to play its role as God's "viceroy" (the authorized representative of a monarch in a town or region) within us. While it retains an ability to recall the "loving memory" of God (Augustine), Donne argues that its natural tendency is now to lock us into that same captivity, rather than to enable us to escape from it.

Despite Donne's concerns, many in western Europe during the eighteenth century came to believe that human beings are perfectly capable of discovering whatever can be known about God through the intelligent use of human reason. There is no need for divine revelation, in that human reason is able to engage and answer the most significant questions concerning human identity and meaning. During the "Age of Reason," Christianity was criticized for needlessly making God the ground and arbiter of truth and justice. Human reason was now seen as the only valid foundation and criterion of true beliefs.

These views remain influential. The movement now generally known as the "New Atheism," which was influential for about a decade following the publication of Richard Dawkins's *God Delusion* (2006), appealed to both reason and science as more reliable authorities than religion. Christopher Hitchens, a leading member of this movement, portrays the Enlightenment as a bold and brilliant period in western culture in which reason and science overthrew the tyranny of religion, tradition, prejudice, and superstition. Humanity, we are told, began to think for itself, and threw out irrational superstitions, such as God. In the concluding chapter of the work, Hitchens appealed for a return to the rationalism of the eighteenth century to recreate a rational world, from which religion would be purged. This led some of its critics to point out that both Dawkins and Hitchens were incorrigibly modernist in their approaches, wedded to an early modern worldview that is now obsolete. Sociologists, it should be noted, have pointed out how the leading figures of the "New Atheism" were elderly white males, suggesting that gender, race, and age were significant factors associated with its leading ideas.

So how should an apologist respond to such bold and confident declarations of the autonomy and omnicompetence of human reason? In what follows, we shall explore some points that might be made in engaging this topic.

Until the middle of the twentieth century, many seem to have believed that the Enlightenment's appeal to unaided reason could sort out all the great questions of life without the need to appeal to a higher authority – or, indeed, to *any* other authority. Rationalism made significant inroads in England, Scotland, Germany, France, and North America during the late eighteenth century and early nineteenth century. Many historians point to an event that took place during the French Revolution as a symbol of the displacement of religion by reason – the "Festival of Reason" held in the Cathedral of Notre-Dame in Paris on 10 November 1793, in which a new "Cult of Reason" was proclaimed as the universal replacement for all forms of religion. Human reason was the same everywhere and at every time. It alone could sustain human well-being and act as the basis of a just society.

Yet this vision faded. One major concern was that the Enlightenment's appeal to reason as the ultimate reliable source of authority could not be verified. Some suggested that reason could demonstrate its own authority. Yet to its critics, this was unpersuasive. Surely such a rational defense of the authority of human reason was ultimately circular and parasitical, assuming and depending upon its own conclusions? If there was a flaw in human reasoning processes, reason itself would not be able to detect this. We would be locked into unreliable patterns of thought, without any means of escape.

The work of the Austrian mathematician and philosopher Kurt Gödel (1906–1978) gave a new rigor to these concerns. Gödel's analysis reinforced the growing realization *that reason cannot be used to establish its own authority and competence.* This point is simply evaded by those who speak loosely and naively of "free-thinking," unaware of the capacity of reason to delude, limit, and imprison. Reason is constrained. The US public philosopher Rebecca Newberger Goldstein, one of Gödel's best recent inter-preters, highlights the importance of his work by considering whether reason can be completely trusted.

> How can a person, operating within a system of beliefs, including beliefs about beliefs, get outside that system to determine whether it is rational? If your entire system becomes infected with madness, including the very rules by which you reason, then how can you ever reason your way out of madness?

The recent rise of postmodernity is thus really not a symptom of irrationalism, but a protest against the existential inadequacy of rationalism, and the cultural authoritarian-ism it has encouraged. People came to realize the manifest deficiencies of an approach to life that is *determined* – as opposed to merely being *informed* – by reason, and pro-tested against those who tried to shoehorn them into what the sociologist Max Weber described as the "Iron Cage" of rationalism. Where many early Enlightenment thinkers saw human reason as liberating, Weber saw it as something that could imprison us within a set of restrictive possibilities.

Others pointed out that while human reason might be capable of proving logical truths, a wide range of *unproven and unprovable* philosophical, moral, and religious beliefs had good claims to be considered as "rational." This point was made with particular force by the philosopher Alasdair MacIntyre, who pointed out that Enlightenment writers, having declared that reason was the foundation of morals, could not agree on what forms of morality were justified by reason. MacIntyre claimed that the "Enlightenment project of justifying morality" could not be sustained: "The legacy of the Enlightenment has been the provision of an ideal of rational justification which it has proved impossible to attain." So if reason is capable of delivering unambivalent, objective judgements, why did so many questions remain unresolved and disputed, even within the Enlightenment itself? For MacIntyre, the only conclusion that can be drawn from this failure is that the notion of a single universal rationality is a myth.

So what do these reflections have to tell us about rationality? Perhaps the most important point is this: *there are multiple valid conceptions of rationality*. The rhetoric of the New Atheism is that the world is neatly divided into the rational (atheism) and irrational or superstitious (religion). Yet this simplistic dichotomist way of thinking is subverted by the realization that there are many ways of being "rational." We have to come to terms with the existence of multiple competing rationalities.

This leads to an important apologetic point. Christianity has its own distinct rationality, which exists alongside – and at points may overlap with – other understandings of rationality. So what does it mean to speak of Christianity as rational? There are two points that can helpfully be explored here. First, a belief can be described as "rational" if there is evidence that it is right. Christian apologetics, particularly forms of evidentialism, have long argued that the evidence of history and reasoned argument point decisively towards the truth of Christianity. Second, a belief can be considered "rational" if it is able to make sense of our observations and experience. Isaac Newton's theory of gravity, for example, was able to make sense of Newton's observations concerning both apples falling to the ground, and the way the planets orbited the sun.

As G. K. Chesterton and others have argued, Christianity offers an interpretative framework, a "big picture," which enables us to make sense of the world within the framework of this Christian rationality. For Chesterton, a "big picture" allows "an arrangement of the pieces by which they remain related, as do the stones arranged in an arch." As we noted earlier in this work (pp. 8–11), this rationality helps us make sense of what we experience within us and observe in the world around us.

Belief and Proof: The Question of Certainty in Faith

The movement that came to be known as the "New Atheism," which emerged with the publication of Richard Dawkins's *God Delusion* (2006), had a simple take on questions of faith. Science proves its beliefs. Science is about *facts* – objective truths that could be proved to be right, resting on unshakeable experimental evidence. Since science is based on evidence, faith is superfluous and doubt is eliminated, in that evidence convinces us of the truth with a compelling clarity. So can religious people prove their belief in God is true *scientifically*? For New Atheist writers, the answer was simple: "No." Faith in God is simply irrational. Faith is about asserting beliefs, rather than offering evidence for them. In his *God is Not Great*, Christopher Hitchens, a leading representative of the "New Atheism," declared that he did not "believe" in anything – he only accepted what was factually correct. Atheism was the default position of a thinking person.

God is Not Great is written with such conviction and confidence that, if self-assurance alone were an indication of truth, Hitchens would win his arguments hands down. Yet his highly superficial analysis of some core religious and philosophical ideas suggests an unwillingness (and possibly an inability) on his part to handle them properly. For example, the chapter of *God is Not Great* boldly entitled "The Metaphysical Claims of Religion Are False" skims the surface of a potentially interesting debate, failing to tell us what those metaphysical claims might be, or what is wrong with them. The New Atheism certainly had an initial novelty value, which appealed to sections of the media – but this appeal lay in the intensity of its ridicule, not the substance of its criticisms, of religion. Bruce DeSilva of Associated Press seemed to capture the consensus on this matter. Commenting on *God is Not Great*, he remarked: "Hitchens has nothing new to say, although it must be acknowledged that he says it exceptionally well."

It soon become clear, however, that the "New Atheism" involved a web of unproven – and probably unprovable – beliefs. The atheist philosopher Julian Baggini complained that the New Atheism seemed to think that it had a monopoly on reason. "With its talk of 'spells' and 'delusions,' it gives the impression that only through stupidity or crass disregard for reason could anyone be anything other than an atheist." We have to recognize the limits of reason, Baggini argued, and accept that reason and evidence play a significant role in religious belief. Shouldn't the New Atheists be a little more skeptical about the reach of reason, Baggini wondered? Dawkins and Hitchens seemed to attribute to reason "a power it does not have." Behind what many consider to be bullying and aggressive rhetoric about a "God delusion" or "blind faith" was a failure to engage with one of the leading questions of philosophy: how do we deal with the fact that most of life's great questions cannot be settled by argument or proof?

The philosopher Karl Popper introduced the phase "ultimate questions" to designate the larger questions about the meaning of life and the nature of the good, which really matter to people, yet which cannot be proved to be true by any known scientific means. It is one thing to prove *shallow* truths; yet, as Popper pointed out, the really significant beliefs in life lie beyond logical or scientific proof. Any answer to such "ultimate questions" ultimately amount to a matter of *what is believed*, rather than *what can be proved*. Proof, in the proper sense of the word, is limited to the worlds of logic and mathematics. In every other area of life – such as questions of meaning, value, ethics, politics, or religion – human beings have to come to terms with accepting ideas that cannot be proven, but may nonetheless be considered to be trustworthy or reliable.

This point is highlighted by the British philosopher and intellectual historian Sir Isaiah Berlin, who suggested that human beliefs fall into three broad groups.

1. Those that can be established by empirical observation;
2. Those that can be established by logical deduction;
3. Those that cannot be proved in either of these ways.

The first two categories of beliefs concern what can be known reliably through the natural sciences on the one hand, and what can be proved through logic and mathematics on the other. The third category, however, concerns the values and ideas that have shaped human culture and given human existence direction and purpose down the ages. These, Berlin insists, cannot be proved by reason or science.

This point is recognized by most philosophers, who are well aware of the fragility of human knowledge. The atheist philosopher Bertrand Russell described the task of philosophy as being to "teach us how to live without certainty." Russell argued that the natural human craving for certainty was a destructive "intellectual vice," which could not be reconciled with the limited capacities of human reason on the one hand, or the complexity of the world on the other. Recognizing the futility of a quest for certitude was, he suggested, essential to responsible philosophizing. Although Russell chose to live as an atheist, he was clear that he could not prove there was no God; like

William James, he believed he could live out his life on the basis of a set of beliefs without being able to demonstrate them with total certainty.

So what are the apologetic lessons to be learned from this brief analysis? Two main points emerge from this. First, accepting *any* worldview – whether religious or secular – involves going beyond what the evidence strictly permits. To believe that there is no God is an opinion, a judgement rather than a proved fact. Secularism is a web of beliefs, not a neutral position. Exploring this point can be very helpful in showing many people quite happily commit themselves to worldviews or beliefs that cannot be *proved* to be true, without causing them any intellectual difficulties. This suggests that the real issue is not believing something that lies beyond proof, but which specific unproven (and potentially unprovable) belief is to be preferred.

Second, these reflections point to the importance of Pascal's famous apologetic advice: we must "make good people wish that [the Christian faith] were true, and then show them that it is true." Pascal's point is that desire is apologetically significant, creating a willingness to consider new options. For Pascal, we ought first to help people long for what the Christian faith promises and then give reasons for believing that it is true and real, not simply desirable.

The Trinity: An Irrational View of God?

Many people find themselves puzzled by the Christian doctrine of the Trinity, which is widely (and rightly) seen as setting out a distinctively Christian way of understanding God. Many, however, find this belief both illogical and pointless. How can God be both three and one? Why not just limit ourselves to the simple vocabulary of the New Testament, and avoid such speculative ways of speaking about God, which seem to amount to mathematical absurdities? Might this be a symptom of some deeper irrationality, which contaminates not simply this one doctrine, but the whole edifice of Christian belief?

Christians believe in one God – but this "God" does not fit the conventional categories of Judaism or Hellenistic philosophy. The Christian vision of God is so rich that it demands a new way of thinking about God as creator, redeemer, and sanctifier. The doctrine of the Trinity does not affirm that there are three Gods; it affirms that there is *one* God, who cannot be adequately described using human categories, and offers a theological framework that safeguards this rich vision of God.

While the Trinitarian language of the church is not present in the New Testament, early Christian theologians found they had to develop these ideas to express the rich account of God that was implicit within it. In the fourth century, Athanasius of Alexandria made the important point that preserving biblical *truth* sometimes required going beyond biblical *terminology*. It wasn't good enough merely to repeat what the New Testament said. Its many insights about God had to be woven together, and the right words found to express the rich and transformative picture of God that emerged from doing so.

Early Christian writers, such as the second-century writer Irenaeus of Lyons, noted that the New Testament's concept of God focused on three main interconnected elements: God as the source of the universe; God as present and active in a focused and concentrated way in the person of Jesus of Nazareth; and God as present and active in both believers and the world through the Spirit. Irenaeus insisted that these three elements needed to be held together as integral elements of the New Testament's vision of God, and were not to be reduced or simplified. The Trinity was a way of holding these insights together, so that the depth and range of the New Testament's vision of God could be preserved.

The Christian understanding of God is that of one God who acts as creator, redeemer, and sustainer – not a God who simply creates the universe and tells us what rules to follow, but a God who having created the world, enters into it in Christ to redeem it, and is present within that world and the lives of believers through the Holy Spirit. Other concepts of God may be simpler and easier to understand, but they fail to affirm and protect the central themes of a distinctively *Christian* understanding of God. The Christian Bible makes it clear that God is not merely a creator and lawgiver; God is also our redeemer and sustainer. The doctrine of the Trinity is an intellectual formalization of these crucial insights. There is only one God – but that God is so rich and complex that we have to use a Trinitarian framework to ensure we do justice to God, rather than simplify (and thus distort) who God *is* and what God *does*. The Trinity maps this Christian vision of God, causing intellectual discomfort precisely because the human mind is incapable of fully taking in this vision, and thus ends up reducing it to what is intellectually manageable.

For many people, the Trinity is problematic. Yet theologians argue this is what we should expect when the finite human mind is confronted with the overwhelming reality of God. Augustine of Hippo offered us one of the finest accounts of the limits of our ability to cope with God in a neat slogan: "If you think you have grasped God, it is not God you have grasped." If you can get your mind around it, it's not God. Anything that we can grasp fully and completely cannot be God, precisely because it would be so limited and impoverished if it can be fully grasped by the human mind.

God simply overwhelms our mental capacities. C. S. Lewis made this point when reflecting on the difficulties that many people experience with the doctrine of the Trinity. We see things from a limiting and constrictive human perspective. He suggests that we think of ourselves as "Flatlanders," two-dimensional people who try – and fail – to visualize three-dimensional objects.

> Flatlanders, attempting to imagine a cube, would either imagine the six squares coinciding, and thus destroy their distinctness, or else imagine them set out side by side, and thus destroy the unity. Our difficulties about the Trinity are of much the same kind.

It is important to notice that Lewis does not offer his readers a defense of the doctrine of the Trinity or any new evidence for believing in it. Instead, he provides a visual framework that allows us to perceive its apparent "irrationality" in a new way, and thus to realize that our previous difficulties with this doctrine arise from seeing it from a limited (and limiting) perspective. The Trinity may be a mystery – but that does not mean it is an irrationality.

Happily, Lewis also uses a more accessible analogy to help his readers think about the Trinity. Imagine, Lewis suggests, someone who is praying. For Lewis, the rich dynamic of prayer is indicative of the complexity of God's actions and presence in the

Christian life, expressed in the Trinity. Christians who pray are aware that God is, in some way, the *goal* of prayer, the *motivating power* for prayer, and the *road* along which they are being propelled in prayer. Lewis thus shows how the Christian experience of prayer maps onto a Trinitarian understanding of God.

Scientism: Only Science Can Answer Life's Big Questions

The natural sciences play an important role in modern western culture. Their cultural authority raises two significant questions, which we shall consider in this and the following section. First, is science the only source of reliable knowledge? And second, are science and religious faith in conflict? Both of these questions are regularly encountered in apologetic debate and discussion. In this section, we shall consider the position known as "scientism," which treats science as a privileged or exclusive source of knowledge.

The biologist and philosopher Massimo Pigliucci suggests that scientism is probably best understood as "a totalizing attitude that regards science as the ultimate standard and arbiter of all interesting questions." Most scientists consider human knowledge to consist of a spectrum of possibilities including scientific knowledge, but extending beyond this to include moral, political, and religious beliefs. Albert Einstein, for example, was quite clear that science was only one form of human knowledge, and that science was not capable of providing satisfactory answers to moral, political, or religious questions. The famous evolutionary biologist Stephen Jay Gould took a similar view:

> Science tries to record and explain the factual character of the natural world, whereas religion struggles with spiritual and ethical questions about the meaning and proper conduct of our lives. The facts of nature simply cannot dictate correct moral behavior or spiritual meaning.

Scientism, however, holds that the only form of valid knowledge results from the application of the scientific method. Two significant atheist writers to take this position are the biologist Richard Dawkins and the philosopher Alex Rosenberg, who both argue (though in different ways) that science makes other forms of knowledge irrelevant and unreliable. In his *Atheist's Guide to Reality* (2011), Rosenberg argues that science is "our exclusive guide to reality." We don't need anything else, and there isn't anything else that counts as secure knowledge. Science alone is able to provide clear and compelling answers to questions that were traditionally seen as ethical, religious, or philosophical. For Rosenberg, these are fundamentally *scientific* questions, and thus can only be answered by scientific methods. Religion has nothing to say to a scientifically informed world.

There are two major questions that many consider to be essential to living well and authentically in this complex world. What is the meaning of life? What is the good life, and how do I lead it? Scientism declares that these are nonquestions that cannot be answered by science – and hence cannot be properly answered at all.

So what sort of questions can science answer, and what answers does it provide? Rosenberg helpfully maps out some of life's more important questions that he believes can be clearly and concisely answered by the natural sciences. He provides four examples of such questions, along with the "reliable" answers, which he asserts that science provides.

Question 1: Is there a God? Answer: No.
Question 2: What is the purpose of the universe? Answer: There is none.
Question 3: What is the meaning of life? Answer: Ditto.
Question 4: What is the difference between right and wrong, good and bad? Answer: There is no moral difference between them.

Let's focus on that answer to the fourth question. For Rosenberg, science cannot tell us what is good or evil. This view is widely held among moral philosophers, who rightly note (following David Hume) that there cannot be a deductively valid argument whose premises take the form of factual or scientific statements, and whose conclusion contains a moral statement. You need some kind of bridging hypothesis to make a connection between facts and values – and science, of course, concerns facts. Yet Rosenberg goes further than most philosophers, and declares that, from the perspective of scientism, "good" and "evil" are essentially *meaningless* terms. There is no difference between them.

Many, however, will feel that Rosenberg's rather rigid approach deprives us of a vital element of the moral framework that we need to challenge evil – to *name* it for what it really is. Rosenberg's unsettling conclusion calls into question the methods he used to derive them. Is there really "no moral difference" between right and wrong? Between good and evil? These simplistic statements seem shallow and empty as we contemplate the many "horrendous evils" of human history – such as Nazi extermination camps, or the mass graves of women and children massacred for belonging to the wrong tribe. Rosenberg has simply demonstrated that science cannot satisfactorily answer moral questions, not that moral questions are invalid or that they cannot be answered.

So if Rosenberg offers us some problematic *answers*, what about the *methods* he uses to get those answers? As Rosenberg himself concedes, the view that that science is "our exclusive guide to reality" is "viciously circular," in that any defense of this approach has to presuppose the reliability of its core beliefs. If science is believed to be the only reliable criterion of judgement, then the only way of confirming this belief is to appeal to science. This means that science functions as both judge and jury in the trial of its own competency.

Yet for any research method to be validated properly, we need an extra-systemic vantage point from which it can be judged. However, if there is a vantage point beyond science by which it may be judged, then the exclusive authority of science is clearly called into question, in that its authority ultimately rests on something else – something that lies *beyond* science. An appeal to any validating authority beyond science effectively concedes that science is not the only reliable source or criterion of knowledge.

For such reasons, most scholars consider scientism – at least in the form set out by Rosenberg and Dawkins – to represent an inflated and unevidenced overstatement. Most would agree with Albert Einstein's clear recognition, based on the philosopher David Hume's critique of moving from the empirical to the ethical realms, that science simply cannot answer moral questions. Scientism is a form of epistemic imperialism, insisting that its methods and criteria are binding for all other disciplines, in effect reducing ethics, politics, and religion to science. Yet there is an alternative approach, already hinted at earlier in this section. This is to think of human knowledge as a spectrum, including a range of forms of knowledge – such as scientific, logical, mathematical, ethical, religious, and political ideas. Each discipline has its own method for investigating the world. The task is to find a way of bringing these different forms of knowledge together, so that we can have a richer and deeper understanding of things that weaves together these many tributaries of human knowledge.

Science and Religious Faith are Incompatible

We now turn to consider an issue that has become particularly important in western culture – namely, the idea that science and religion are "incompatible" or exist in a state of permanent warfare, which has become widely accepted within the media and popular culture, despite a significant lack of evidence for this statement. It is certainly true that science and religion are *different*; that does not, however, entail that they are *incompatible*. Cultural studies of the relation of science and religion in different global regions has shown that the incompatibility of science and religion (especially when this is developed into the idea of a permanent warfare between science and religion) is a peculiarly western idea, which is not replicated in other major cultural contexts (such as India).

Three main attitudes towards the relation of science and religious faith are found in contemporary discussion in western culture. I shall summarize these very briefly, and give a leading representative of each of these positions.

1. Science and religion are at war with each other. This position, exemplified by Richard Dawkins, argues that science is simply polluted or contaminated if it enters into dialogue with religious faith.
2. Science and religion are different forms of knowledge, each of which is important – but no dialogue between them is necessary or possible. This position, exemplified by Albert Einstein, holds that science and religion are different yet compatible, but that they have no common themes of discussion. Science explains how the world functions, where religious faith is concerned with questions of meaning or value. These are neither inconsistent nor in conflict.
3. Science and religion represent different forms of human knowledge, yet can enrich each other through discussion and dialogue. This position, exemplified by Francis S. Collins, recognizes the limitations of both science and religion, and sees mutual dialogue as a way of expanding our understanding of the world.

It is clearly important for apologetics to engage the assumption, explicitly stated in the writings of most "New Atheist" writers, that science makes religious belief both redundant and intellectually untenable. Although this way of thinking was dominant in the 1960s, since about 1990 there has been growing recognition of its inadequacies. During the early modern period, when the "scientific revolution" began to develop, many used what is known as the "Two Books" metaphor to explore how science and faith could be held together constructively. This metaphor invites us to see God as the author or creator of two distinct yet related "books" – the natural world, and the Bible – and thus to imagine nature as a readable text that requires interpretation, in a manner comparable to the Christian interpretation of the Bible.

According to the historian of science Thomas Dixon, the myth of the "warfare" of science and religion was a self-serving myth that was invented by Enlightenment rationalists in the late 1700s, propagated by Victorian free-thinkers in the late 1800s, and is defended today by "scientific" atheists and many influential voices competing for authority within western popular culture. The idea that the history of the relationship between science and religion is in the first place simple, and in the second marked by a permanent and necessary conflict of ideas and methods has been comprehensively refuted by historians of science. Many would agree with the philosopher Alvin Plantinga's argument that the fundamental conflict is not between "science" and "Christianity," but between a dogmatic metaphysical naturalism and belief in God.

The origins of the myth of the warfare of science and religious belief lie in the later nineteenth century, in which two US works – John William Draper's *History of the Conflict between Religion and Science* (1874) and Andrew Dickson White's *Warfare of Science with Theology in Christendom* (1896) – caused the crystallization of the "warfare" metaphor in popular culture. The "warfare" model of science and religion arose during a period when professional scientists wished to distance themselves from their amateur colleagues, and when changing patterns in academic culture necessitated demonstrating its independence from the church and other bastions of the establishment. Academic freedom demanded a break with the church; it was a small step towards depicting the church as the opponent of learning and scientific advance in the late nineteenth century, and the natural sciences as its strongest advocates. This naturally led to earlier incidents – such as the Galileo debate – being read and interpreted in the light of this controlling paradigm of the warfare of science and religion.

The idea that science and religion are in permanent conflict thus clearly reflects the agendas and concerns of a specific period. Yet that moment is now past, and its agendas can be set to one side, allowing a more informed and dispassionate assessment of things. The study of history allows us both to account for the origins of this deeply problematic understanding of the relation of science and religion, and to assess its reliability. Above all, it allows us to move beyond it, and construct more informed and positive approaches to the interaction of these two distinct domains of thought.

It is now widely agreed that there is no "master narrative" that reliably frames the historical relation of science and faith. The relationship of science and faith is complex, and varies from one historical location to another. In a series of important and influential historical studies of science and religion in the 1990s and beyond, focusing especially on the nineteenth century, John Hedley Brooke has argued that serious scholarship in the history of science has revealed "so extraordinarily rich and complex a relationship between science and religion in the past that general theses are difficult to sustain. The real lesson turns out to be the complexity."

This point was developed further by the intellectual historian Peter Harrison, who concluded that study of the historical relations between science and religion "does not reveal any simple pattern at all," such as the "conflict" narrative. It does, however, disclose a "general trend" – that for most of the time, religion has *facilitated* scientific inquiry. For Harrison, there is no "right" or privileged way of understanding the relationship of Christianity – or any other religion – to the natural sciences. Harrison is critical of the tendency to essentialize both "science" and "religion" – in other words, to suggest that both have fixed and permanent identities – which he argues has led many to neglect the importance of historical and cultural context in shaping perceptions about how Christianity and the natural sciences relate to each other.

So what is the relation of science and religious faith, if they are not at war with each other? It is not difficult for an apologist to make the point that the myth of some perennial or essential warfare between science and faith is a recent invention, whose social origins can be accounted for in terms of competing claims for cultural authority and influence. Yet there is a second apologetic point that needs to be made: it is certainly correct to suggest that science and religion are *different* – but they are not incompatible for that reason. "Difference" and "incompatibility" are not equivalent notions. Science, ethics, politics, and religious faith occupy different positions on the spectrum of human knowledge, as we noted earlier in this chapter (p. 159). Albert Einstein, perhaps the twentieth century's most celebrated scientist, felt it was important for human beings to somehow hold together science, religion, politics, and ethics. Einstein recognized that these were intellectually *distinct*, but was quite clear that did not mean they were *incompatible*.

Apologetically, two helpful ways of thinking about the relation of science and religious faith may be noted. Each offers an intellectual framework that respects the differences between science and faith, yet allows them to contribute to a richer and deeper understanding of reality. They are different, but compatible, when seen within an appropriate intellectual framework.

The first, advocated by the British public philosopher Mary Midgley, is the "multiple maps" approach. Midgley argues that we need "many maps, many windows" if we are to represent the complexity of reality, reflecting the fact that "there are many independent forms and sources of knowledge." She suggests that it is helpful to think of the world as a "huge aquarium."

> We cannot see it as a whole from above, so we peer in at it through a number of small windows ... We can eventually make quite a lot of sense of this habitat if we patiently put together the data from different angles. But if we insist that our own window is the only one worth looking through, we shall not get very far.

Midgley's basic principle of using multiple maps – such as a *scientific* map and a *theological* map – to represent a complex reality opens up some important possibilities for integration and enrichment of our vision. We need a rich palette of colors to represent the complexities of our observations of the world around us, and our experience within us.

Midgley's image can be used apologetically to emphasize the importance of values and meaning in life – in other words, using a religious or theological map alongside others. Science maps our world at one level, explaining how it functions; religion maps our world at another level, explaining what it means. We need to superimpose those maps, so that all this information is at our disposal. Each map is to be respected, but it depends on a specific way of exploring our world, and is incomplete. It needs supplementation with other maps. A scientific map helps us understand how we, as human beings, function – and that's important medically. Yet a theological map helps us understand our deeper needs – and that's important spiritually.

A second approach is to think of science and religious belief as answering questions at different levels. The geologist Frank H. T. Rhodes, who served as President of Cornell University from 1977 to 1995, made this point using the analogy of a boiling kettle. Rhodes invited his readers to answer this question: why is this kettle boiling? Rhodes notes that two types of explanation might be given. At the scientific level, energy is being supplied, which raises the temperature of the water to its boiling point. Yet another answer can be given – an answer that is teleological in nature. "The kettle is boiling because I put it on to make a cup of tea." Rhodes makes the point that this second answer is different from the first – but that does not mean it is incompatible with it. Taken together, both these answers give a richer answer to the original question.

> Now these are different answers … But both are true, both are complementary and not competitive. One answer is appropriate within a particular frame of reference, the other within another frame of reference. There is a sense in which each is incomplete without the other.

The apologetic point that both Midgley and Rhodes bring out is that while science and religion may answer our questions in different ways, taken together they can give us a richer and fuller account of reality. Science helps us understand how our world *works*; religion adds depth to this functional account by helping us understand what it *means*. These are complementary, not competing; both are part of the larger and more satisfying picture of reality that human beings need if they are to inhabit this world meaningfully, and flourish within it. Rhodes makes the point that a scientific answer to the question of why a kettle is boiling does not invalidate other answers – such as the desire to make a cup of tea. Nor is the scientific answer incompatible with the second. Both answers are part of a bigger picture, allowing a richer account of explanation.

The Question of Miracles

A question that is often debated in apologetics relates to miracles – such as the resurrection. How can we take miracles seriously in a scientific age? Since the early modern period, this debate is often framed in terms of the intellectual difficulties that might accompany thinking of God violating the laws of nature. The Dutch rationalist philosopher Baruch Spinoza (1632–1677) argued that miracles were impossible, in that the "laws of nature" are decrees of God that are expressions of the necessity and perfection of the divine nature. The concept of a "law of nature" is here understood as a divinely established rule that certain things shall happen, and others shall not. Since a miracle represents a violation or contravention of these divinely ordained laws of nature, anyone suggesting that God performed miracles would have to accept that God here contradicted his own nature, which seems deeply problematic.

It is important to note that Spinoza here assumes that a miracle is defined in terms of violating the laws of nature. Yet many twenty-first century philosophers of science are highly critical of philosophical overinterpretation of the idea of a "law of nature." Natural "laws" are really little more than summaries of what seems to happen in the universe. They are to be understood as incomplete inductive generalizations, summarizing what has been observed to date, rather than the philosophical absolutization proposed by Spinoza. This definition became problematic with the rise of statistical approaches to thermodynamics in the late nineteenth century, and to quantum mechanics in the twentieth century. We must speak of a range of probabilities that certain things may happen, rather than absolute declarations that certain things will always happen.

Historians point out that the term "laws of nature" only came to be used around 1650, so that earlier discussions of miracles did not involve framing them as violations of these "laws of nature." Thomas Aquinas, writing in the thirteenth century, described a miracle as something that "surpasses the capabilities of nature," making no reference to *violating* the laws of nature. For Aquinas, a miracle is an event whose occurrence exceeds the natural capacities of visible and physical nature. This view was widespread at this time.

The British philosopher David Hume (Figure 8.2) is widely considered to have shaped the terms of modern discussions of miracles. For Hume, a miracle is "a violation of the laws of nature" or "a transgression of a law of nature by particular volition of the Deity, or by the interposition of some invisible agent." Hume's definition of a miracles

Figure 8.2 Statue of the Scottish philosopher David Hume (1711–1776) on Edinburgh's Royal Mile. Adobe Stock Image 106703224.

remains influential and is often the starting point for contemporary discussions of the notion. For example, in his *Concept of Miracle* (1970), the philosopher of religion Richard Swinburne follows Hume in defining a miracle as "a violation of a law of nature by a god."

Yet Hume's appeal to "laws of nature" in his discussion of miracles is inconsistent with his discussion of the inductive processes that lead to the formulation of "laws of nature" in the first place. Hume saw induction as a process that summarized observations, allowing certain patterns or "rules" to be proposed. If the laws of nature are simply summative statements of natural regularities, however, an apparent "violation" of those laws could be seen as a miracle – but would more reasonably be taken as an indication that what had hitherto been assumed to be a "law of nature" was actually nothing of the sort. Furthermore, Hume was emphatic that induction was not conclusive, in that the possibility that a future observation might not fit in with existing observations could not be excluded. Induction summarizes known observations; but what of *future* observations? Can we be sure that these will not call the certainties of the past into question?

Others have highlighted the importance of this point, most notably the British philosopher Bertrand Russell (Figure 8.3). In his 1912 work *The Problems of Philosophy*, Russell raised some difficult questions concerning the scientific method, noting that the scientific enterprise apparently depended on certain unjustifiable assumptions.

Figure 8.3   Bertrand Russell (1872–1970), the British philosopher and Nobel Prize winner in literature. Alamy Image GG2GJW.

"The belief in the uniformity of nature is the belief that everything that has happened or will happen is an instance of some general law to which there are *no* exceptions." But what are the grounds of this belief, which is arguably foundational to the scientific method? For Russell, this "inductive principle" is not capable of being either *proved* or *disproved* by an appeal to experience. The analogy that Russell uses in making this point is often cited in philosophical textbooks: "The man who has fed the chicken every day throughout its life wrings its neck instead, showing that more refined views as to the uniformity of nature would have been useful to the chicken."

In his *Miracle and Its Philosophical Presuppositions*, the philosopher F. R. Tennant argued that "until we shall have arrived at something like omniscience as to Nature's constitution and intrinsic capacities, we cannot affirm any marvel to be beyond them." In many ways, Tennant echoes approaches to miracles that emerged in Christian thinking before the Enlightenment. For writers such as Augustine of Hippo, writing in the fifth century, a miracle is not something that is "contrary to *nature*," but rather is something that is "contrary to *our understanding of nature*." Augustine, like Isaac Newton, took the view that a given event might seem miraculous to one observer and natural to another, depending upon our present understandings of the workings of the universe.

A similar point is made by C. S. Lewis in his important work *Miracles*. "Nothing can seem extraordinary until you have discovered what is ordinary. Belief in miracles, far from depending on an ignorance of the laws of nature, is only possible in so far as those laws are known." Yet Lewis makes a deeper point. Developing Aquinas's idea of miracles as events that transcend the productive power of nature, Lewis emphasizes the fundamental continuity of divine action in creating and inhabiting the world. Miracles are not about an external God pulling strings within a world that has no connection or relation to him. Rather, God is a "Power which is not alien," who works at a deeper level within the world to achieve its ultimate aims and goals. The Christian way of looking at things, he suggests, leads us to believe in the "total harmony of all that exists." Everything that happens within nature – including miracles, if they do indeed occur – must reflect and disclose that harmony. While miracles must, by definition, interrupt the 'usual course of Nature,' they nevertheless reflect the "unity and self-consistency of total reality at some deeper level." There is indeed a "total harmony" within the universe, which is only partially accessible to science. "In Science we have been reading only the notes to a poem; in Christianity we find the poem itself."

Finally, we need to consider a point made by Isaac Newton in the late seventeenth century. Suppose that something happened that was miraculous, in that it could not be explained on the basis of an existing understanding of the natural order. Now suppose that this event happened frequently. Would not the frequency of its occurrence lead us to consider that it was "natural"?

[M]iracles are so called not because they are the works of God but because they happen seldom and for that reason create wonder. If they should happen constantly according to certain laws impressed upon the nature of things, they would be no longer wonders of miracles but would be considered in philosophy as part of the phenomena of nature notwithstanding that the cause of their causes might be unknown to us.

Reductionism: Human Beings are Nothing but Atoms

In 1935, the noted physiologist J. S. Haldane declared his support for the view of many "biologists and numerous popular writers that life must ultimately be regarded as no more than a complicated physico-chemical process," a controlling assumption that now seemed to have gained the ascendancy within the natural sciences. Haldane's analysis highlights how scientific advance often involves clarifying how complex systems – such as human beings – function, leading some to suggest that human beings can be reduced to mechanical accounts of their individual components. A good example of this is found in the writings of the biologist Francis Crick, who defines human beings in strongly reductionist terms.

> "You," your joys and your sorrows, your memories and your ambitions, your sense of personal identity and free will, are in fact no more than the behaviour of a vast assembly of nerve cells and their associated molecules. … You're nothing but a pack of neurons.

For Crick, human beings can be defined simply and neatly in terms of our physical components. This highly reductive approach to human identity assumes that a complex system is no more than the sum of its parts.

Another familiar example of scientific reductionism is found in Richard Dawkins's account of human nature, which centers on the idea of a "selfish gene." For Dawkins, human beings are machines that are controlled and determined by our DNA – the complex biological molecule that transmits genetic information from one generation to another. "DNA neither cares nor knows. DNA just is. And we dance to its music." Our sole purpose in existing is to pass on our genes to future generations. Human beings are just gene-perpetuating machines.

These influential reductive views of humanity present a single aspect of human existence as if it were the totality (or the only important aspect) of that existence. Yet they have been widely criticized by both religious and secular thinkers, who rightly point out that this diminishes human distinctiveness by treating human identity simply in terms of our physical, chemical, and biological components. Yes, human beings are made up of atoms and molecules – but they are far more than this. The clinical neuroscientist Raymond Tallis is one of many leading atheists who regards such views as indefensible and dehumanizing. "I am an atheist humanist; but this does not oblige me to deny what is staring me in the face – namely, that we are different from other animals, and that we are not just pieces of matter."

A helpful way of countering such reductionist accounts of human nature lies to hand in the "critical realism" developed by the social philosopher Roy Bhaskar, which recognizes the "stratification of reality." Human nature is understood to consist of different levels or strata. Humanity can be – and, indeed, ought to be – investigated at the physical, chemical, biological, and sociological levels (to mention a few of the obvious possibilities); yet none of these multiple levels is to be regarded as normative or definitive, but rather is to be considered part – and only part – of the complex reality that we know as humanity.

The natural sciences make extensive use of the notion of "levels of explanation," a stratified approach to the natural world that counters inappropriate reductionism by emphasizing that some explanations might be offered of *some* aspects of systems that could not be applied to *every* aspect of that system, or to the system *as a whole*. The interaction of such levels is complex, and it is becoming increasingly clear that causation exists and operates at multiple levels and in multiple directions within complex biological systems. Whereas reductionist approaches prematurely argue that the more fundamental levels – such as physical reality – determine the properties and behaviors of higher levels, it is now clear that such "bottom-up" approaches need to be modified by recognizing the importance of "top-down" mechanisms.

Until recently, modern biology was more likely to emphasize reductionism than holism; yet this is now being challenged, as the complexity of biology is reasserted, and holistic approaches begin to recover the ground lost to mechanistic approaches in the twentieth century. Reductionist approaches on their own are simply inadequate to account for our complex world; we need a more complex account to do justice to reality.

A "multiple levels" approach affirms that we are indeed made up of atoms and molecules, while insisting that this does not mean that we are "nothing but" atoms and molecules. This hopeless oversimplification just confuses a component or level within a system with the system as a whole. We must learn to consider human beings as complex totalities, which cannot be defined or described in terms of any one of their constituent parts. It is particularly important to challenge the depersonalization of identity arising from simplistic statements about humanity being "nothing more than atoms." The Jewish philosopher Martin Buber argued that purely scientific accounts of humanity reduced people to objects – to an "it," rather than a "you." The essence of personal identity, for Buber, was an ability to exist in relationships with other people, and with God. We are not *defined* by our chemical or genetic make-up, but by our social and personal relationships. Human beings are indeed made up of atoms and molecules – and so are robots, washing machines, and coffee cups. Yet this does not mean that human beings are identical to robots or coffee cups. It fails completely to understand what is different about human beings – above all, their ability to think about life. Marilynne Robinson captures this point well: "We are very remarkable. We alone among the creatures have learned a bit of the grammar of the universe."

In this chapter, we have reflected on 10 questions that are often raised in apologetic discussions. They are illustrative, not exhaustive. In developing your own approach to apologetics, you may find them useful in mapping out responses to these questions, adapted to your audiences, to your own experience and knowledge, and to the time available to engage them. Other such questions can easily be added. Part of the art of apologetics is crafting such responses, based on a good knowledge of the field, and an empathy for the audience. You may find it helpful to prepare lists of questions you anticipate engaging and the points you would like to make, as you develop your own distinct "voice" as an apologist. In the final chapter of this work, we shall consider some figures of apologetic wisdom, who may help you craft your own approach and ministry.

Study Questions

1. Set out in your own words the argument for God being a wish-fulfilment. Then outline how you would challenge this argument.

2. Which do you think is more important: to explain why there is suffering in the world, or to show how Christianity enables people to cope with suffering?
3. What do you think is the most effective criticism of the assertion that science is able to answer all of life's important questions?
4. Sketch the outline of a brief talk you might give on whether science and faith are compatible. Who might you use as dialogue partners? What are the main options you would want to explore?

For Further Reading

Bamford, Greg. "Popper and His Commentators on the Discovery of Neptune: A Close Shave for the Law of Gravitation?" *Studies in History and Philosophy of Science Part A* 27, no. 2 (1996): 207–32.

Brooke, John Hedley. *Science and Religion: Some Historical Perspectives.* Cambridge: Cambridge University Press, 1991.

Buckley, Michael J. *At the Origins of Modern Atheism.* New Haven, CT: Yale University Press, 1987.

Cauchi, Francesca. *Zarathustra's Moral Tyranny: Kant, Hegel and Feuerbach.* Edinburgh: Edinburgh University Press, 2022.

Cavanaugh, William T. *The Myth of Religious Violence: Secular Ideology and the Roots of Modern Conflict.* Oxford: Oxford University Press, 2009.

Cumming, Richard P. "Revelation as Apologetic Category: A Reconsideration of Karl Barth's Engagement with Ludwig Feuerbach's Critique of Religion." *Scottish Journal of Theology* 68, no. 1 (2015): 43–60.

Dahl, Espen. *The Problem of Job and the Problem of Evil.* Cambridge: Cambridge University Press, 2019.

Douglas, Christopher. "This Is the Shack that Job Built: Theodicy and Polytheism in William Paul Young's Evangelical Bestseller." *Journal of the American Academy of Religion* 88, no. 3 (2020): 505–42.

Gleeson, Andrew. "On Letting Go of Theodicy: Marilyn McCord Adams on God and Evil." *Sophia* 54 (2015): 1–12.

Haidt, Jonathan. "The Emotional Dog and its Rational Tail: A Social Intuitionist Approach to Moral Judgment." *Psychological Review* 108, no. 4 (2001): 814–34.

Haidt, Jonathan. *The Righteous Mind: Why Good People Are Divided by Politics and Religion.* New York, NY: Pantheon Books, 2012.

Harrison, Peter. "Laws of God or Laws of Nature? Natural Order in the Early Modern Period." In *Science without God? Rethinking the History of Scientific Naturalism*, edited by Peter Harrison and Jon Roberts, 59–77. Oxford: Oxford University Press, 2019.

Horst, Steven W. *Beyond Reduction: Philosophy of Mind and Post-Reductionist Philosophy of Science.* Oxford: Oxford University Press, 2007.

Kelhoffer, James A. "Suffering as Defense of Paul's Apostolic Authority in Galatians and 2 Corinthians 11." *Svensk Exegetisk Årsbok* 74 (2009): 127–43.

Keller, Tim. *Walking with God through Pain and Suffering.* New York, NY: Dutton, 2013.

Kenny, Dianna T. *God, Freud and Religion: The Origins of Faith, Fear and Fundamentalism.* London: Routledge, 2015.

Laverda, Alessandro. "Revising the Supernatural: Prospero Lambertini's Reconsideration of the Concept of Miracle." *Church History* 90, no. 1 (2021): 45–67.

Lennox, John. *Can Science Explain Everything?* Epsom, UK: Good Book Company, 2019.

McGrath, Alister E. *Dawkins' God: From The Selfish Gene to The God Delusion.* 2nd ed. Oxford: Wiley-Blackwell, 2014.

McGrath, Alister E. *Enriching Our Vision of Reality: Theology and the Natural Sciences in Dialogue.* West Conshohocken, PA: Templeton Press, 2017.

McGrath, Alister E. *The Territories of Human Reason: Science and Theology in an Age of*

Multiple Rationalities. Oxford: Oxford University Press, 2019.

McGrath, Alister E. "The Owl of Minerva: Reflections on the Theological Significance of Mary Midgley." *Heythrop Journal* 61, no. 5 (2020): 852–64.

McGrath, Alister E. "A Consilience of Equal Regard: Stephen Jay Gould on the Relation of Science and Religion." *Zygon* 56, no. 3 (2021): 547–65.

Miller, Jon. "Spinoza and the Concept of a Law of Nature." *History of Philosophy Quarterly* 20, no. 3 (2003): 257–76.

Millican, Peter. "Earman on Hume on Miracles." In *Debates in Modern Philosophy: Essential Readings and Contemporary Responses,* edited by Stewart Duncan and Antonia Lordo, 271–84. New York, NY: Routledge, 2013.

Nicholi, Armand M. *The Question of God: C. S. Lewis and Sigmund Freud Debate God, Love, Sex, and the Meaning of Life.* New York, NY: Free Press, 2002.

Numbers, Ronald L., ed. *Galileo Goes to Jail and Other Myths About Science and Religion.* Cambridge, MA: Harvard University Press, 2009.

O'Neil, Mary Kay, and Salman Akhtar. *On Freud's the Future of an Illusion.* London: Routledge, 2018.

Orr-Ewing, Amy. *Where is God in All the Suffering? Questioning Faith.* Epsom, UK: The Good Book Company, 2020.

Pearson, Christopher H., and Matthew P. Schunke. "Reduction, Explanation, and the New Science of Religion." *Sophia* 54 (2015): 47–60.

Reiss, Michael J., and Michael Ruse. *The New Biology: The Battle between Mechanism and Organicism.* Cambridge, MA: Harvard University Press, 2023.

Ryrie, Alec. *Unbelievers: An Emotional History of Doubt.* London: Collins, 2019.

Schönbaumsfeld, Genia. "On the Very Idea of a Theodicy." In *Wittgenstein, Religion and Ethics: New Perspectives from Philosophy and Theology,* edited by Mikel Burley, 93–112. London: Bloomsbury Academic, 2018.

Shaw, Jamie. "Duhem on Good Sense and Theory Pursuit: From Virtue to Social Epistemology." *International Studies in the Philosophy of Science* 33, no. 2 (2020): 67–85.

Shortt, Rupert. *The Hardest Problem: God, Evil and Suffering.* London: Hodder & Stoughton, 2022.

Stump, Eleonore. *Wandering in Darkness: Narrative and the Problem of Suffering.* Oxford: Clarendon Press, 2010.

Sumney, Jerry L. "Salvific Suffering in Paul: Eschatological, Vicarious, and Mimetic." In *Let the Reader Understand: Essays in Honor of Elizabeth Struthers Malbon,* edited by Edwin K. Broadhead, 195–212. London: Bloomsbury Publishing, 2018.

Swinton, John. *Raging with Compassion: Pastoral Responses to the Problem of Evil.* Grand Rapids, MI: Eerdmans, 2007.

Tallis, Raymond. *Aping Mankind: Neuromania, Darwinitis and the Misrepresentation of Humanity.* London: Routledge, 2014.

Ward, Keith. "Believing in Miracles." *Zygon* 37, no. 3 (2002), 741–50.

Wykstra, Stephen. "The Humean Obstacle to Evidential Arguments from Suffering: On Avoiding the Evils of 'Appearance.'" *International Journal for the Philosophy of Religion* 16 (1984): 73–93.

9

Learning from the Wise
Case Studies in Apologetics

In this introduction to apologetics, we have focused on some representative intellectual approaches to apologetics, engaging a number of writers who have made significant contributions to Christian apologetics – such as Thomas Aquinas, Blaise Pascal, C. S. Lewis, and J. R. R. Tolkien. We have also considered how some other influential apologists – such as Tim Keller – put apologetics into practice by relating to specific audiences. Yet there are other voices that merit attention. In what follows, we shall consider the approaches of five other apologists, focusing not simply on the intellectual foundations of their approach, but their practical outworking. Each of the writers discussed in this chapter can be seen as a figure of wisdom, someone who is concerned not merely with thinking about apologetics, but its implementation in the life of the church.

In these vignettes of significant apologists, we shall focus not simply on the arguments and affirmations that they offer in defending and commending the faith, but the manners in which they do this. Apologetics, as we have stressed throughout this work, is both a science and an art. Each of the individuals we will be considering is an artist, a reflective practitioner, someone who has something that they can teach us. The object of this chapter is not simply to learn about these individuals, but to learn from them. How does each of them ensure the core realities of the Christian faith connect up with their audiences? What particular gifts does this writer bring to the apologetic task? What is the problem that needs to be solved? What solution is developed? And what can we learn from this?

Although most of the writers we shall consider in this chapter were active in the past 100 years, it is important to appreciate that many earlier writers still have much to teach us about the apologetic task. For example, Augustine of Hippo was active in the fifth century, more than 1,500 years ago – but he can still help us develop a robust

Christian Apologetics: An Introduction, First Edition. Alister E. McGrath.
© 2024 John Wiley & Sons Ltd. Published 2024 by John Wiley & Sons Ltd.

and compelling approach to apologetics. In their important recent study *The Augustine Way: Retrieving a Vision for the Church's Apologetic Witness*, Joshua D. Chatraw and Mark D. Allen develop what we might call "an apologetics of retrieval," which enriches and informs the present. They rightly point out that this involves wise insights concerning the communication of faith, and engaging a changing – even disintegrating – social order, showing how Christianity offers stability in the midst of an uncertain world. It is helpful to be reminded that our own age is not the only period of history during which the seemingly secure cultural context in which it is embedded seemed to be on the point of collapsing.

Yet Augustine also offers challenges to the present, particularly the historically conditioned and apologetically vulnerable emphasis on abstractly intellectual defenses of the faith. "Augustine might want to have a word with many present-day pastors and theologians, who, though inheritors of his tradition, have sold off their apologetic birthright, mistakenly assuming apologetics is synonymous with a flattened Enlightenment-style rationality and seeing it as irrelevant to their ministry." For Augustine, faith makes human existence meaningful, livable, and comprehensible.

C. S. Lewis is perhaps one of the most eloquent advocates of learning from the past, reminding us that the most recent approaches are not necessarily the best or most appropriate, and that we have much to learn from those who have practiced apologetics in the past. All too often, we assume that modernist rational modes of persuasion are the norm; in reality, however, modes of persuasion are often shaped by historical circumstances. Where the Enlightenment favored rational demonstrations of logical truth, earlier generations developed more affective approaches to persuasion, linked with the recognition of beauty, or the capacity of faith to transform life. This reflection neatly leads us into the first of the writers we shall consider: the seventeenth century English religious poet George Herbert, who used powerful affective and imaginative imagery to help his readers grasp the transformational impact of the Christian gospel, and demonstrate that Christianity offers both an intellectually capacious way of *thinking* and an existentially satisfying way of *living*.

George Herbert: Apologetics through Poetry

In this work thus far, we have focused mainly on argument and narratives as means of presenting the Christian faith. But what about other literary forms – such as poetry? The English poet George Herbert (1593–1633) studied at Trinity College, Cambridge, where he was elected as a Fellow of his college and later a Reader in Rhetoric. He served as Cambridge University's Public Orator before entering the ministry of the Church of England, and serving as parish priest in the village of Bemerton, near Salisbury. This allowed him time to develop and revise his collection of poems, *The Temple*, and his guide to rural ministry entitled *A Priest to the Temple*. Herbert died at Bemerton in 1633, and was buried in the local churchyard. On his deathbed George Herbert entrusted the manuscript of *The Temple* to his long-time friend Nicholas Ferrar, asking him to arrange for it to be published if he thought it was good enough. It is now one of the most highly regarded collections of English-language poetry.

So what particular skills does Herbert bring to his apologetics? Two may be noted. First, Herbert was theologically informed, having a good understanding of some of the leading Protestant theologians of the late sixteenth century. Yet although Herbert was richly steeped in and informed by the theological tradition of the European Reformation, he also possessed a rare ability to transform this theology into rhetorical forms capable of captivating the imagination. This second skill is reflected in his Cambridge University appointment as Public Orator. Herbert possesses a rare mastery of both a significant theological tradition and the English language as a means of communicating its insights using images, analogies, and verbal tropes. Underlying Herbert's poetry is a profound understanding of how words can be used to bridge the gap between heaven and earth, between the believer and Christ.

And what is the problem that needed to be solved? As many studies of the Church of England in this period indicate, a major problem was how to help Christians appreciate and apprehend the living realities at the heart of the Christian faith. Herbert's agenda in *The Temple* was not to convince his readers that Christianity was *true*, but rather to help his readers grasp and inwardly digest its spiritual significance. In an age in which Christianity could easily become a nominal social convention, Herbert allowed his readers to grasp and experience its imaginative breadth and spiritual depth, penetrating beneath the surface of conventional religious practice and language. Or, to put this another way, Herbert realized that a notional acceptance of Christianity needed to be converted into a living faith, nourished by deep spiritual insights, such as the ability of Christ to transform even the most inadequate individual. Herbert thus uses the imagination to convey the deep affective impact of Christ on the believer.

So how does Herbert practice the *art* of apologetics? Like Augustine of Hippo before him, Herbert uses familiar mundane signs, embedded in the worlds of nature or culture, as emblems capable of engaging the imagination, and helping individuals internalize the realities of faith. To illustrate how Herbert does this, we shall focus on one single poem within *The Temple* – "The Elixir," with its famous opening lines "Teach me my God and King/In all things Thee to see." In this poem, which is often sung as a hymn, Herbert uses what we now know was a familiar image to help him communicate the core ideas of acceptance and transformation by grace – the image of the "Philosopher's Stone" that could convert base metals such as lead into gold.

This image was used by many preachers and religious poets in the early 1600s. It was familiar to their audiences, and could easily be developed to emphasize the transformative aspects of the Christian faith. Herbert appeals to this "famous stone" in one of the best-known stanzas of this poem:

> This is that famous stone
> That turneth all to gold:
> For that which God doth touch and own
> Cannot for less be told.

The basic message is simple: just as the Philosopher's Stone converts lead to gold by touching it, so God makes the worthless, inadequate, and inferior into worthy people by *touching* them, and owning them. Anyone who is touched by God is special, important, and valued. Faith is not limited to notional acceptance of the teachings of the

Creeds (a common perception at this time); rather, faith is about allowing God to accept, renew, and transform people, despite their obvious imperfections and failings.

So what can be learned from Herbert? How can his practice of the art of apologetics help those reflecting on how this might be done today? The stand-out theme is Herbert's connection of a central Christian theme with the concerns of ordinary human beings – namely, the question of whether God is concerned with ordinary people, conscious of their weaknesses, failings, and shortcomings. Herbert addresses this theme at multiple points in *The Temple*, especially in the poem "Love (III)," with its well-known opening lines:

> Love bade me welcome: yet my soul drew back,
>   Guilty of dust and sin.

The central anxiety is that God, knowing someone's true nature, cannot possibly accept or embrace them; Herbert's response is that God already knows this, and has acted to "bear the blame" for this situation. The proper response is to accept and embrace God's love.

The second point to note is Herbert's use of a culturally familiar image to convey a significant apologetic point. Recent studies of early seventeenth-century English culture have shown how alchemical imagery was widely used and accepted, and seen as consistent with Christian ideas. Robert M. Schuler has noted how a "spiritual alchemy" emerged in England around this time, seeing a parallel between the physical transmutation of base metals into gold and the spiritual transmutation of believers through God's grace. This imagery was culturally plausible at that time, and Herbert found it helpful in bearing the weight of his theological reflections. Today, of course, alchemy is seen in a rather more negative way. Yet Herbert's approach invites modern apologists to ask what cultural artefacts, practices, and images might be used *today*, as Herbert used alchemy in his own period.

Third, Herbert's use of this poetic imagery uses the imagination – rather than reason – as the gateway to spiritual discernment and growth. Rather than invite his readers to memorize catechisms, Herbert uses memorable images – such as God lovingly touching and transforming individuals – which can become the basis of a theologically expanded vision of both the form and the outcome of the Christian life. Herbert invites us to reflect on what images and analogies might be used to capture the imagination of our audiences, and enable them to reflect on deeper questions.

G. K. Chesterton: Christianity as a Hypothesis

The English journalist G. K. Chesterton (1874–1936) is widely regarded as one of the most effective apologists of the first half of the twentieth century. We have already made use of his ideas at several points in this work; it is time to draw them together, so that the coherence of Chesterton's overall approach can be appreciated, and set within its historical context. Chesterton belonged to the golden generation of popular writers in the first decade of the twentieth century, at a time when increased literacy had created a growing demand for serious yet accessible reflection on the issues of the day in

England. Chesterton developed his writing skills in his weekly columns for the *Daily News* and *The Illustrated London News*, and became a familiar voice on the British Broadcasting Corporation during the 1930s. Although Chesterton later converted to Catholicism, he is widely recognized as an effective apologist for Christianity as a whole.

After a period of agnosticism, Chesterton rediscovered the intense intellectual seriousness of Christianity in 1903. His famous article "The Return of the Angels" expresses his central belief that Christianity offers "an intelligible picture of the world." Chesterton realized that testing a theory meant checking it out against observation. "The best way to see if a coat fits a man is not to measure both of them, but to try it on." Chesterton explained the point he has in mind as follows.

> Numbers of us have returned to this belief; and we have returned to it, not because of this argument or that argument, but because the theory, when it is adopted, works out everywhere; because the coat, when it is tried on, fits in every crease ... We put on the theory, like a magic hat, and history becomes translucent like a house of glass.

Chesterton's argument, as we noted earlier (pp. 9–10; 26–7), is that it is the Christian vision of reality *as a coherent and interconnected whole* – rather than any of its individual components – that proves imaginatively and intellectually compelling. It is not that individual observations of nature or experiences "prove" that Christianity is true; rather, Christianity validates itself by its ability to make sense of those observations, providing a framework that is able to coordinate them convincingly. "The phenomenon does not prove religion, but religion explains the phenomenon." For Chesterton, a good theory – whether scientific or religious – is to be judged by its capacity to accommodate what we see in the world around us and experience within us. "With this idea once inside our heads, a million things become transparent as if a lamp were lit behind them."

Yet while Chesterton insists that Christianity *is* rational, and can be *shown* to be rational, this does not mean that it is a *rationalist* way of thinking that limits reality to what can be proved by reason. In a brilliant phrase, he declares that "by the rejection of rationalism, the world becomes suddenly rational." The point that Chesterton is making is that we cannot limit reality to what reason discloses, as the materialism of George Bernard Shaw and other naturalist writers of this period suggested. The journalist Adam Gopnik explains Chesterton's appeal in the Edwardian period as follows:

> A certain kind of fatuous materialist progressivism was ascendant – the progressivism of Shaw and Wells and Beatrice and Sidney Webb, which envisaged a future of unending technological advance. The illusions of faith would be dispelled in an empire of slow-chewed spinach, rational spelling, and workers' reading circles. Against this, the young Chesterton's themes, the superiority of the local and the primacy of the imaginary, were irresistible.

Chesterton insisted that there was more to life than could be captured by the human reason. Rationalism was a needlessly impoverished and inadequate account of our world. For Chesterton, the paradox of going beyond the limits of human reason is that we develop a more satisfying and adequate understanding of our world, an "architecture of meaning" that allows us to connect God with the particularities of our lives. By acknowledging one thing to be mysterious, everything else becomes lucid and rationally transparent. Yet Chesterton makes a further point: Christianity, by offering a coherent view of the world, makes life *livable*. "I believe life to be logical and workable with these beliefs and illogical and unworkable without them." We see here a key theme from early Christian apologetics: that Christianity articulates a coherent way of thinking, which leads to a meaningful way of living.

One of Chesterton's most striking characteristics is his ability to use words effectively to convey complex arguments. As a journalist, Chesterton knew that effective communication often demanded well-chosen phrases, memorable analogies, and simple prose. His reflections on the Fall, for example, bring out this point clearly. For Chesterton, the Fall is both "the only enlightening" and "the only encouraging view of life," holding that "we have misused a good world, and not merely been entrapped into a bad one." Indeed, some suggest that Chesterton might be better at constructing neat aphorisms rather than sustained arguments.

Yet perhaps the most distinctive feature of Chesterton's apologetics is how he presents himself. He does not come across as someone who wants to force Christianity upon his readers, but someone who wants them to accompany him on a journey of discovery, as he reflects on how they can make sense of the strange complexities of their world and experience. He wants his readers to see what he has seen, believing it to be right and transformative. Time and time again, Chesterton appeals to "experience," to what can be learned by "merely living in this world," and to making decisions that can be "more or less tested by experience." It is striking how rarely Chesterton appeals to religious texts; he rather presents Christianity as a theory, a way of seeing things, which convinces us by its ability to fit things in. A good case can be made that Chesterton adopts a form of natural theology, which begins from our experience of our own world, and allows us to discern a viable pathway to another.

As a successful Edwardian journalist and novelist, Chesterton developed a way of expressing himself that was both clear and engaging, ensuring that he was one of the most accessible and widely read British public intellectuals of the first three decades of the twentieth century. He had his flaws, most notably an incorrigible anti-Semitism that cannot be entirely explained in terms of his cultural context. Yet his humorous, nondogmatic style of writing won him a large following, and established him as a leading public representative of Christianity. Though his reputation has now faded, he remains an important role model for apologists.

So what can be learned from Chesterton? Perhaps the most obvious starting point is the clarity and brilliance of his writing style, which gained his accessible and engaging accounts of faith a large and sympathetic readership. It is worth observing how many of the most effective recent British apologists (such as C. S. Lewis, Dorothy L. Sayers, and Francis Spufford) were well-established authors who were able to use their literary skills in an apologetic context.

Chesterton's apologetic style is also distinctive. While he offers a coherent defense of Christianity as a way of understanding the world, his approach is not technical or dogmatic. He offers a winsome articulation of faith for ordinary people, using his skills as a journalist to avoid theological terms on the one hand, while on the other using rich analogies and metaphors that allow him to make persuasive connections between the common human experience of the world and Christianity. Like C. S. Lewis after him,

Chesterton began with everyday experience of the world – rather than with the Christian Bible or Creeds – and used this as a gateway for faith. Chesterton's approach involves the construction of an apologetic *persona* – in other words, an understanding of his identity and role as an apologist, which shapes how he does apologetics. As we have seen, Chesterton presents himself as an ordinary person who has found a great way to make sense of things, and wants to share it with his readers.

Yet while Chesterton emphasizes that Christianity makes sense of things, he studiously avoids the superficial rationalism that declares that reason can understand everything; that there is nothing that lies beyond what the human mind can master. Where secular rationalism declares everything can be understood through unaided human reason, Chesterton argues that we need something that lies beyond human reason to make sense of the world. God cannot be proved by experience or reason; yet God is able to make sense of what we experience and reason.

Chesterton's point can best be understood by comparing it with Isaac Newton's theory of universal gravitation. Newton was deeply uneasy about his own theory, particularly the idea of "action at a distance." Yet by proposing something that he could not prove to be true, he was able to make sense of a vast range of hitherto disconnected observations – such as the falling of apples from a tree to the ground, and the rotation of the planets around the sun. Chesterton's point is that, by accepting one thing that is mysterious, everything else becomes lucid.

> The whole secret of mysticism is this: that man can understand everything by the help of what he does not understand. The morbid logician seeks to make everything lucid, and succeeds in making everything mysterious. The mystic allows one thing to be mysterious, and everything else becomes lucid.

Something that we do not – and perhaps cannot – fully understand allows us to understand everything else. Paradoxically, as Chesterton insisted, mysteries have a remarkable capacity to illuminate.

Dorothy L. Sayers: Apologetics and Detective Novels

Christianity makes sense of life, and provides us with a moral, imaginative, and existential framework within which we can flourish. Although there is more to the Christian gospel than its ability to make sense of things, this is widely regarded as one of its main apologetic virtues, corresponding to the deep built-in human instinct to try to make sense of things. Many theologians link this with the idea of bearing the "image of God"; we are created with a desire and ability to make sense of our lives. Perhaps this helps us to understand why detective novels are so popular. Writers such as Arthur Conan Doyle, Agatha Christie, and Earl Stanley Gardner mastered the art of assembling a body of evidence, challenging their readers to find the hidden pattern that makes sense of all the clues.

G. K. Chesterton, who we considered in the previous section, developed the "Father Brown" series of detective novels, realizing how these narratives linked the human love of sense-making with deeply religious questions. In this section, we shall consider one of the leading writers of the "golden age" of crime fiction, who saw her own detective

Figure 9.1   The British novelist and lay theologian Dorothy L. Sayers (1893–1957). Alamy Image GPTB60.

fiction as appealing to our implicit belief in the intrinsic rationality of the world around us, and our own ability to discover its deeper patterns.

Dorothy L. Sayers (1893–1957; Figure 9.1) studied modern languages at Oxford University shortly before the First World War, before turning her attention to writing detective novels featuring the aristocratic amateur sleuth Lord Peter Wimsey. These novels, written between 1923 and 1935, can be seen as elegant literary applications of what is now known in the philosophy of science as "inference to the best explanation," which we considered earlier (pp. 51–4). For every set of observations, there are several competing explanations. So which of these is the best? To use the famous image of the philosopher of science William Whewell, which explanatory thread best connects the pearls of our observations?

For Sayers, life was a quest for a pattern of meaning in life. In her *Mind of the Maker* (1941), Sayers suggests that we should think of the "image of God" in humanity as a kind of imaginative template, which predisposes human beings to think and imagine in certain ways. We are *meant* to think in this way, and the God who is the *origin* of this way of thinking is also its *goal*. Sayers was convinced that Christianity was "the only explanation of the universe that is intellectually satisfactory." It gave her a tool by which she might "make sense of the universe," disclosing its otherwise hidden patterns. For Sayers, Christianity was a discovery of the way things really are, not an invention of the way we would like things to be. We find happiness by uncovering the deep logic of the world, which is disclosed in Christ. The apologist is thus like a detective, who follows the trail of those clues and is led to their final destination, in which all the clues converge in a satisfying manner.

In a lecture on the enduring appeal of crime fiction, Sayers appealed to the image of "Ariadne's thread" in trying to explain its essence and appeal. The reference here is to a trope of Greek mythology – a ball of thread that Ariadne gave to the Greek hero Theseus as he entered the labyrinth of Knossos in pursuit of the Minotaur, so that he could find his way out again afterwards. Sayers uses this evocative image to express the process of connecting clues to solve a mystery, in which we "follow, step by step, Ariadne's thread, and finally arrive at the centre of the labyrinth."

This process of reflection is particularly evident in Sayer's novel *The Unpleasantness at the Bellona Club* (1928), set in London's high society during the 1920s. Sayers opens her chapter describing Peter Wimsey's breakthrough in the mystery surrounding the puzzling death of General Fentiman by reflecting on the criteria that might be used in choosing one theory over another:

> "What put you on to this poison business," [Detective Inspector Parker] asked.
>
> "Aristotle, chiefly," replied Wimsey. "He says, you know, that one should always prefer the probable impossible to the improbable possible. It was possible, of course, that the General should have died off in that neat way at the most confusing moment. But how much nicer and more probable that the whole thing had been stage-managed."

So what can be learned from Sayers? The key thing to take away from Sayers is her fundamental belief that there is a deeper pattern to the world that we can grasp – not through the certain proofs of mathematics, but rather by finding the best way of holding together the "clues" that emerge from our experience of the world. What otherwise seems a chaotic and meaningless set of observations can become meaningful and coherent when seen from the right perspective. Sayers saw the assembling of evidence, the gathering of clues, and the finding of the pattern to be creative and rewarding, bringing the "satisfaction of plaiting and weaving together innumerable threads."

Many commentators on Sayers's apologetics have highlighted this theme, particularly her appeal to the "craft of detective fiction" – the art of weaving together evidential threads to find the pattern that lies beneath them, and the sense of achievement that this creates. Indeed, John Thurmer, one of Sayer's more perceptive interpreters, suggested that we can see her work as a "detection of the Trinity," neatly capturing both her theological emphasis on this doctrine and her preferred literary mode of engaging it. The apologist is the one who points out these clues, taking delight in their diversity, yet showing how they converge and combine into a single larger picture and pattern – which for Sayers was the Christian faith, which alone made intellectual and existential sense of the complexities of life.

Sayers, however, realized that the analogy between making sense of clues in a detective novel and discovering the meaning of life was incomplete, and potentially flawed. It is one thing to work out who committed a fictional crime; it is quite another to step into a pattern of meaning in the universe, and thus find personal fulfilment. As Janice Brown points out, Sayers's focus in her detective novels gradually "shifted away from shallow mysteries of crime to the profound mysteries of the human spirit," as her interest shifted from "developing the intricacies of plot" to "exploring the intricacies of the soul."

Yet there is another point that apologists can learn from Sayers. In a helpful account of Sayer's popular defense of Christianity, Jane Craske suggests that Sayers's real significance lies in her ability to speak to audiences who did not know about Christian theology, not merely telling them what Christians believe, but presenting these beliefs in a new manner, emphasizing its capacity to connect with the deepest themes of human existence. Sayers was "not simply repeating but re-presenting, so that those who did not know anything about Christian doctrine could better understand it." Apologetics is thus "a discipline of re-presentation, especially as directed towards audiences beyond the Church." Sayers herself saw detective novels and drama as effective and artful ways of "re-presenting" the Christian faith in a way that enhanced its accessibility, and opened up new ways of presenting its core themes. There is surely something to be learned from this!

Francis Schaeffer: Worldview Apologetics

Francis Schaeffer (1912–1984; Figure 9.2), probably the most important evangelical apologist of the twentieth century, was a leading representative of what is known as "worldview apologetics" – an approach that commends Christianity primarily by

Figure 9.2   The US apologist Francis Schaeffer (1912–1984) at the L'Abri Conference, Urbana, Illinois, in 1981. Alamy Image RPJ77C.

critiquing its alternatives, aiming to expose their underlying presuppositions, and demonstrate their ultimate incoherence. Schaeffer's apologetics involves exposing the presuppositions or assumptions that control the way in which individuals understand the world, and calling their reliability into question. Secularism is not a neutral worldview, but one which is grounded on a set of controlling assumptions. This approach can also be found in the apologetic writings of the Swiss theologian Emil Brunner, who developed an "eristic" approach to apologetics that involved an assessment of the vulnerabilities and deficiencies of rival ways of thinking, as a prelude to affirming the superior capacity of a Christian approach. Although Schaeffer's apologetic ministry primarily concerned the critique of various forms of rationalism and materialism that were widespread in the 1960s, his approach has a wider application.

In his *Escape from Reason* (1968), Schaeffer argued that western thought had allowed itself to be trapped within a narrow and constricting rationalist worldview, which excluded religious beliefs as a matter of principle. Yet this worldview was intellectually problematic and existentially deficient.

> Christianity has the opportunity, therefore, to say clearly that its answer has the very thing modern man has despaired of – the unity of thought. It provides a unified answer for the whole of life. True, man has to renounce his rationalism; but then … he has the possibility of recovering his rationality.

Christianity is in no sense irrational; indeed, its own system of rationality is remarkably coherent. Yet it is critical of a rationalist approach to the world that holds that the world can be known totally by reason alone.

Schaeffer argues that worldviews – whether implicit or explicit – embed a series of presuppositions, controlling assumptions that need to be challenged and assessed. "The more logical a man who holds a non-Christian position is to his own presuppositions, the further he is from the real world; and the nearer he is to the real world, the more illogical he is to his own presuppositions." Christian apologetics aims to identify the vulnerabilities of rival worldviews, partly by demonstrating their internal contradictions, and partly by arguing that Christianity provides a more reliable account of things. He sets out to debate the inner logical consistency of belief systems. Observations and experiences need to be interpreted for their significance to be appreciated; the question for Schaeffer is which worldview offers the best and most reliable interpretation. This question can be partly answered by assessing the coherence of the presuppositions on which such worldviews are based.

> Every person we speak to … has a set of presuppositions, whether he or she has analyzed them or not … It is impossible for any non-Christian individual or group to be consistent to their system in logic or in practice … A man may try to bury the tension and you may have to help him find it, but somewhere there is a point of inconsistency.

Apologetics thus involves identifying these problematic presuppositions, and showing how they create an irresolvable intellectual tension, a cognitive dissonance that sooner or later will lead to the collapse of the worldview in question, in that it cannot be lived out without self-contradiction.

Schaeffer provides a number of examples of how this general principle can be put into practice, offering narrative accounts of how exposing contradictions and tensions within worldviews has important (and negative) implications for their credibility. We may note two representative examples. The first relates to a discussion group Schaeffer was leading at Cambridge University, attended by a young critic of Christianity who Schaeffer variously describes as a "Sikh" and a "Hindu."

> He started to speak strongly against Christianity, but did not really understand the problems of his own beliefs. So I said, "Am I not correct in saying that on the basis of your system, cruelty and noncruelty are ultimately equal, that there is no intrinsic difference between them?" He agreed. ... The student in whose room we met, who had clearly understood the implications of what the Sikh had admitted, picked up his kettle of boiling water with which he was about to make tea, and stood with it steaming over the Indian's head. The man looked up and asked him what he was doing, and he said with a cold yet gentle finality, "There is no difference between cruelty and noncruelty". Thereupon the Hindu walked out into the night.

Schaeffer's point is that the young man realized that his worldview was unviable, in that it was both self-contradictory and that it could not sustain a meaningful life.

The same technique of searching for incoherence within a rival worldview underlies Schaeffer's criticism of the ethical nihilism of the French philosopher Jean-Paul Sartre. Sartre argued that the moral component of an action lay in the individual's exercise of free choice, not the actual moral decision that was reached. But could this view be sustained in the real world? Schaeffer thought not, and pointed out that Sartre signed the 1960 "Manifesto of the 121" – a protest by leading French intellectuals against the brutal attempts by the French army to suppress a revolt in its African colony of Algeria. As Schaeffer pointed out, events in the real world called into question Sartre's ethical views, forcing him to realize that the ethical decisions did matter after all. Sartre "took up a deliberately moral attitude and said it was an unjust and dirty war. His left-wing political position which he took up is another illustration of the same inconsistency."

So how can an apologist expose these contradictions and inadequacies? Schaeffer argues that secularism is not a neutral or uncommitted position; it rests on a series of vulnerable and unacknowledged presuppositions, which are open to challenge. Aware of their intellectual fragility, advocates of secular worldviews therefore construct shields to protect themselves against the external world of public, objective reality, which calls their fundamental presuppositions into question. For Schaeffer, apologetics is about getting inside someone else's worldview and dismantling its seemingly secure foundations from within. It is about "taking the roof off" a worldview, exposing its vulnerability and proposing an alternative.

Drawing on an analogy that was familiar to him from his time in Switzerland, Schaeffer suggested that apologetics is like "taking the roof off" the shelters constructed on some Alpine roads to protect travelers and vehicles against falling rocks. Apologetics removes the ideological shields that people construct to protect themselves from the realities of the external world, and experience the tension between reality and their presuppositions.

> It is like the great shelters built upon some mountain passes to protect vehicles from the avalanches of rock and stone which periodically tumble down the mountain. The avalanche, in the case of the non-Christian, is the real and the abnormal fallen world which surrounds him. The Christian, lovingly, must remove the shelter and allow the truth of the external world and of what man is to beat upon him.

Where evidentialism appeals to theistic arguments in preparing the ground for evangelism, Schaeffer undermines the foundations of existing belief systems, and thus making people receptive to their Christian alternative.

But Schaeffer is important for another reason – his appreciation of the importance of listening to his audiences, and aiming to understand their concerns and questions. Schaeffer is perhaps best known for his self-supported apologetic ministry at L'Abri, a chalet in the Swiss village of Huémoz-sur-Ollon, which began in 1955 and continued until the 1980s. Schaeffer and his wife Edith hosted intellectually curious US students who were visiting Europe who wanted to talk about the meaning of life, often through the lens of the literature and films of the day. Schaeffer listened to their reflections on the new philosophies of the 1960s, and realized he was then able to engage with them on their own level and in their own language, using illustrations drawn from their cultural world to appreciate the plausibility of the Christian faith.

Schaeffer himself was not familiar with the youth culture of the 1960s. knowing little about the movies that people were watching, or the novels they were reading. Yet his extended interactions with student visitors at L'Abri both introduced him to this cultural world and its controlling assumptions, and helped him formulate critical and informed responses to it. While Schaeffer's grasp of philosophy and art was, in the view of some of his critics, less than compelling, he nevertheless knew enough about them to grasp two fundamental points. First, that contemporary culture embodies a set of presuppositions, whether implicitly or explicitly. And second, that it was possible to disentangle these presuppositions from their cultural forms, and challenge their reliability. Many would argue that Schaeffer's work can be seen as encouraging an apologetic engagement with art, literature, and cinema – a theme that has become of increasing importance in the twenty-first century, as the potential of novels and movies to open up deep questions of meaning and value becomes more fully appreciated.

So what can we learn from Schaeffer? Schaeffer tends to engage with apologetic questions that were important back in the 1960s. Although rapid cultural change in the west has diminished familiarity with some of the issues he engaged, this has not blunted the utility of his apologetic method, which can still be used to engage some questions that are relevant today. In what follows, we shall consider how Tim Keller's apologetic ministry in Manhattan clearly draws on some of Schaeffer's insights – for example, that modern secularism operates within an unacknowledged fiduciary framework, which shapes its collective reasoning. You may find it helpful to read the section in Chapter 7 dealing with Keller (pp. 132–34) in preparation for what follows.

Keller follows Schaeffer in stressing the impossibility of someone being able to "just look at the facts" in a neutral and objective manner. "Secularism is its own web of beliefs that should be open to examination." Like Schaeffer, Keller's apologetic includes a critical probing of secularism, alongside a positive commendation of the intellectual, emotional, and imaginative aspects of Christianity. Keller's influential *Making Sense of God* opens by pointing out that its readers are already trapped within their own unacknowledged and uninterrogated assumptions, and suggests that some kind of faith commitment is built into most secular worldviews. This, as Keller points out, has important consequences for apologists. He channels Alasdair MacIntyre's account of tradition-mediated rationality in arguing for apologists to develop an intellectual empathy with their audience.

> First they must "come to understand what it is to think in the terms prescribed by that particular rival tradition." They must do everything they can to sympathetically put themselves in the shoes of the other viewpoint. … Second, in both their own worldview and the one they are assessing, they should identify "unresolved issues and unsolved problems— unresolved and unsolved *by the standards of that tradition.*" One kind of problem is inconsistency, so that some beliefs of the worldview contradict others. Another kind of problem is unlivability, so that some beliefs are impossible for the bearer to actually practice.

Keller's reformulation of Schaeffer's presuppositionalism is a telling indication of the potential of reappropriating apologetic insights from the past. In many ways, Keller is an excellent example of a contemporary apologist whose approach was enriched and informed by earlier figures of wisdom. Yet, as we shall see, Keller also drew on some more recent scholarly accounts of the emergence of the secular world – including the Canadian philosopher Charles Taylor, to whom we now turn. While Tim Keller's apologetic method is important in its own right (pp. 131–32), it is helpful to see it as a refocusing of Taylor's ideas with the needs and language of a new audience in mind.

Charles Taylor: Apologetics in a Secular Age

Many recent Christian apologists have drawn on the work of the Canadian Catholic philosopher Charles Taylor (born 1931; Figure 9.3), especially his substantial work *A Secular Age* (2009). In his *How (Not) To Be Secular*, J. K. A. Smith walks his readers through *A Secular Age*, making helpful apologetic connections and applications – perhaps most importantly, encouraging us to avoid the rational overreach that is so evident in certain types of theodicy (see pp. 149–50).

Taylor's analysis of the origins and nature of the secular age, and its obvious existential inadequacies has enormously significant apologetic implications, and offers twenty-first century apologists a rigorous framework for engaging secular culture. By framing secularism in a certain way, Taylor gives apologists a set of tools to affirm Christian ideas effectively. He also offers the notion of a "social imaginary," a notion that in some ways parallels the notion of a worldview, but which is more attuned to the role of the imagination in human self-understanding. In this section, we shall consider some of Taylor's insights and explore their apologetic application.

In one of his most-quoted passages, Taylor explores how a cultural shift has apologetic implications. "Why was it virtually impossible not to believe in God in, say,

Figure 9.3   The Canadian philosopher Charles Taylor (born 1931) speaking at a philosophy conference in Cologne, Germany, in 2015. Alamy Image ERHJ3A.

1500 in our Western society, while in 2000 many of us find this not only easy, but even inescapable?" Taylor's answer is this: it is not that evidence has emerged discrediting the intellectual plausibility of God; rather, there has been a shift in culturally regnant metanarratives which changes a society's understanding of what is to be considered as "reasonable." Our views on rationality are shaped by our social imaginary. For Taylor, this helps us understand why affirming patterns of thought that run counter to a deeply embedded cultural mindset is potentially to be seen or judged as being "irrational." This underlies Taylor's observation that, on the basis of a "subtraction" account of secularism, which holds that secularism is basically about the removal or suppression of transcendence, religion can only be seen as a social construction. Yet, Taylor argues, it is actually the "secular" (not the "religious") that is socially constructed.

So how this analysis this help an apologist? We have already noted several ways in which Taylor's cultural analysis is apologetically useful (pp. 7–8; 54–5). Perhaps most importantly, Taylor helps us to understand how our secular culture has arisen, and what an apologist might do to engage it critically and intelligently. One of Taylor's concerns is to "define and trace" the critical change "which takes us from a society in which it was virtually impossible not to believe in God, to one in which faith, even for the staunchest believer, is one human possibility among others." What has changed? In the past, many apologists assumed this was due to a shift in criteria of rationality. Taylor, however, suggests that how we understand rationality is not primary, but is rather something that emerges from a wider shift, best described as a "social imaginary." By this, Taylor means something that is "deeper than the intellectual schemes people may entertain when they think about social reality in a disengaged mode." The social imaginary is primary; what is thought to be reasonable or desirable is secondary.

Taylor's analysis of the origins of the "immanent frame" can be supplemented apologetically by noting the widespread anxiety over whether this can ever have the capacity to satisfy the deepest human moral and spiritual aspirations. Framing human existence without reference to the transcendent results in what Taylor terms the "malaise of modernity" – a pervasive sense of flatness and meaninglessness. Taylor uses the phrase "neutral self" to describe the detached position of those who do not recognize the existence or authority of any frameworks of meaning or backgrounds of intelligibility.

> A human being exists inescapably in a space of ethical questions; she cannot avoid assessing herself in relation to some standards. To escape all standards would not be a liberation but a terrifying lapse into total disorientation. It would be to suffer the ultimate crisis of identity.

For Taylor, the moral issue is not simply that of doing the right thing; it is that of being authentically who and what we are. "From Taylor's perspective, our identity is ultimately determined by what we consider to be of utmost value, by a hypergood that not only structures our choices but shapes the fundamental orientations of our lives."

The point Taylor makes is clearly significant and applicable apologetically: we need a "frame or horizon within which things can take on a stable significance," allowing us to decide what is "good and meaningful," or "bad or trivial." He suggests that those people who are unanchored and unattached to any transcendent vision of reality are "at sea" when it comes to issues of moral values – questions concerning "what is good, or worthwhile, or admirable, or of value." Something more than the immanent order is needed; human beings seem to be intrinsically oriented toward transcendence. Our moral values presuppose frameworks and horizons of meaning (and ultimately theism).

Justin Ariel Bailey offers one of the best summaries of the significance of Taylor for apologetics, succinctly identifying what Taylor sees as the aim of his ambitious project:

> Taylor is clearing a space, challenging the habits of closed minds, trying to reopen a conversation that has for years been cut short by subtraction stories. He seeks to achieve epistemic permission (to show that it is reasonable and good to believe) rather than to argue for epistemic obligation (to prove that you must believe).

So having created and argued for the legitimacy of this apologetic space, what does Taylor want us to do with it? As Bailey points out, Taylor offers us an *imaginative* apologetic. And to make the most of Taylor's approach, we need to turn to consider his idea of the "social imaginary." Instead of persuading people to change their modes of reasoning, we need to bring about a shift in the way they *imagine* the world, which ultimately shapes the forms of their reasoning – and which allows Christianity to be seen as epistemically permissible. Much more needs to be said, but it is a good point of departure for apologetics.

Let's go back to Taylor's insistence that we need a "frame or horizon within which things can take on a stable significance," allowing us to decide what is "good and meaningful," or "bad or trivial." How does this emerge? For the Enlightenment, this arose through a recalibration and redirection of human reason; for Taylor, however, it involves a change in "the ways people imagine their social existence, how they fit together with others, how things go between them and their fellows, the expectations that are normally met, and the deeper normative notions and images that underlie these expectations." This imaginative framework shapes our understanding of our world, providing our thoughts and practices with a sense of legitimacy. To change that understanding, we need first to offer culture a new way of *imagining* our world. This process of reimagination runs counter to the Enlightenment narrative of the supremacy of reason. Yet Taylor's analysis suggests that our ways of thinking are secondary to a "world picture," a way of *seeing* reality.

With this point in mind, we are in a position to develop his approach in an explicitly apologetic way. Consider this famous statement from Wittgenstein: "a *picture* held us captive. And we can't get outside it." Wittgenstein's point is that a "world picture" traps us, predisposing us to interpret experience in certain manners as natural or self-evidentially correct, while blinding us to alternative ways of understanding it. This "picture" is assumed to be the "natural" or "objective order" of the world, which does not require justification, but which rather justifies our moral and rational values. So how can be break free from its imaginative thrall? Wittgenstein's answer is to find another picture – a *better* picture. (This idea can supplement the idea of Christianity telling a better story, considered earlier: p. 112.)

Wittgenstein's approach can be helpfully compared to visiting a worldview gallery, in which we are able to look at ourselves and the world through a variety of controlling pictures. Apologetics is about liberating individuals from captivity to a particular way of thinking, partly by showing them that there are alternatives, and particularly through helping them appreciate how things look when seen through a Christian world picture. In my own case, I was held captive for some years as a teenager by a form of Marxism. I escaped from its thrall partly by realizing its intellectual weaknesses and its internal inconsistencies, but mainly because I came to see how a Christian "big picture" seemed much more satisfying and resilient.

The process towards which Taylor and Wittgenstein both point involves determining which "imaginary" or "picture" seems to give the best account of our world. Rather than allowing ourselves to be trapped by any specific inherited or culturally dominant imaginary, we are invited to assemble a group of possible imaginaries, and determine which is the most reliable and satisfying. Taylor himself is quite clear that an imaginary can be a self-serving fiction, something that is dangerously false. The problem lies in recognizing this possibility, and being open to considering alternatives. For Taylor we need to find the 'best account' of things. Human beings are continuously engaged in a process of understanding themselves, one another, and the world they live in; inevitably, this leads to at least a concern for finding the "best account," which is able to make sense of significant aspects of life, such as the moral sources of human meaning.

Apologetically, this means showing how Christianity is able to offer a better account of everything that really matters in life, avoiding the shallow rationalism of the "Age of Reason" and being more attentive to the imaginative, emotional, and intuitive aspects of human existence, which have often been overlooked by apologists. Taylor himself uses the essentially descriptive notion of "fullness" to express what comes close to the biblical idea of *shalom*, the goal of the spiritual life: "Somewhere, in some activity, or condition, lies a fullness, a richness; that is, in that place (activity or condition), life is fuller, richer, deeper, more worthwhile, more admirable, more what it should be."

Taylor's gift to Christian apologetics is a framework for articulating human "fullness," and inviting us to find the "best account" of how such fullness is to be achieved, and on what it is grounded. It is not necessary (and, Taylor would add, not *possible*) to prove that this is the "best account"; the question is whether it is found to be authentic and workable.

The apologist can use Taylor's framework to engage this "immanent social imaginary," which is haunted by the sense of loss created by disenchantment, and show that there are alternative ways of imagining and inhabiting this world. Taylor's core narrative is that of the loss of a cosmos of transcendent meaning, which has now been displaced by a closed universe. Meaning is now relocated to the individual human mind, which constructs an "immanent frame" that denies transcendence and is bereft of intrinsic meaning. The apologist needs to show both that this "immanent frame" is unable to meet (or explain) our deepest needs – and that a "better account" of life is available and that it is reasonable. Again, this is where developing the *art* of apologetics becomes critically important: it is essential to be able to draw on Taylor's insights and approach to inform apologetic approaches to audiences that lie far beyond Taylor's intended academic readership.

Conclusion: Moving On

This book has aimed to introduce Christian apologetics as both a theoretical discipline and a practical art, aiming to convey, explain, and justify Christianity as a meaningful and life-giving faith. Inevitably, limits on space have restricted the scope and depth of discussion and analysis that is possible. However, this book is best seen as a resource to begin a process of exploration. In this brief concluding section, I shall make some suggestions about how you can take this further, and develop your own distinct approach to apologetics, adapted to your own particular gifts and situations.

1. This work has drawn on a wide range of apologists, aiming to allow you to taste a variety of approaches, and see what you make of them. Most apologists are very alert to the cultural assumptions of their time, and often present and defend Christianity in ways that are attuned to their historical contexts and audiences. While some students of apologetics aim to model themselves on past apologists, there are risks of being trapped in a cultural mindset of the past in doing so. We can learn from past apologists, however, without becoming the prisoners of a rapidly receding past. You need to learn to read them in order to inform and stimulate your own approach *in the present*. It is, for example, quite possible to learn from Francis Schaeffer without being trapped in the evangelical rationalism of the 1960s – think of the ways in which Tim Keller used Schaeffer's approach in postmodern Manhattan. You can develop your own apologetic approach and voice in dialogue with such writers, without being limited by the specifics of their historical location. Among younger apologists, I would highlight the work of Justin Ariel Bailey, Joshua Chatraw, Rebecca McLaughlin, and Holly Ordway. All these writers

are attuned to the cultural realities of the twenty-first century, and engage these thoughtfully from an orthodox Christian perspective.

2. Although a familiarity with the approaches of other apologists is helpful, it is important that you develop your own apologetic method, adapted to your own personal gifts and professional credentials on the one hand, and to the kind of audiences you might expect to engage on the other. While reading other apologists will help you do this, you need to develop your own answers to the kind of questions about faith we have been exploring in this work. No apologist can live on borrowed answers. You need to develop your own – ones that you yourself find convincing, and can use with intellectual integrity.

Throughout this work, I have engaged a *representative* but not *exhaustive* set of apologetic issues and individual apologists. Limits on space mean that we cannot hope to offer a comprehensive account of the issues that apologetics needs to engage, or individual apologists who can stimulate and inform your own approach. The idea is that wrestling with these representative questions and individuals will help you grow in confidence and wisdom, and allow you to progress to consider others in a way that works for you. It's important that you develop approaches to questions that you feel comfortable with, rather than simply and uncritically repeating the positions of other writers. You can adapt and channel the approaches of other writers, especially in making sure that they connect up with live questions of today rather than the historic questions of the past.

3. This work is nothing more than an *introduction*, which maps the territory of Christian apologetics, and will help you get a good sense of its main writers, approaches, and issues. You will, however, need to go further and deeper, for the following reasons:

   a. New apologetic issues often arise, which require the repurposing or reformulation of older approaches, or perhaps the opening up of new approaches. In this work, I have engaged the "New Atheist" movement, which was highly influential in the west for about a decade from 2006. This has now faded, and has largely ceased to be discussed. But we can still learn from this movement, even as it recedes into the background – both in terms of the questions that it raised, and the answers that Christian apologists developed in response to them.

   b. While recent trends in the social sciences, philosophy, and psychology may raise challenges for faith that will need to be addressed, they often offer new insights and apologetic possibilities that can be explored and applied. The writings of the Canadian social philosopher Charles Taylor, engaged at several points in this work, offer a particularly good example of this synergy. Christian theologians and apologists have always drawn on cultural voices to help them articulate and communicate the gospel; that task continues, and it is hoped that the material presented in this work may be helpful in doing so.

   c. Many apologists find that they develop a focus on certain specific topics (such as the relation of science and faith, or the problem of suffering), which leads them to speak and write on these matters. This requires both a good knowledge of a specialist literature, and an ability to translate this into the "cultural vernacular." While this introduction to apologetics will provide you with some useful material, specialization requires you to go far beyond the necessarily brief discussion presented in this work.

4. Although apologetics is often understood as engaging an audience outside the Christian community, helping answer their questions and concerns about faith, it is essential to realize that there is a need for an apologetic ministry *within* the community of faith. Many Christians need help and reassurance in thinking through their faith. Preachers can play an especially important role here by incorporating some apologetic themes into their sermons, helping their congregations to deal with questions that concern some – such as the problem of suffering, or the (apparent) illogicality of the doctrine of the Trinity.

5. Finally, and perhaps most importantly, remember that apologetics is a *science* and an *art*. This introduction has provided material that will help you develop your own understanding about the nature and purpose of apologetics; you will need to turn this into your own distinct way of *practicing* apologetics, such as developing writing and speaking skills. Hopefully, this work will have given you enough pointers to allow you to progress on your own!

Study Questions

1. Some of the writers discussed in this chapter are located in the past. Set out, in your own words, the problems that this historical location creates. Yet each of these writers is widely used in contemporary apologetics. What can be learned about the value of past apologists from this observation?

2. Dorothy L. Sayers stresses the importance of clues in solving mysteries. How can this be applied to making sense of life?

3. Francis Schaeffer and Tim Keller both identify the unacknowledged controlling presuppositions that shape secular visions of the world. What can we learn from this insight? How can it enable a critical engagement with secularism?

4. In what ways might Charles Taylor's analysis of our secular age help Christian apologists as they minister in this context?

For Further Reading

Baum, Gregory. "The Response of a Theologian to Charles Taylor's *A Secular Age*." *Modern Theology* 26, no. 3 (2010): 363–81.

Braman, Brian J. "Epiphany and Authenticity: The Aesthetic Vision of Charles Taylor." In *Beauty, Art, and the Polis*, edited by A. Ramos, 224–36. Washington, DC: Catholic University of America Press, 2000.

Craske, Jane. "Dorothy L. Sayers: Apologist for Her Time – and Ours?" *Theology* 122, no. 6 (2019): 412–19.

Follis, Bryan A. *Truth with Love: The Apologetics of Francis Schaeffer*. Wheaton, IL: Crossway Books, 2006.

Keller, Timothy. *The Reason for God: Belief in an Age of Skepticism*. New York, NY: Dutton, 2008.

Keller, Timothy. *Making Sense of God: An Invitation to the Skeptical*. New York, NY: Viking, 2016.

Logsdon, M. J. "George Herbert and C. S. Lewis." *The Lamp-Post of the Southern*

California C. S. Lewis Society 16, no. 1 (1992): 3–7.

Long, D. Stephen. "How to Read Charles Taylor: The Theological Significance of a Secular Age." *Pro Ecclesia* 18, no. 1 (2009): 93–107.

McGrath, Alister E. "The Famous Stone: The Alchemical Tropes of George Herbert's 'The Elixir' in their Late Renaissance Context." *George Herbert Journal* 42, no. 1–2 (Fall 2018/Spring 2019): 114–27.

Orr-Ewing, Amy. "Dorothy L. Sayers: Proving Truth through Stories and Patterns." In *The History of Apologetics: A Biographical and Methodological Introduction*, edited by Benjamin Forrest, Joshua D. Chatraw, and Alister E. McGrath, 584–603. Grand Rapids, MI: Zondervan, 2020.

Peters, James R. *The Logic of the Heart: Augustine, Pascal, and the Rationality of Faith*. Grand Rapids, MI: Baker Academic, 2009.

Pickering, David. "Chesterton, Natural Theology, and Apologetics." *Chesterton Review* 44, no. 3 (2018): 495–508.

Pickering, David. "New Directions in Natural Theology." *Theology* 124, no. 5 (2021): 349–57.

Schuler, Robert M. "Some Spiritual Alchemies of Seventeenth-Century England." *Journal of the History of Ideas* 41, no. 2 (1980): 293–318.

Morris, Thomas V. *Making Sense of It All: Pascal and the Meaning of Life*. Grand Rapids, MI: Eerdmans, 1992.

Schrotenboer, Paul G. *A New Apologetics: An Analysis and Appraisal of the Eristic Theology of Emil Brunner*. Kampen, The Netherlands: Kok, 1955.

Sire, James W. *Naming the Elephant: Worldview as a Concept*. Downers Grove, IL: InterVarsity Press, 2004.

Smith, James K. A. *How (Not) to Be Secular: Reading Charles Taylor*. Grand Rapids, MI: Eerdmans, 2014.

Taylor, Charles. *Modern Social Imaginaries*. Durham, NC: Duke University Press, 2004.

Taylor, Charles. *A Secular Age*. Cambridge, MA: Belknap Press, 2007.

Thurmer, John. *A Detection of the Trinity*. Exeter: Paternoster Press, 1984.

Acknowledgments

The vision for this textbook was due to Clelia Petracca, my editor at John Wiley & Sons, Inc., who commissioned me to write it in response to many requests from colleges and seminaries for an introductory textbook to the field of apologetics that would find wide acceptance across the Christian world. The material on which this book is based was developed over the past 20 years, primarily in the form of lectures given at the Oxford Centre for Christian Apologetics, supplemented by material that I developed for recent lectures and courses in apologetics in Asia and North America. I am grateful to many in those audiences for their comments and feedback, which have helped me ensure that the approach set out in this book is viable and helpful. While there are far too many to acknowledge these people individually, it is important for readers to appreciate that the material in this textbook has been tested against multiple audiences, and that it has been improved considerably as a result of this feedback. I am also indebted to four anonymous readers of the first draft of this work, who made comments that were enormously helpful in developing and improving its focus, scope, and overall approach. Both the publisher and author will welcome further feedback, which will help in developing the next edition of this work.

Sources of Citations

How to Use this Book

p. xi
Francis Spufford, *Unapologetic*. London: Faber & Faber, 2013, 22.

Chapter 1

p. 1
Avery Dulles, *A History of Apologetics*, 2nd ed. San Francisco, CA: Ignatius Press, 2005, xix.

p. 2
Charles Taylor, *A Secular Age*. Cambridge, MA: Belknap Press, 2007, 556–7. Taylor bases this idea on the writings of the sociologist Robert Wuthnow.

p. 4
Francis Schaeffer, *Trilogy: The God Who Is There*. Wheaton, IL: Crossway, 1990, 151.

p. 4
Frederick G. Lawrence, "The Human Good and Christian Conversation." In *Communication and Lonergan: Common Ground for Forging a New Age*, edited by Thomas J. Ferrell and Paul A. Soukup, 248–68. Kansas City, MO: Sheed & Ward, 1993; quote at p. 249.

p. 7
Austin Farrer, "The Christian Apologist." In *Light on C. S. Lewis*, edited by Jocelyn Gibb, 23–43. London: Geoffrey Bles, 1965; quote at p. 26.

p. 7
James K. A. Smith, *How (Not) to Be Secular: Reading Charles Taylor*. Grand Rapids, MI: Eerdmans, 2014, 141.

p. 7
John G. Stackhouse, *Humble Apologetics: Defending the Faith Today*. Oxford: Oxford University Press, 2002, 228.

p. 8
Charles Taylor, *A Secular Age*. Cambridge, MA: Belknap Press, 2007, 225.

p. 8
Charles Taylor, *A Secular Age*. Cambridge, MA: Belknap Press, 2007, 232.

p. 8
Francis Spufford, *Unapologetic*. San Francisco, CA: HarperOne, 2013, xii. [Note: this sentence comes from the preface that Spufford added to the US edition of the original UK edition of this work.]

p. 8
Keith Yandell, *Philosophy of Religion: A Contemporary Introduction*. London: Routledge, 1999, 16.

p. 9
G. K. Chesterton, *Collected Works*, 35 vols. San Francisco, CA: Ignatius Press, 1986, vol. 3, 156.

p. 9
G. K. Chesterton, "The Return of the Angels." First published in the *Daily News*, 14 March 1903. Text in *G. K. Chesterton at the Daily News: Literature, Liberalism and Revolution, 1901–1913*, edited by Julia Stapleton, 8 vols. London: Pickering & Chatto, 2012, vol. 2, 24–6.

p. 10
W. V. O. Quine, *From a Logical Point of View*, 2nd ed. Cambridge, MA: Harvard University Press, 1951, 20–46.

p. 11
C. S. Lewis, "Is Theology Poetry?" In *Essay Collection*. London: HarperCollins, 2000, 21. *Essay Collection* by C. S. Lewis copyright © 1960 C. S. Lewis Pte. Ltd. Extracts reprinted by permission.

p. 11
Francis Schaeffer, *Trilogy*. Leicester: Inter-Varsity Press, 1990, 262–3.

p. 11
C. S. Lewis, Letter to Arthur Greeves, 18 October, 1931, in *The Collected Letters of C. S. Lewis*, edited by Walter Hooper, 3 vols. San Francisco: HarperOne, 2004–6, vol. 1, 977. *Collected Letters* by C. S. Lewis copyright © 1942 C. S. Lewis Pte. Ltd. Extracts reprinted by permission.

p. 11
David J. Bosch, *Transforming Mission: Paradigm Shifts in Theology of Mission*. Maryknoll, NY: Orbis Books, 1991, 11.

p. 13
John Calvin, *Institutes of the Christian Religion*, III.ii.7.

p. 13
Mark McIntosh, *Mysteries of Faith*. Cambridge, MA: Cowley Publications, 2000, 11.

Chapter 2

p. 16
F. F. Bruce, "Paul's Apologetic and the Purpose of Acts." *Bulletin of the John Rylands University Library* 89, no. 2 (1987): 379–93; quote at 389–90.

p. 17
Tertullian, *de poenitentia* I, 2.

p. 19
Athanasius, *On the Incarnation*, 3.

p. 27
Marilynne Robinson, *What Are We Doing Here?* New York: Farrar, Straus & Giroux, 2018, 271.

Chapter 3

p. 32
Pierre Hadot, "La philosophie est-elle un luxe?" *Le Monde de l'Education* 191 (1992): 90–3; quote at p. 92.

p. 33
Francis Spufford, *Unapologetic*. London: Faber & Faber, 2013, 21.

p. 34
Marilynne Robinson, *Gilead*. London: Virago, 2005, 203.

p. 34
Alasdair C. MacIntyre, *Whose Justice? Which Rationality?* London: Duckworth, 1988, 350.

p. 34
Alasdair C. MacIntyre, *Whose Justice? Which Rationality?* London: Duckworth, 1988, 6.

p. 35
Jonathan Edwards, *Treatise on the Religious Affections*. New Haven, CT: Yale University Press, 1959, 305.

p. 35
A. C. Grayling, *The God Argument*. London: Bloomsbury, 2013, 66.

p. 36
Charlton T. Lewis and Charles Short, *A Latin Dictionary*. Oxford: Oxford University Press, 1891, 479.

p. 36
Teresa Morgan, *The New Testament and the Theology of Trust*. Oxford: Oxford University Press, 2022, 8.

p. 36
Faustus of Riez, *On the Holy Spirit*, I, 1.

p. 36
C. S. Lewis, "On Obstinacy in Belief." in *C. S. Lewis: Essay Collection*. London: HarperCollins, 2000, 206–15; quote at p. 214. *Essay Collection* by C. S. Lewis copyright © 1960 C. S. Lewis Pte. Ltd. Extracts reprinted by permission.

p. 36
William H. Griffith-Thomas, *The Principles of Theology*. London: Longmans, Green & Co., 1930, xviii.

p. 36
John Calvin, *Institutes of the Christian Religion*, III.ii.7.

p. 38
Martin Luther, "The Babylonian Captivity of the Church (1520)." In *D. Martin Luthers Werke: Kritische Ausgabe*. Weimar: Böhlau, 1888, vol. 6, 513–14.

p. 38
William Kingdon Clifford, *The Ethics of Belief and Other Essays*. Amherst, NY: Prometheus, 1999, 70.

p. 38
Richard Dawkins, *The Selfish Gene*. Oxford: Oxford University Press, 1976, 198.

p. 39
Terry Eagleton, "Lunging, Flailing, Mispunching: A Review of Richard Dawkins' *The God Delusion*." *London Review of Books*, 19 October 2006.

p. 39
Bertrand Russell, *A History of Western Philosophy*. London: George Allen & Unwin, 1950, 2.

p. 39
Isaiah Berlin, "The Pursuit of the Ideal." In *The Crooked Timber of Humanity*. New York, NY: Knopf, 1991, 1–19; quote at p. 14.

p. 39
John Stackhouse, *Can I Believe? Christianity for the Hesitant*. Oxford: Oxford University Press, 2020, 15–16.

p. 40
Francis Darwin, ed., *The Life and Letters of Charles Darwin*, 3 vols. London: John Murray, 1887, vol. 2, 155.

p. 40
Charles Darwin, *Origin of Species*, 6th ed. London: John Murray, 1872, 444. This comment is not present in the five earlier editions of the work.

p. 41
John Polkinghorne, *The Way the World Is: The Christian Perspective of a Scientist*. London: Triangle, 1983, 2.

p. 41
John Polkinghorne, *Theology in the Context of Science*. New Haven, CT: Yale University Press, 2009, 125–6.

p. 44
John Henry Newman, Letter to William Robert Brownlow, 13 April 1870. In *The Letters and Diaries of John Henry Newman*. Oxford: Clarendon Press, 1973, vol. 25, 97.

p. 45
Anselm, *Proslogion*, XX.

p. 46
C. S. Lewis, *The Pilgrim's Regress*. London: HarperCollins, 2018, xii. *Pilgrims Regress* by C. S. Lewis copyright © 1933 C. S. Lewis Pte. Ltd. Extracts reprinted by permission.

p. 47

William Lane Craig and Quentin Smith. *Theism, Atheism, and Big Bang Cosmology.* Oxford: Clarendon Press, 1993, 63.

p. 48

Ludwig Wittgenstein, *Culture and Value,* edited by G. H. von Wright, translated by Peter Winch. Oxford: Blackwell, 1980, 82–6.

p. 48

Blaise Pascal, *Pensées.* Minneola, NY: Dover Publications, 2003, 190.

p. 48

Blaise Pascal, *Pensées.* Minneola, NY: Dover Publications, 2003, 110.

p. 48

G. K. Chesterton, "The Return of the Angels." *Daily News,* 14 March, 1903. For the full text, see *G. K. Chesterton at the Daily News,* edited by Julia Stapleton, 8 vols. London: Pickering & Chatto, 2012, vol. 2, 22–6.

p. 49

C. S. Lewis, "Is Theology Poetry." In *Essay Collection.* London: HarperCollins, 2002, 10–21; quote at p. 21. *Essay Collection* by C. S. Lewis copyright © 1960 C. S. Lewis Pte. Ltd. Extracts reprinted by permission.

p. 50

C. S. Lewis, *Mere Christianity.* London: HarperCollins, 2002, 21.

p. 50

Augustine of Hippo, *Confessions,* translated by Henry Chadwick. Oxford: Oxford University Press, 2008, 3.

p. 50

C. S. Lewis, *Mere Christianity.* London: HarperCollins, 2002, 25.

p. 51

C. S. Lewis, *Mere Christianity.* London: HarperCollins, 2002, 136–7.

p. 53

Richard Swinburne, *The Existence of God,* 2nd ed. Oxford: Oxford University Press, 2004, 121.

p. 53

Charles Taylor, *A Secular Age.* Cambridge, MA: Belknap Press, 2007, 222.

p. 56

Gary Wolf, "The Church of the Non-Believers" (1 November 2006). https://www.wired.com/2006/11/atheism/ (accessed 10 March 2023).

p. 57
Linda Zagzebski, "Recovering Understanding." In *Knowledge, Truth, and Duty: Essays on Epistemic Justification, Responsibility, and Virtue*, edited by Matthias Steup, 235–52. Oxford: Oxford University Press, 2001; quote at p. 241.

Chapter 4

p. 61
Augustine of Hippo, *Confessions*, translated by Henry Chadwick. Oxford: Oxford University Press, 2008, 3.

p. 61
Hans-Georg Gadamer, *Truth and Method*. London: Continuum, 2013, 316.

p. 63
John M. G. Barclay, "Interpretation, Not Repetition: Reflections on Bultmann as a Theological Reader of Paul." *Journal of Theological Interpretation* 9, no. 2 (2015): 201–9; quote at 205.

p. 63
John Warwick Montgomery, *Evidence for Faith*. Dallas, TX: Probe Books, 1991, 319.

p. 64
Ludwig Wittgenstein, *Notebooks, 1914-1916*. New York, NY: Harper, 1961, 74.

p. 64
Albert Einstein, *Ideas and Opinions*. New York, NY: Crown Publishers, 1954, 41–9.

p. 64
Ludwig Wittgenstein, *Tractatus Logico-Philosophicus*. London: Routledge & Kegan Paul, 1992, 6.52.

p. 64
Hendrik Kraemer, *The Christian Message in a Non-Christian World*. London: Edinburgh House Press, 1938, 303.

p. 66
C. S. Lewis, "Christian Apologetics." In C. S. Lewis, *Essay* Collection. London: HarperCollins, 2000, 151, 155. *Essay Collection* by C. S. Lewis copyright © 1960 C. S. Lewis Pte. Ltd. Extracts reprinted by permission.

p. 65
Iain McGilchrist, *The Master and His Emissary: The Divided Brain and the Making of the Western World*. New Haven, CT: Yale University Press, 2012, 93.

p. 67
Mary Midgley, *What is Philosophy For?* London: Bloomsbury Academic, 2018, 193.

p. 67
Mary Midgley, "Mapping Science: In Memory of John Ziman." *Interdisciplinary Science Reviews* 30, no. 3 (2005): 195–7.

p. 68
J. G. van der Watt, "Introduction." In *Salvation in the New Testament: Perspectives on Soteriology*, edited by J. G. van der Watt. Leiden: Brill, 2005, 1–3; quote at p. 1.

p. 69
Anselm of Canterbury, "Prayer to Christ." In *The Prayers and Meditations of St Anselm*, translated by Benedicta Ward. London: Penguin, 1973, 97, lines 31–4.

p. 69
C. S. Lewis, *Surprised by Joy*. London: HarperCollins, 2002, 267. *Surprised by Joy* by C. S. Lewis copyright © 1955 C. S. Lewis Pte. Ltd. Extracts reprinted by permission.

p. 71
H. Richard Niebuhr, *The Meaning of Revelation*. New York: Macmillan, 1960, 59–60.

p. 71
James McTavish, "Jesus the Divine Physician." *Linacre Quarterly* 85, no. 1 (2018): 18–23; quote at p. 19.

p. 71
Philip Melanchthon, *Commentary on Romans*, translated by Fred Kramer. St. Louis, MO: Concordia Publishing House, 1992, 18.

p. 70
Roger Scruton, *The Face of God: The Gifford Lectures 2010*. London: Continuum, 2014, 45.

p. 79
Albert Einstein, *Ideas and Opinions*. New York: Crown Publishers, 1954, 255.

p. 79
Roger Scruton, *The Face of God: The Gifford Lectures 2010*. London: Continuum, 2014, 9.

p. 80
Paul Elmer More, *Pages from an Oxford Diary*. Princeton, NJ: Princeton University Press, 1937, section XV (the work is unpaginated).

p. 80
Paul Elmer More, *Pages from an Oxford Diary*. Princeton, NJ: Princeton University Press, 1937, section XVIII (the work is unpaginated).

p. 80
Neil MacGregor with Erika Langmuir, *Seeing Salvation: Images of Christ in Art*. London: BBC, 2000, 13.

p. 80
Nicholas of Cusa, *De visione Dei*, IV, 10.

p. 80
Katherine Sonderegger, "Christ's Mystery." In *The Bond of Peace: Exploring Generous Orthodoxy Today*, edited by Graham Tomlin and Nathan Eddy, 48–61. London: Society for the Promotion of Christian Knowledge (SPCK), 2021; quote at 53.

p. 81
Jeanette Winterson, *Why Be Happy When You Could Be Normal?* London: Vintage, 2012, 68.

p. 81
Michael F. Steger, "Meaning in Life." In *Oxford Handbook of Positive Psychology*, edited by Shane J. Lopez, 679-87. Oxford: Oxford University Press, 2009; quote at p. 682.

p. 81
Salman Rushdie, *Is Nothing Sacred? The Herbert Read Memorial Lecture*. Cambridge: Granta, 1990, 8–9.

p. 82
Augustine of Hippo, *Confessions*, translated by Henry Chadwick. Oxford: Oxford University Press, 2008, 3.

p. 83
Steven Weinberg, *The First Three Minutes: A Modern View of the Origin of the Universe*. New York: Harper, 1993, 154.

p. 83
Raymond Carver, "Late Fragment." In *All of Us: The Collected Poems*. London: Harvill Press, 1996, 294.

p. 85
Marilynne Robinson, *The Death of Adam: Essays on Modern Thought*. New York: Picador, 2005, 240.

Chapter 5

p. 87
Peter L. Berger, *A Rumor of Angels: Modern Society and the Rediscovery of the Supernatural*. New York: Doubleday, 1969, 24.

p. 87
Peter L. Berger, *A Rumor of Angels: Modern Society and the Rediscovery of the Supernatural*. New York: Doubleday, 1969, 53.

p. 88
Augustine of Hippo, *de Trinitate*, VIII.vi.12.

p. 89
Augustine of Hippo, *Confessions*, translated by Henry Chadwick. Oxford: Oxford University Press, 2008, 3.

p. 89
John Calvin, *Institutes of the Christian Religion*, I.iii.2; I.iv.1.

p. 91
Bertrand Russell, Letter to Lady Constance Mary Malleson (Colette O'Niel), 23 October 1916. In *The Selected Letters of Bertrand Russell: The Public Years 1914–1970*, edited by Nicholas Griffin. London: Routledge, 2001, 85.

p. 91
Julian of Norwich, *Showings*. New York: Paulist Press, 1978, 296.

p. 91
C. S. Lewis, *Surprised by Joy*. London: HarperCollins, 2001, 16. *Surprised by Joy* by C. S. Lewis copyright © 1955 C. S. Lewis Pte. Ltd. Extracts reprinted by permission.

p. 91
C. S. Lewis, "The Weight of Glory." In *Essay Collection*. London: HarperCollins, 2002, 103. *Essay Collection* by C. S. Lewis copyright © 1960 C. S. Lewis Pte. Ltd. Extracts reprinted by permission.

p. 92
R. W. L Moberly, "To Hear the Master's Voice: Revelation and Spiritual Discernment in the Call of Samuel." *Scottish Journal of Theology* 48 (1995): 443–68; quote at p. 458.

p. 92
Joseph Pieper, *On Hope*. San Francisco, CA: Ignatius Press, 1986, 38.

p. 92
Alexander Wood, *In Pursuit of Truth: A Comparative Study in Science and Religion.*
London: Student Christian Movement, 1927, 102.

p. 93
Bonaventure, *The Soul's Journey into God*, translated by Philotheus Boehner, OFM. Saint
Bonaventure, NY: The Franciscan Institute of Saint Bonaventure University, 1956, 61.

p. 93
Jonathan Edwards, *Miscellanies*, no. 108; in *Works*, 26 vols. New Haven, CT: Yale
University Press, 1977–2009, vol. 13, 279.

p. 94
C. S. Lewis, "The Weight of Glory." *Essay Collection.* London: HarperCollins, 2001,
98–9. *Essay Collection* by C. S. Lewis copyright © 1960 C. S. Lewis Pte. Ltd. Extracts
reprinted by permission.

p. 94
C. S. Lewis, "The Weight of Glory." *Essay Collection.* London: HarperCollins, 2001,
104. *Essay Collection* by C. S. Lewis copyright © 1960 C. S. Lewis Pte. Ltd. Extracts
reprinted by permission.

p. 95
John Polkinghorne, *Science and Creation: The Search for Understanding.* London:
SPCK, 1988, 20–1.

p. 96
Thomas F. Torrance, *The Christian Frame of Mind: Reason, Order, and Openness in
Theology and Natural Science.* Colorado Springs, CO: Helmers & Howard, 1989, 40.

p. 96
Thomas F. Torrance, "Divine and Contingent Order." In *The Sciences and Theology in
the Twentieth Century*, edited by A. R. Peacocke, 81–97. Notre Dame, IN: University
of Notre Dame Press, 1981; quote at 84.

p. 98
David Brewster, *Life of Sir Isaac Newton*, new ed., revised by W. T. Lynn. London:
Tegg, 1875, 303.

p. 98
Immanuel Kant, *Gesammelte Schriften*, 30 vols. Berlin: Reimer, 1902, vol. 5, 161.

p. 98
C. S. Lewis, *Mere Christianity.* London: HarperCollins, 2001, 21.

p. 98
C. S. Lewis, *Mere Christianity.* London: HarperCollins, 2001, 25.

p. 99
Paul Kurtz, *Forbidden Fruit: The Ethics of Humanism*. Buffalo, NY: Prometheus Books, 1988, 65.

p. 100
Richard Rorty, *Consequences of Pragmatism*. Minneapolis, MN: University of Minneapolis Press, 1982, xlii.

p. 100
Richard Rorty, *Consequences of Pragmatism*. Minneapolis, MN: University of Minneapolis Press, 1982, xlii.

p. 100
Blaise Pascal, *Pensées*. Mineola, NY: Dover, 2003, 61 (no. 205).

p. 101
Peter Berger, *A Rumor of Angels: Modern Society and the Rediscovery of the Supernatural*. New York, NY: Doubleday, 1969, 30.

p. 101
G. K. Chesterton, *Tremendous Trifles*. London: Methuen, 1909, 209.

p. 102
Cyprian of Carthage, *On Mortality*, 7; 25.

Chapter 6

p. 107
Christian Smith, *Moral, Believing Animals: Human Personhood and Culture*. Oxford: Oxford University Press, 2009, 64.

p. 107
H. Richard Niebuhr, *The Meaning of Revelation*. New York, NY: Macmillan, 1960, 93.

p. 107
Edward T. Oakes, "Apologetics and the Pathos of Narrative Theology." *Journal of Religion* 72, no. 1 (1992): 37–58; quotes at pp. 37–8.

p. 108
John Milbank, "Foreword." In *Imaginative Apologetics: Theology, Philosophy and the Catholic Tradition*, edited by Andrew Davison, xiii–xiv. London: SCM Press, 2011.

p. 108
Paul Fiddes, "Story and Possibility: Reflections on the Last Scenes of the Fourth Gospel and Shakespeare's 'The Tempest.'" In *Revelation and Story: Narrative Theology and the*

Centrality of Story, edited by Gerhard Sauter and John Barton, 29–52. London: Routledge, 2000.

p. 109
Christian Smith, *Moral, Believing Animals: Human Personhood and Culture*. Oxford: Oxford University Press, 2009, 67.

p. 110
J. R. R. Tolkien, *Tree and Leaf*. London: HarperCollins, 2001, 56.

p. 111
C. S. Lewis, Letter to Arthur Greeves, 18 October, 1931. In C. S. Lewis, *Collected Letters*, edited by Walter Hooper, 3 vols. London: HarperCollins, 2004–06, vol. 1, 976. *Collected Letters* by C. S. Lewis copyright © 1942 C. S. Lewis Pte. Ltd. Extracts reprinted by permission.

p. 111
J. R. R. Tolkien, *Tree and Leaf*. London: HarperCollins, 2001, 71.

p. 111
C. S. Lewis, Letter to Arthur Greeves, 18 October, 1931. In C. S. Lewis, *Collected Letters*, edited by Walter Hooper, 3 vols. London: HarperCollins, 2004–06, vol. 1, 977. *Collected Letters* by C. S. Lewis copyright © 1942 C. S. Lewis Pte. Ltd. Extracts reprinted by permission.

p. 111
C. S. Lewis, "Myth became Fact." In C. S. Lewis, *Essay Collection*. London: HarperCollins, 2000, 142. *Essay Collection* by C. S. Lewis copyright © 1960 C. S. Lewis Pte. Ltd. Extracts reprinted by permission.

p. 111
Gilbert Meilaender, "Theology in Stories: C. S. Lewis and the Narrative Quality of Experience." *Word and World* 1, no. 3 (1981): 222–30; quote at p. 228.

p. 111
J. R. R. Tolkien, *Tree and Leaf*. London: HarperCollins, 2001, 56.

p. 111
J. R. R. Tolkien, *Tree and Leaf*. London: HarperCollins, 2001, 71.

p. 111
The Letters of J. R. R. Tolkien, edited by Humphrey Carpenter. New York: Houghton Mifflin Company, 2000, 100–101.

p. 113
Christian Smith, *Moral, Believing Animals: Human Personhood and Culture*. Oxford: Oxford University Press, 2009, 85–6.

p. 113
J. B. S. Haldane, *Possible Worlds and Other Essays*. London: Chatto and Windus, 1927, 209.

p. 113
C. S. Lewis, "The Weight of Glory." In *Essay Collection*. London: HarperCollins, 2002, 96–106; quote at p. 99. *Essay Collection* by C. S. Lewis copyright © 1960 C. S. Lewis Pte. Ltd. Extracts reprinted by permission.

p. 113
C. S. Lewis, *Surprised by Joy*. London: HarperCollins, 2002, 249. *Surprised by Joy* by C. S. Lewis copyright © 1955 C. S. Lewis Pte. Ltd. Extracts reprinted by permission.

p. 114
Alasdair MacIntyre, *Three Rival Versions of Moral Enquiry: Encyclopedia, Genealogy, and Tradition*. Notre Dame, IN: University of Notre Dame Press, 1990, 81.

p. 114
N. T. Wright, *The New Testament and the People of God*. Minneapolis, MN: Fortress Press, 1992, 132.

p. 115
N. T. Wright, *The New Testament and the People of God*. Minneapolis, MN: Fortress Press, 1992, 132.

p. 116
John R. W. Stott, *The Cross of Christ*. Downers Grove, IL: InterVarsity Press, 1986, 174.

p. 118
Christopher P. Scheitle and Elaine Howard Ecklund, "The Influence of Science Popularizers on the Public's View of Religion and Science: An Experimental Assessment." *Public Understanding of Science* 26, no. 1 (2017): 25–39, especially 33–4.

Chapter 7

p. 122
John Stott, *Christian Mission in the Modern World*. Downers Grove, IL: InterVarsity Press, 2008, 65–5.

p. 128
John A. Mackay, *A Preface to Christian Theology*. London: Nisbet, 1942, 29–30.

p. 128
Charles Taylor, *A Secular Age*. Cambridge, MA: Belknap Press, 2007, 232.

p. 129
C. S. Lewis, *The Problem of Pain*. London: Bles, 1940, 91.

p. 129
C. S. Lewis, *The Problem of Pain*. London: Bles, 1940, xii.

p. 130
C. S. Lewis, "Christian Apologetics." In *Essay Collection*. London: HarperCollins, 2000, 147–60; quotes at pp. 153–5. *Essay Collection* by C. S. Lewis copyright © 1960 C. S. Lewis Pte. Ltd. Extracts reprinted by permission.

p. 130
C. S. Lewis, "Christian Apologetics." In *Essay Collection*. London: HarperCollins, 2000, 147–60; quote at p. 151. *Essay Collection* by C. S. Lewis copyright © 1960 C. S. Lewis Pte. Ltd. Extracts reprinted by permission.

p. 131
Robert Wuthnow, *After Heaven: Spirituality in America since the 1950s*. Berkeley, CA: University of California Press, 1998, 4.

p. 133
Tim Keller, cited in Eleanor Barkhorn, "How Timothy Keller Spreads the Gospel in New York City, and Beyond." *New Atlantic* 21 February 2011.

p. 133
Anthony Sacramone, "An Interview with Timothy Keller." *First Things*. 25 February 2008. https://www.firstthings.com/web-exclusives/2008/02/an-interview-with-timothy-kell (accessed 10 March 2023).

p. 135
Eric Mason, *Woke Church: An Urgent Call for Christians in America to Confront Racism and Injustice*. Chicago, IL: Moody, 2018, 106.

p. 137
Tomáš Halík, *Patience with God: The Story of Zacchaeus Continuing in Us*. New York, NY: Doubleday, 2009, 6.

p. 137
Tomáš Halík, *Patience with God: The Story of Zacchaeus Continuing in Us*. New York, NY: Doubleday, 2009, 9.

p. 137
Adela Muchova, "Pastoral Practice of the Academic Parish of Prague." *Studia Universitatis Babeş-Bolyai Theologia Catholica Latina* 66 (2021): 56–91; quotes at pp. 66–8.

p. 138
Tomáš Halík, "Befriending the Nonbeliever Within." In *Is God Absent? Faith, Atheism, and Our Search for Meaning*, edited by Anselm Grün, Tomáš Halík, and Winfried Nonhoff. New York, NY: Paulist Press, 2019, 123–38.

p. 138
John Stott, *Between Two Worlds: The Challenge of Preaching Today*. Grand Rapids, MI: Eerdmans, 1982, 154.

Chapter 8

p. 143
Sigmund Freud, *Complete Psychological Works*, 24 vols. London: Hogarth Press, 1953–74, vol. 21, 30.

p. 145
Sigmund Freud, *The Future of an Illusion*. New York, NY: W.W. Norton and Co., 1990, 40.

p. 145
Aldous Huxley, *Ends and Means: An Inquiry into the Nature of Ideals*. New Brunswick, NJ: Transaction Publishers, 2012, 312.

p. 145
Thomas Nagel, *The Last Word*. Oxford: Oxford University Press, 1997, 130.

p. 146
Czesław Miłosz, "Discreet Charm of Nihilism." *New York Review* 19 November 1998.

p. 148
Michael Shermer, *How We Believe: Science, Skepticism, and the Search for God*. New York, NY: Freeman, 2000, 71.

p. 149
J. K. A. Smith, *How (Not) To Be Secular: Reading Charles Taylor*. Grand Rapids, MI: Eerdmans, 2014, 52.

p. 149
William J. Abraham, *Among the Ashes: On Death, Grief, and Hope*. Grand Rapids, MI: Eerdmans, 2017, 16.

p. 150
Nicholas Wolterstorff, *Lament for a Son*. Grand Rapids, MI: Eerdmans, 1987, 68.

p. 150
Frances M. Young, *Brokenness and Blessing: Towards a Biblical Spirituality*. London: Darton, Longman and Todd, 2007, 47.

p. 151
Stanley Hauerwas, *Naming the Silences: God, Medicine and the Problem of Suffering*. London: Continuum, 2004, 53.

p. 151
John Swinton, *Raging with Compassion: Pastoral Responses to the Problem of Evil*. London: SCM Press, 2018, 4.

p. 152
Thomas S. Kuhn, *The Structure of Scientific Revolutions*, 2nd ed. Chicago, IL: University of Chicago Press, 1970, 146.

p. 153
John Donne, *Divine Sonnet* XIV. In *John Donne: Complete English Poems*. London: Dent, 1994, 347–8.

p. 154
Rebecca Goldstein, *The Proof and Paradox of Kurt Gödel*. New York, NY: Norton, 1995, 204.

p. 154
Alasdair MacIntyre, *Whose Justice? Which Rationality?* Notre Dame, IN: University of Notre Dame Press, 1988, 6.

p. 155
G. K. Chesterton, "Is Humanism a Religion?" In *The Collected Works of G. K. Chesterton*. San Francisco: Ignatius Press, 1986, vol. 3, pp. 146–56; quote at p. 156.

p. 156
Bruce DeSilva, "Pundit Christopher Hitchens Picks a Fight in Book, 'God is Not Great.'" *Rutland Herald* [Vermont], 25 April 2007.

p. 156
Julian Baggini, "The New Atheist Movement is Destructive." *Fri Tanke*. 19 March 2009. https://fritanke.no/the-new-atheist-movement-is-destructive/19.8484. Accessed 10 March 2023.

p. 156
Isaiah Berlin, *Concepts and Categories: Philosophical Essays*. New York, NY: Viking Press, 1979, 2–5, 161–2.

p. 156
Bertrand Russell, *A History of Western Philosophy*. London: Routledge, 1950, 2.

p. 157
Blaise Pascal, *Pensées*. Minneola, NY: Dover Publications, 2003, 52.

p. 158
Augustine, *Sermon* 117.3.5.

p. 158
C. S. Lewis, "The Poison of Subjectivism." In *Christian Reflections*. Grand Rapids, MI: Eerdmans, 1974, 79–80. *Christian Reflections* by C. S. Lewis copyright © 1967 C. S. Lewis Pte. Ltd. Extracts reprinted by permission.

p. 159
Massimo Pigliucci, "New Atheism and the Scientistic Turn in the Atheism Movement." *Midwest Studies in Philosophy* 37, no. 1 (2013): 142–53; quote at p. 144.

p. 159
Stephen Jay Gould, *The Hedgehog, the Fox, and the Magister's Pox: Mending and Minding the Misconceived Gap between Science and the Humanities*. London: Jonathan Cape, 2003, 87.

p. 159
Alexander Rosenberg, *The Atheist's Guide to Reality: Enjoying Life without Illusions*. New York, NY: W.W. Norton, 2011, 7–8.

p. 162
Alvin Plantinga, *Where the Conflict Really Lies: Science, Religion, and Naturalism*. New York, NY: Oxford University Press, 2011, 168–74.

p. 162
John Hedley Brooke, *Science and Religion: Some Historical Perspectives*. Cambridge: Cambridge University Press, 1991, 6.

p. 162
Peter Harrison, "Introduction." In *The Cambridge Companion to Science and Religion*, edited by Peter Harrison, 1–18. Cambridge: Cambridge University Press, 2010; quote at p. 4.

p. 163
Mary Midgley, *The Myths We Live By*. London: Routledge, 2003, 26–7.

p. 164
Frank H. T. Rhodes, "Christianity in a Mechanistic Universe." In *Christianity in a Mechanistic Universe and Other Essays*, edited by D. M. MacKay, 11–48. London: InterVarsity Fellowship, 1965; quote at p. 42.

p. 165
David Hume, *An Enquiry Concerning Human Understanding*. Oxford: Clarendon Press, 2007, 62.

p. 166
Richard Swinburne, *The Concept of Miracle*. London: Macmillan, 1970, 23.

p. 167
Bertrand Russell, *The Problems of Philosophy*. London: Oxford University Press, 1912, 98–9.

p. 167
F. R. Tennant, *Miracle & Its Philosophical Presuppositions*. Cambridge: Cambridge University Press, 1925, 33.

p. 167
Augustine, *The City of God*, XXI, 8.

p. 167
C. S. Lewis, *Miracles: A Preliminary Study*. London: HarperCollins, 2002, 87–98.

p. 167
Isaac Newton, as cited in Richard Westfall, *Science and Religion in Seventeenth Century England*. New Haven, CT: Yale University Press, 1970, 203–4.

p. 168
J. S. Haldane, *The Philosophy of a Biologist*. Oxford: Oxford University Press, 1935, 16.

p. 168
Francis Crick, *The Astonishing Hypothesis: The Scientific Search for the Soul*. London: Simon & Schuster, 1994, 3; 11.

p. 168
Richard Dawkins, *River Out of Eden: A Darwinian View of Life*. London: Weidenfeld & Nicholson, 133.

p. 168
Raymond Tallis, *Aping Mankind: Neuromania, Darwinitis and the Misrepresentation of Humanity*. London: Routledge, 2014, 349.

p. 169
Marilynne Robinson, *What Are We Doing Here?* New York, NY: Farrar, Straus & Giroux, 2018, 271.

Chapter 9

p. 173
Joshua D. Chatraw and Mark D. Allen, *The Augustine Way: Retrieving a Vision for the Church's Apologetic Witness*. Grand Rapids, MI: Baker Academic, 2023, 8.

p. 174
The Works of George Herbert, edited by F. E. Hutchinson. Oxford: Clarendon Press, 1945, 184–5.

p. 175
The Works of George Herbert, edited by F. E. Hutchinson. Oxford: Clarendon Press, 1945, 188.

p. 176
G. K. Chesterton, "The Return of the Angels." *Daily News*, 14 March, 1903. For the full text, see *G. K. Chesterton at the Daily News*, edited by Julia Stapleton, 8 vols. London: Pickering & Chatto, 2012, vol. 2, 22–6.

p. 176
Adam Gopnik, "The Back of the World." *The New Yorker*, 7 July and 14 July 2008.

p. 177
Cited in Dudley Barker, *G. K. Chesterton: A Biography*. London: Constable, 1973, 169.

p. 177
G. K. Chesterton, *Collected Works*, 37 vols. San Francisco, CA: Ignatius Press, 1986–2012, vol. 3, p. 311.

p. 177
David Pickering, "Chesterton, Natural Theology, and Apologetics." *Chesterton Review* 44, no. 3 (2018): 495–508; quote at p. 504.

p. 178
G. K. Chesterton, *Orthodoxy*. San Francisco, CA: Ignatius Press, 1995, 33.

p. 179
William Whewell, *The Philosophy of the Inductive Sciences*, 2 vols. London: John W. Parker, 1847, vol. 2, 36.

p. 179
Letter to William Temple, Archbishop of Canterbury, 7 September 1943. In *The Letters of Dorothy L. Sayers: Volume II, 1937 to 1943*, edited by Barbara Reynolds. New York: St Martin's Press, 1996, 429.

p. 180
Dorothy L. Sayers, *Les origines du roman policier*. Hurstpierpoint: Dorothy L. Sayers Society, 2003, 14.

p. 180
Dorothy L. Sayers, *The Unpleasantness at the Bellona Club*. London: Hodder & Stoughton, 1968, 155.

p. 180

Dorothy L. Sayers, letter to L. T. Duff, 10 May 1943. In *The Letters of Dorothy L. Sayers: Volume II, 1937 to 1943*, edited by Barbara Reynolds. New York: St Martin's Press, 1996, 401.

p. 180

The Letters of Dorothy L. Sayers: Child and Woman of Her Time, edited by Barbara Reynolds. Hurstpierpoint: Dorothy L. Sayers Society, 2002, 97.

p. 180

Janice Brown, *The Seven Deadly Sins in the Work of Dorothy L. Sayers*. Kent, OH: Kent State University Press 1998, 213.

p. 181

Jane Craske, "Dorothy L. Sayers: Apologist for Her Time – and Ours?" *Theology* 122, no. 6 (2019): 412–19; quote at p. 414.

p. 182

Francis A. Schaeffer, *Trilogy*. Wheaton, IL: Crossway Books, 1990, 262–3.

p. 182

Francis A. Schaeffer, *Trilogy*. Wheaton, IL: Crossway Books, 1990, 134.

p. 182

Francis A. Schaeffer, *Trilogy*. Wheaton, IL: Crossway Books, 1990, 132–3.

p. 183

Francis A. Schaeffer, *Trilogy*. Wheaton, IL: Crossway Books, 1990, 110.

p. 183

Francis A. Schaeffer, *Trilogy*. Wheaton, IL: Crossway Books, 1990, 58.

p. 184

Francis A. Schaeffer, *Trilogy*. Wheaton, IL: Crossway Books, 1990, 140.

p. 184

Timothy Keller, *Preaching: Communicating Faith in an Age of Skepticism*. New York: Penguin, 2015, 126.

p. 184

Timothy Keller, *Making Sense of God: An Invitation to the Skeptical*. New York: Viking, 2016, 280.

p. 185

Charles Taylor, *A Secular Age*. Cambridge, MA: Belknap Press, 2007, 25.

p. 186
Charles Taylor, *A Secular Age*. Cambridge, MA: Belknap Press, 2007, 3.

p. 186
Charles Taylor, *Modern Social Imaginaries*. Durham, NC: Duke University Press, 2004, 23.

p. 187
Charles Taylor, "The Dialogical Self." In *Rethinking Knowledge: Reflections Across Disciplines*, edited by R. F. Goodman and W. R. Fisher, 57–68. Albany, NY: State University of New York Press, 1995; quote at p. 58.

p. 187
Brian J. Braman, "Epiphany and Authenticity: The Aesthetic Vision of Charles Taylor." In *Beauty, Art, and the Polis*, edited by Alice Ramos, 224–236. Washington, DC: Catholic University of America Press, 2000; quote at p. 225.

p. 187
Charles Taylor, *Sources of the Self: The Making of the Modern Identity*. Cambridge, MA: Harvard University Press, 1989, 26–31.

p. 187
Justin Ariel Bailey, *Reimagining Apologetics: The Beauty of Faith in a Secular Age*. Downers Grove, IL: InterVarsity, 2020, 53.

p. 188
Charles Taylor, *Modern Social Imaginaries*. Durham, NC: Duke University Press, 2004, 23.

p. 188
Ludwig Wittgenstein, *Philosophical Investigations*, 4th ed. Oxford: Wiley-Blackwell, 2009, §115 (emphasis in original).

p. 188
Charles Taylor, *A Secular Age*. Cambridge, MA: Belknap Press, 2007, 5.

Index

Abraham, William J.   149
Abū Qurrah, Theodore   22
"Age of Reason"   24–6, 33, 152–5
Allen, Mark D.   173
Al-Ghazālī   46–7
Anomalies and theoretical fragility   152
Anselm of Canterbury   22, 44–6, 69
Apologetics
  in "Age of Reason"   24–6
  as an art   2–3, 127–9, 174
  and beauty   93–4
  as a defense of faith   3
  and divine grace   12–13
  in early church   15–20
  in early Islamic era   20–2
  as finding the "Best Account" of life
    (Charles Taylor)   189
  in Enlightenment period   24–6
  evangelism, relation to   11–12
  evidentialist approaches to apologetics   5,
    63–4
  as an explanation of faith   3–4, 57
  history of development of   15–30
  and Holy Spirit   12–13
  and the imagination   xi, 26, 27, 34,
    109–11, 131, 174–5, 188–9

  as making sense of reality   8–11, 78–9,
    112–15, 176–8, 179–80
  in Middle Ages   22–4
  narrative approaches to apologetics   6,
    106–20
  in patristic period   15–20
  presuppositionalist approaches to
    apologetics   5, 182–3
  retrieving older approaches   173, 185
  schools of   4–6
  as a science   2–3, 127
  as telling a "better story" about
    life   112–15
  theology, relation to   12–13
  as cultural translation of the key ideas of
    faith   4, 65, 138–40
  types of   4–6
  worldview apologetics   181
Aquinas, Thomas   22–3, 41–4, 144–5, 165
Aratus   125
Areopagus address in Athens (Acts 17:22–31)
    16, 89, 125–6
Arguments for the Existence of God   41–9
  Aquinas's Five Ways   41–4
  Anselm of Canterbury's Ontological
    Argument   44–6

Christian Apologetics: An Introduction, First Edition. Alister E. McGrath.
© 2024 John Wiley & Sons Ltd. Published 2024 by John Wiley & Sons Ltd.

The argument from beauty   93–4
The argument from desire   49–51
Kalām Arguments   46–7
The argument from morality   98–100
The argument from order   95–7
Utility of such arguments in apologetics
      47–9
Aristides of Athens   17
Aristotle   12
Arnobius of Sicca   17
Arnold, Matthew   91
Athanasius of Alexandria   19, 157
Audience, apologetic importance of   122–40
Augustine of Hippo   17, 19–20, 55, 61, 69,
      71, 75, 82, 83, 149, 158, 167, 172–3

Babylonian Exile, as apologetic
      framework   116–17
Baggini, Julian   156
Bailey, Justin Ariel   187, 189
Balcony and Road, as framework for
      apologetics   128–9, 149–50
Barclay, John   63
Barth, Karl   144–5
Baucham, Voddie T.   135
Beauty, apologetic importance of   93–4
Benedict of Nursia   131
The "benefits of Christ" in
      apologetics   67–8, 70, 71–2
Berger, Peter   87
Berlin, Isaiah   39, 156
Bernstein, Richard   100
Best Explanation, Inference to the   50,
      51–4, 92, 99, 112–13, 134, 152, 179
Better Story, Christianity as a   112–15
Bhaskar, Roy   168
"Big Picture" approaches to apologetics
      8–11, 78–9, 176–8
Bonaventura of Bagnoregio   93
Bosch, David   11
Bowlby, John   82
Brooke, John Hedley   162
Bruce. F. F.   16
Brueggeman, Walter   101
Brunner, Emil   182
Buber, Martin   169

Calling of Samuel (1 Samuel 3:4–20)   91–2
Calvin, John   13, 24, 36–7, 82, 89

Carnell, Edward John   27, 62
Carr, Bernard   38
Carver, Raymond   83
Chatraw, Joshua D.   173, 189
Chesterton, G. K.   1, 9–10, 26, 76, 154,
      176–8
Christ and apologetics
      The "Benefits of Christ" in apologetics
            67–8, 70, 71–2
      Incarnation and apologetics   78–80
      Salvation and apologetics   71–8
Christie, Agatha   178
Clement of Alexandria   8, 17
Clifford, William K.   38–40
Collins, Francis C.   118–19
Colson, Charles   62
Constantine, Roman emperor   20
Copernicus, Nikolaus   52
Craig, William Lane   28, 46–7
Crick, Francis   168
Cyprian of Carthage   102

Dante Alighieri   83
Darwin, Charles   40–1
Davie, Grace   132
Dawkins, Richard   28, 32–3, 38, 52, 55, 56,
      156, 159, 168
Deism, as diminished account of God   8, 24–5
Dennett, Daniel   56
DeSilva, Bruce   156
Desire, argument from   49–51
Detective fiction, as analogue of
      apologetics   26–7, 179–80
Diogenes Laertius   126
Dirac, Paul   52
Donne, John   152–3
Doyle, Arthur Conan   178
Draper, John William   162
Dulles, Avery   1

Eagleton, Terry   39
Edwards, Jonathan   26, 34–5, 93
Einstein, Albert   52, 64, 79, 95, 159,
      160, 163
Enlightenment rationalism   24–6, 33, 152–5
"Epistemic Pelagianism"   54, 149
European Wars of Religion, impact on
      apologetics   25, 33
Eusebius of Caesarea   15

Evidentialist approaches to apologetics
    5, 63–4
Evil, problem of   32, 128, 129–30, 148–52
Exile in Babylon, apologetic application of
    116–17

Face of God   79–80
Faith   37–8, 139, 155–7
    as justified belief   35–8
    and uncertainty   38–41
Farrer, Austin   7
Faustus of Riez   36
Feuerbach, Ludwig   144–5
Fiddes, Paul   108–9
Fine tuning of the universe   96–7
Five Ways (Thomas Aquinas)   41–4
Frei, Hans   107
Freud, Sigmund   76, 83, 143–5

"God of the Gaps", as apologetic
    approach   95
"God of the Philosophers"   48, 77, 78, 79
Gödel, Kurt   154
Goldstein, Rebecca Newberger   154
Gould, Stephen Jay   159
Graham, Billy   75
Gregory of Nyssa   19
Griffith–Thomas, W. H.   36
Gadamer, Hans–Georg   61
Gaunilo of Marmoutiers   45
Geworfenheit ("being thrown" into
    the world)   101
Gide, André   76
Graham, Billy   75
Gray, John   34, 56, 147
Grayling, A. C.   35
Grotius, Hugo   24

Hadot, Pierre   32
Haldane, J. S.   113, 168,
Haley, Alex   101
Halík, Tomáš   132, 136–8
Harris, Sam   28, 56, 146
Harrison, Peter   19, 162–3
Hauerwas, Stanley   151
Heidegger, Martin   8, 101
Herbert, George   84, 114, 173–5
Hick, John   149
Hitchens, Christopher   35, 55, 56, 146,
    147, 155–6

Hume, David   40, 160, 65–6
Huxley, Aldous   145

Ignatius of Antioch   70
Image of God, as apologetic motif   88–9,
    109–11
Imagination, apologetic significance of   xi, 26,
    27, 34, 109–11, 131, 174–5, 188–9
"Immanent frame" (Charles Taylor)   187
Incarnation, apologetic aspects of   78–80
Inference to the Best Explanation   50, 51–4,
    92, 99, 112–13, 134, 152, 179
Irenaeus of Lyons   18, 149, 157
Islam   20–22, 23
    and early Christian apologetics   20–2
    critique of Trinity   20–1

James, William   39, 157
Job, Book of   150
John of Damascus   21
Julian of Norwich   84, 91
Justin Martyr   8

Kant, Immanuel   97–8
Keller, Tim   5, 27, 132–4, 152, 184–5
Kepler, Johann   52
Kraemer, Hendrik   64
Kuhn, Thomas   152
Kurtz, Paul   99

Laws of nature   164–5
Leibniz, Gottfried Wilhelm   149
Lennox, John   28
Lessing, Doris   76
Levels of explanation   168–9
Lewis, C. S.   1, 5, 10, 12, 27, 36, 46,
    49–51, 57, 65, 69, 79, 91, 94, 98–9,
    103, 104, 110–14, 133, 158–9, 167,
    173, 177
Lindbeck, George   144
Longing, sense of   49–51, 69–70
Llull, Ramon   23
Luther, Martin   24, 38, 82
Lyotard, Jean–François   109

MacGregor, Neil   80
MacIntyre, Alasdair   34, 114, 154, 185
Mackay, John A.   128
Mapping a complex reality   67–70, 163–4
Marty, Martin   147

Mason, Eric   134–5
Marxism   12
McGilchrist, Iain   65
McGrath, Alister E.   28
McIntosh, Mark   13
McLaughlin, Rebecca   189
McTavish, James   71
Meaning in life, apologetic significance of
    81–5
    As finding fulfilment   82
    As finding a secure base in life   82
    As inhabiting a coherent world   82–3
    As having a proper sense of self–worth
        83–4
Meilaender, Gilbert   111, 145
Melanchthon, Philip   67–8, 70, 71–2
Melito of Sardis   17
"Mere Christianity" (C. S. Lewis)   12
Metanarratives and apologetics   109
Midgley, Mary   67, 163–4
Milbank, John   108
Miłosz, Czesław   146
Miracles   96, 164–7
Moberley, Walter   92
Montgomery, John Warwick   27, 63
More, Paul Elmer   79–80
Morgan, Teresa   36
Morse, Christopher   115
Multiple maps of a complex reality   67–70,
    163–4
Murdoch, Iris   82, 99
Myth, as literary form   110–11
Mythology and apologetics   110–12

Nagel, Thomas   145
Narrative approaches to apologetics   106–20
    Christianity as a metanarrative   109
    In C. S. Lewis   110–14
    Marginalized during "Age of
        Reason"   106–7
    Parables as examples of   93–4
    Realism of narrative approaches   119
    Rediscovery of   106–9
    In J. R. R. Tolkien   109–11
"New Atheism"   28, 32, 146–7, 152,
    155–6
Newton, Isaac   66–7, 97–8, 154, 167
Nicholas of Cusa   80
Niebuhr, H. Richard   71, 107
Oakes, Edward   107–8

Ockham's Razor   52
Ontological argument   44–6
Ordway, Holly   189
Origen   17, 19

Pain, problem of   32, 128, 129–30, 148–52
Palamas, Gregory   20
Paley, William   44
"Parable of the Pearl of Great Price"
    (Matthew 13:45–46)   93–4
Parsimony, Principle of   52
Pascal, Blaise   5, 24, 69, 100–1, 157
Paul's Areopagus address in Athens
    (Acts 17:22–31)   16, 89, 122, 124-6
Penicillin, as analogue for salvation   72
Peter's Pentecost sermon in Jerusalem
    (Acts 2:14–36)   16, 124
Pigliucci, Massimo   159
Plantinga, Alvin   27, 36, 45, 61, 89,
    113, 162
Plato's Cave, as framework for
    apologetics   102–4, 117
Platonism   8, 79–80
Points of contact   87–9
    In Augustine of Hippo   88–9
    In Calvin   89
    Grounded in the "image of God"   88–9
Points of contact, apologetic significance of
    87–104
    The beauty of the world   93–4
    Existential anxiety and alienation   100–2
    The ordering of nature   95–7
    A sense of longing   90–2
    A sense of moral obligation   98–100
    A sense of wonder   97–8
Polkinghorne, John   41, 95, 119
Popper, Karl   156
Postmodernism   109, 155
Postrationalism   33–5
Presuppositionalist approaches to apologetics
    5, 182–3
Proof, limits of   32–3, 35–7, 38–41, 155–7

Quine, W. V. O.   10

Rationality of faith   6–7, 8–11, 78–9, 112–15,
    152–5, 176–8, 179–80
Redemption   74–5
Reductionism   168–9
Religion as the cause of violence?   146–8

Religion, as natural kind?   146–7
Rhodes, Frank H. T.   164
Ricci, Matteo   24
Road and Balcony, as framework for
    apologetics   128–9, 149–50
Robinson, Marilynne   27, 34, 84–5, 169
Roots, importance of   101–2, 117
Rorty, Richard   100
Rosenberg, Alex   159–60
Ruggieri, Michele   24
Rushdie, Salman   81
Russell, Bertrand   39, 91, 156–7, 166–7

Salvation, apologetic aspects of   70–5,
    139–40
    Salvation as adoption   73–4, 123–4, 140
    Salvation as healing   70–2
    Salvation as liberation   74–5
    Salvation as redemption   74–5
    Salvation and sacrifice   72–3
Sartre, Jean–Paul   183
Sayers, Dorothy L.   26–7, 31, 177, 178–81
Schaeffer, Francis A.   5, 11, 27, 133, 181–5
Schleiermacher, F. D. E.   144
Schuler, Robert M.   175
Science and faith, apologetic approaches to
    118–19, 159–61, 161–4
Scientism, apologetic critique of   159–61
Scruton, Roger   79
"Seekers–Dwellers" Paradigm   131–2
Self–Worth and apologetics   83–4
Sehnsucht in apologetics   90–1
Shaw, George Bernard   113
Shermer, Michael   148
"Signals of transcendence" (Peter Berger)   87
Sin, explaining the nature of   75–7
Sin, noetic impact of   55
Smith, Christian   109, 113
Smith, James K. A.   7, 54, 149
Sonderegger, Katherine   80
Spinoza, Baruch   164
Sproul, R. C.   27
Spufford, Francis   8, 123, 177
Stackhouse, John   39
Steger, Michael F.   81
Stories as a form of apologetics   106–20
Stott, John R. W.   116, 122, 132
Suffering, problem of   32, 128, 129–30,
    148–52

Swinburne, Richard   27–8, 41, 51–4, 57,
    96, 166
Swinton, John   151

Tallis, Raymond   168
Taylor, Charles   2, 7, 8, 54, 101, 131–2,
    149, 185–9
Tennant, F. R.   167
Tertullian   17, 18–19,
Theodicy   128, 129–30, 148–52
Thomas Aquinas see Aquinas, Thomas
Timothy of Baghdad   21
Tolkien, J. R. R.   27, 94, 109–11
Torrance, Thomas F.   95
Translation, cultural, as apologetic
    theme   138–40
Trinity, apologetic approaches to
    157–9, 180
    Islamic critique of   20–1

Ultimate questions   3, 156
Urban Apologetics   134–6

van Til, Cornelius   27

Weber, Max   34, 154
Weil, Simone   117
Weinberg, Steven   83
Wells, H. G.   113
Whewell, William   179
White, Andrew Dickson   162
William of Ockham   52
Winterson, Jeanette   81
Wiseman, Jennifer   119
Wish–fulfilment, God as?   143–5
Wittgenstein, Ludwig   36, 47, 64, 76, 188
Wolf, Gary   56
Wolterstorff, Nicholas   150
Wonder, apologetic significance of   97–8
Wood, Alexander   92
Worldview apologetics   181
Wright, N. T. (Tom)   5, 114–15
Wuthnow, Robert   131–2
Wykstra, Stephen   149

Yandell, Keith   8
Young, Frances   150

Zagzebski, Linda   57

Printed and bound by CPI Group (UK) Ltd, Croydon, CR0 4YY

21/05/2024

14504558-0001